P9-CRE-645

# HOW TO GROW UP

Photo by Lydia Daniller

MICHELLE TEA is the author of four memoirs, one novel, a collection of poetry, and a young adult fantasy series. She is the creator and editor of Muthamagazine.com, and she blogs regularly about her attempts to get pregnant at Getting Pregnant with Michelle Tea on xoJane.com. She is founder and artistic director of RADAR Productions, a literary organization that produces monthly reading series, the international Sister Spit performance tour, the Sister Spit Books imprint on City Lights, and other events.

---

### Praise for *How to Grow Up*

"Full of insights and weirdness, crazy hope and transcendent humor and despair, *How to Grow Up* is a riveting read for anyone who's clawed their way into adulthood kicking and screaming, or knows someone who's still clawing. I can't recommend it enough."
—Jerry Stahl, author of *Happy Mutant Baby Pills*

"If this is your first introduction to the force of nature known as Michelle Tea, get ready for a new hero in your world. Her ferociously wild life has served up some of the juiciest stories in memoir and now she reflects on that life with her singular humor and brazen honesty at full tilt. Few writers come off so scrappy and so elegant at the same time."
—Beth Lisick, author of *Yokohama Threeway*

# How to Grow Up

*A Memoir*

Michelle Tea

A PLUME BOOK

PLUME

Published by the Penguin Group
Penguin Group (USA) LLC
375 Hudson Street
New York, New York 10014

USA | Canada | UK | Ireland | Australia | New Zealand | India | South Africa | China
penguin.com
A Penguin Random House Company

First published by Plume, a member of Penguin Group (USA) LLC, 2015

LIBRARY OF CONGRESS CATALOGING-IN-PUBLICATION DATA
Tea, Michelle.
 How to grow up : a memoir / Michelle Tea.
  pages cm
 ISBN 978-0-14-218119-5
 1. Tea, Michelle. 2. Authors, American—20th century—Biography.   I. Title.
 PS3570.E15Z46 2015
 813'.6—dc23
 [B]          2014032902

Printed in the United States of America
10  9  8  7  6  5  4  3  2  1

Set in Goudy Old Style Std.
Designed by Eve L. Kirch

# Contents

# Introduction

Perhaps some of you have glided into adulthood with all the grace of a swan, skimming lightly into an adult living situation, adult relationships, adult jobs and income, and, most important, an adult sense of confidence, of a solid place in the world, of stability.

Who *are* you people? I'm not sure you actually exist.

If you are not yet an adult and fear you may never be one; if you suspect you in fact *may* be an adult, but your grasp on both the concept and the lifestyle is shaky enough to wake you up at night; if you spend too much time longing for items you can't quite afford and break into a cold sweat whenever you do part with some of your hard-earned cash; if your sliding-scale therapist has diagnosed you with post-traumatic stress disorder from the dysfunctional formative years you're clambering out of; if you are slowly learning how to clean your house; if you are slowwwwwwwly learning how not to date narcissists; if you've spent too much time with too much booze in your belly; if you never went to college; if you have embarrassing spiritual inclinations that lead you to whisper affirmations under your breath and hiss occasional desperate prayers to unknown unicorn goddesses; if you have a stack of unread self-help books under your bed; if some of your most ridiculous, irresponsible choices have turned out to be some of the best decisions you've ever made; if your path into so-called adulthood has been more meandering and counterintuitive than fast-tracked, then this is a book for all of you, my darlings. And as for those graceful individuals who swanned themselves effortlessly into adulthood, you, too, might find something that interests you, even if it's just a juicy bit of voyeurism.

I have spent the past decades alternately fighting off adulthood with the gusto of a pack of Lost Boys forever partying down in Neverland, and timidly, awkwardly, earnestly stumbling toward the life of a grown-ass woman: healthy, responsible, self-aware, stable. At forty-three years old, I think I've finally arrived, but my path has been via many dark alleys and bumpy back roads. Along the way I've managed to scrawl a slew of books—memoirs about growing up a persecuted Goth teen in a crappy town, or a love-crazed party person getting my heart smashed up again and again; about the creepy secrets my family was harboring; about my time working in the sex industry. That I got these books published was a shocker—I hadn't gone to college or studied writing or anything. That people read them, and liked them, felt like a total miracle. Because of these books I've been able to cobble together something of an adult life, writing and producing literary events, blogging and running a nonprofit of my own creation.

It is from this somewhat trembling, hard-won perch of adulthood that I type to you now. I type to you from a marginally clean home—no longer do roaches scamper under cover of darkness! No longer do stubbed-out cigarette butts stud my floors! No longer will hungover twentysomething roommates vomit in *my* toilet! I type to you as one who has, amazingly, learned to fix my "broken picker"—you know, the terrible radar that sends a person fluttering in the direction of the cad most likely to trample your heart. After a lifetime of flat-broke-ness that includes many dips into full-on poverty, there is enough cash in my bank account to occasionally blow on pricey perfumes and other useless but beautiful items. And, after nearly killing my life with drugs and alcohol, I have more than a decade sober, and all the oddball spiritual wisdom that comes with it. After a lifetime spent writing memoirs that detail the struggles that I and countless other girls experience when they're born broke, or weird, into tricky families and unsafe towns, it seemed like time to write a book about how that struggle can actually, with luck and grit, lead you straight into a life you didn't know you wanted and never thought you'd have.

Getting from there to here is a story that will take us to Paris Fashion Week and the punishing halls of blue-collar all-girl Catholic high schools; to the bingo games of Las Vegas casinos and a New England bus station where an Internet-sourced date peddled her pills; from a yacht on the French Riviera to a rundown San Francisco apartment with a persimmon tree in the backyard; from Buddhist meditation halls to the magnificent Pacific Ocean. Like life, these tales rise up out of nowhere and leave you shaking your head and changed from the experience. Through repeat failures and moments of bruised revelation, I have mastered the art of doing things differently and getting different results. If you can't quite relate, I do hope you enjoy the wild ride. And if you do relate, I hope that what I've lived and what I've learned serve to make your own messy journey to adulthood a little less rocky, a little less lonely. At the end of it all, we're all just kids playing dress-up in our lives, some a little more convincingly than others.

# How to Grow Up

# 1.

## You Deserve This

I chose the apartment because of the persimmon tree outside the bedroom window.

I haven't always selected my residences based on special magical details—more like, if I was lucky to score a room in an apartment that was a cheap-o price, I snagged it. Never mind if people were shooting up between the cars parked outside my door, or if an anal yet ambitious roommate attempted to charge me an hourly rate for the housekeeping she did (true stories). Never mind if a nation of cockroaches scattered when a light flicked on and roommates responded to my horror with a snotty directive to "learn to cohabit peacefully with another species" (true story). Never mind if the shower was a tin can with a floor so rusted that one had to stand upon a milk crate in a pair of Tevas in order to bathe (like everything you will read in this book, true, true, true). This was the landscape of my twenties. I was flat broke and planned on spending the rest of my life as an

1

impoverished writer; cheap rent was a must. I was a little funny-looking, with tattoos sprawling across my body; choppy, home-cut hair that was dyed a color not found in nature; and thrifted clothes that fit strangely and bore many holes and stains. If all this was overlooked and I was permitted entry to a household, it was always in my best interest to grab it, roaches and rotting showers be damned.

In my twenties I spent seven years living in the Blue House, a crumbling Victorian so infamous for its lawlessness and squalor it had its own name, and its name was legend. The rent was ridiculously cheap, cheap enough for even the worst slacker/artist/alcoholic/addict to scrounge it up without having to clean up their lives too much. And speaking of clean—we didn't, as a rule, and we would state this as baldly as possible to new roommates. "You don't clean?" a prospective cohabitant would ask, a bit incredulous.

"Just look around," I would invite them. Cigarette butts covered the floor, mashed there by a shoe, as if it were not a house but a bar after closing, before the cleaning crew came in. The beer cans and bottles rolling into the corners also suggested not a home but a tavern, or alternately, a frat house. Dishes were stacked in the sink, unless they were stacked in the bathtub, where they were piled when the sink stack rose too high. Heaps of trash bags mounded at the top of the stairs, where feng shui practice suggests you have an altar to peacefully greet you as you arrive home. And the kitchen floor—how interesting, the potential cohabitants probably thought, to see a mud floor in an American home in 1997! How unexpected! But no, it was not an actual mud floor; we simply hadn't cleaned the kitchen in quite a while. We were busy doing other things, *man*! Like, um, getting drunk! And in my case, at least, writing a book about it.

Although the Blue House was by any standard a total wreck of a place, it served me well. I simply didn't know how to take care of myself in my twenties. I was feral, and I needed a feral cave that allowed me to live in my simple ways. Because my rent was cheap, I didn't have to work very hard, and because I wasn't spending all my time at a J-O-B, I had plenty of time to write, and I did. I woke hungover every morning (okay, well, afternoon) and would wobble down to the bagel shop to spend the next four hours scribbling into notebooks. I wrote my first few books in this way, back when my alcoholism was, as they say, "working." Sure, there were consequences, but I lived so low I didn't notice them. In fact, my low living *was* a consequence of my drinking, but I didn't see that then. I just saw, and felt, the thrill of the constant party. So there were some nights spent with my head in the toilet, some baffling inebriated fights with lovers and friends, some roaches in the kitchen. There were also my notebooks, filling up and piling up, and the exhilarating feeling that I was *living*. I'd missed out on the East Village in the eighties, that heyday of decadent art and culture. I felt like I was getting a second chance in the Mission District of 1990s San Francisco.

At the dramatic finale of that wild decade, I hooked up with a man I would spend the next eight years with. Or, to be real, a man-child. He was nineteen years old when I met him, a Teen Poetry Slam champion. He moved straight from his parents' house into my own squalor palace, much to the alarm of my roommates, who I'd believed were beyond feeling alarmed about anything. I guess even a punk house has its limits, and a jobless teen slumped on the couch watching *Unsolved Mysteries* and smoking pot all day is one of them. I was twenty-nine, coming down from my Saturn return, that infamous, dreaded moment when, if you believe in astrology, you feel the often brutal effects of Saturn, planet of limits and responsibility, returning to the place it sat at your moment of birth. This completion of the planet's orbit around the sun syncs up with the end of your twenties. It also roughly corresponds to the frontal lobe of your brain—the place that comprehends risk and empathy—finally developing. The frontal lobe gets damaged by alcohol abuse, so maybe that was why, so close to the moment when one is meant to comprehend her limits and get her shit together, I embarked upon a long-term cohabitation with a teenager.

When he and I moved out of the Blue House at the end of my seventh year in residence, I hadn't expected that it would be the start of eight years of house hopping together. But the both of us were a mess, and it was easier to scan our low-rent apartments and declare, "This—this is the reason we are so miserable," than to look at the root causes of our unhappiness. It was as if each new apartment would elicit from us the harmony we lacked, each new house key a metaphorical key, too, the elusive key to making this thing work. Maybe here we would stop squabbling like children. Maybe here my boyfriend would find a job he wasn't compelled to quit, bringing in some grown-up income. Maybe here would be the place where I would stop agonizing over whether mine was an "unhealthy relationship," stop daydreaming about running away with whatever doe-eyed creature happened to glance my way on the bus.

Our first apartment was a studio plagued with roaches; our next one was so crooked that fallen items rolled south. Eventually we scored an apartment that had not a single strike against it—it was clean and spacious, affordable, and bug-free. Of course, we needed a roommate in order to make rent, and so we endured a parade of lunatics to make it work: the compulsive liar who smuggled a pet Chihuahua into the apartment, as if we wouldn't hear it barking; the guy whose girlfriend left strange notes in the common spaces hysterically declaring how super sexy he was, as if she needed us to be aware of their powerful amour; my boyfriend's twin sister, the both of them engaging in the sort of psychotic fighting that only twins from dysfunctional families engage in. Our final home was in San Francisco's Italian North Beach neighborhood. It was as if the clouds had parted and angels had shoved it out of heaven and onto busy Columbus Avenue, bustling with tourists and the young Italian men who worked the restaurants, Chinese grandmothers clutching pink bags of produce, and drunkards on their way to the strip clubs over on Broadway. The North Beach apartment held such promise: no roommates, but bigger than a studio; two bedrooms, yet affordable enough that even I with my freelancer's erratic income and my boyfriend with his underachiever's erratic employment could make rent, no problem. Sure, our building manager, Mr. Fan, strangled ducks for dinner on his back porch right behind our bedroom. But he was always handy with a set of keys when I locked myself out, and I supposed I preferred witnessing the occasional murder of waterfowl to participating in the daily murder of vermin—our new little apartment was bug-free.

The special magical detail of this apartment was the old-fashioned funeral band that played outside the mortuary across the street each weekend. At first, we were both enchanted by it. The apartment would suddenly fill with horns and drums— "Amazing Grace" and some wrenchingly dramatic melodies lifted from Italian opera. The sound would invade the space and, just as abruptly, be gone, like a plane traveling overhead. It was so majestic that we forgot it was in honor of someone's passing.

Anyone who believes in omens knows that a funeral band and a procession of mourners outside your window every weekend is not a good one. The songs were like odes to this dying relationship, one I'd started nearly a decade ago. A lot had happened since then. I'd gotten sober, hadn't had a drink in years. I'd gotten published, and a photographer from the daily news came to take my picture. He snapped my photo against a brightly painted mural in my neighborhood, the wind blowing my hair around, a chunky strand of fake pearls around my neck. In the picture I'm looking off in the distance, as if at my own future— which, now that I was sober, I actually had a shot at. I'd felt so old before I'd quit drinking. The damage and drama that accompanies a downward spiral weighs on your body and mind like age. The longer I stayed sober, the younger I felt, as if emerging from a chrysalis.

Even though my boyfriend had also gone through significant changes during our eight years together, eventually dealing with his own addictions, our personal transformations hadn't made our relationship any easier. I'd read somewhere that people's patterns are established very early on, and if that's the case, my ex and I had gotten off to some brutally bad starts, back when I was still drinking and he was a deadbeat teen. But for eight long years we continued. And at the end of every fight, when we made up, we would dissect what had happened and feel like we'd solved the mystery—the mystery of why, when we loved each other so much, we couldn't get along. Armed with knowledge, we'd pledge to never, ever do it again.

But of course it would happen again. All of it.

Our apartment in North Beach should have been the best ever—both of us the best, sober versions of ourselves, living without the annoyance of other people. Playing house. But our days began in anxiety and too often ended with me crying and us making promises of peace we seemed incapable of keeping.

By the end, I knew one thing for sure. Whatever relationship you are in right now, *that* is the relationship you're in. You're not in the future awesome relationship that may never happen. You're not in the possibility of it; you're in the reality of it. When my ex brought his mother to help move his stuff out, I sat downstairs at the French patisserie and ate my feelings. I promised myself that I wouldn't let the dream of a better, more harmonious connection allow me to stay in an exhausting relationship ever again.

I wanted to make my life work in that North Beach apartment, solo. Living alone sounded great in my mind, the epitome of adulthood. But that house felt haunted to me now, empty, lacking the ruckus of my and my boyfriend's habits—our fights,

7

sure, and the blaring of his reality television shows, but of our laughter, too, and our conversations. The silence was creepy. I barely used the kitchen, just snacked at the table. I never watched the TV, so there was no reason to sit on the futon. The little room I'd kept as an office, a tiny spot of privacy and quiet, was unnecessary now that the whole place was so private, so quiet. Not even the bedroom was a comfort; I'd paid for the mattress but had allowed my ex to select it, and it was hard as a rock to accommodate his aching back. I didn't want to be a grown-up if it meant being lonely and isolated, living in a tiny haunted house.

I put the word out to the people around me that I was looking for a new place in my old stomping ground, the Mission. I knew the chance of finding another affordable apartment to live in alone was unlikely in San Francisco with my fluctuating writer's income. I was in a tender, lonely state from the demise of my relationship. Even though it had been no good, we'd worked so hard and for so long. When I shared about it at a support group, an older, gray-haired woman took my hand. "It's like a death," she said knowingly.

Maybe roommates wouldn't be so bad, I thought. Maybe it would be nice to not be the only body in a house, stuck with my downer thoughts and aching heart. Maybe being a grown-up wasn't about the total independence of living alone, capable of paying 100 percent of the bills yourself. Maybe being a grown-up could be more about knowing what you really need and letting yourself have it. Even if what you need is to live in a household full of people half your age, in a bedroom meant to be a dining room, with a window that looks out onto the most beautiful, fiery persimmon tree you have ever seen in your life. Have you ever seen a persimmon tree? As all the other trees lose their leaves and begin their winter dying, the persimmon flares up brighter than any of them have ever been, bearing fruit, even. That was me. I wasn't on the same timetable as the other trees in the garden, but I was alive, coming into a certain prime, even. It wasn't starting over, no. It was just the newest chapter.

So, at thirty-seven, the most adult I'd ever been, I moved into a home that looked suspiciously like a lighter, slightly cleaner version of the Blue House.

Know what's a grown-up thing to do? Having movers move your shit for you. It cost me three hundred dollars for a trio of dudes to come and heft my vintage kitchen table, my flea market desk with the Bakelite handles, and my boxes and boxes and boxes of books from my apartment in North Beach to my new home in the Mission.

My new roommate Bernadette, a twentysomething writer, stood at the top of the stairs as the movers lugged my belongings into the house. "It's so cool that you're moving in," she gushed. "You have furniture!" In the kitchen, my yellow Formica table gleamed, the only piece of furniture in the room.

Bernadette took me on a tour. She brought me to the back door off the kitchen, where shambly stairs led to a tiny yard crammed with a billion plants that had gone to weedy seed in cracked pots and sawed-off milk jugs.

"The hoarder who lives in the garage took over the yard,"

Bernadette explained. "But people hang out here on the stairs. And smoke, obviously." She pointed to a dessert plate being used as an ashtray. There were so many spent cigarettes on it that at first glance, it didn't look like an ashtray at all. A grotesque installation, it resembled a Bloomin' Onion from the Outback Steakhouse, a circular configuration of butts rising out from the plate. It was absolutely disgusting, if somewhat fascinating.

Off a narrow hallway sat my new roommate Christopher's room. Christopher was a twink. He was as skinny as a string bean, with those undeserved muscles boys get simply for being boys, with wide blue eyes and a scoop of golden hair on his head. Christopher had grown up on a farm in the middle of nowhere, cultivating a fierce bitchiness to get by. He was sort of the "head roommate"— his name was the only one on the lease, and he was the only one who had the landlord's phone number.

Bernadette's bedroom was lined with books. A collection of feathered jewelry hung on the wall, and a giant broken mirror sat on the floor. Much of what I saw in the house appeared to have been dragged in from the street, a look I was familiar with. Back in the Blue House all of our furniture had been found on the street. The realization hit me: Everything the movers were lifting into the house was stuff I'd actually *bought*. Things I'd selected because they were what I desired, and I'd paid for them. None of them were pieces I'd pulled into my life because I just needed something—a table, a chair—and there it was, right there on the street, and it was free, and I had no money. I hadn't intended to weed out my curbside finds and replace them with nicer pieces; I just had, slowly, over time.

10

It was a breath of fresh air to leave my secluded North Beach apartment with its funeral dirges and memories of a broken relationship and land in this house, with young people for whom life was still new. Nightclubs were still exciting; bars were not drab. Music was something to be endlessly discovered, as were people, as was everything. My new roomies would be invigorating. The persimmon tree promised.

"It is cool that I'm moving in," I agreed with Bernadette. "I'm really excited to be here."


I referred to this new apartment as the Blue House Light, and in many ways it was. There was partying, for sure, but no all-night cocaine parties. If my roommates indulged, they did so at other people's houses, which seemed like the best you could hope for when cohabiting with twentysomethings who made their living bartending or enacting drag performances. The place was dirty, but there were no bugs, no mysterious fungi sprouting on moldering dish towels. And rather than a rebellious refusal to clean, there were sporadic, optimistic stabs at spiffing the house up, mostly by Christopher. Perhaps as part of his head roommate duties, he would sometimes wake early on a weekend, smoke a bowl of weed, and cheerfully mop the kitchen floor, scrub the crust off the stove, toss leftovers from the fridge, episodes of *Ab Fab* blaring from his computer all the while. Of course, no one's erratic attempts at cleanliness made much of a difference in the long run; what the shabby place needed was really a deep, *deep* cleaning, probably by professionals. I tried to stay out of the scant common space, in an effort to both avoid the yuck and not add to it. I kept to my bedroom.

Something about how roomy my bedroom was made it feel not so much like I was living with some twenty-year-olds and more like I had my own studio apartment in an old-timey building where I had to share the toilet and kitchen with other renters down the hall. I kept my room neat, even swept the hardwood floors, and cultivated the illusion that it was unconnected to the general mess outside the door. Working from home while Christopher and Bernadette were at their day jobs, I enjoyed the silence, punctuated only by the birds in the backyard. I'd sprawl on my bed during breaks throughout the day, flipping through magazines, or sit on the floor and make crush crafts for whatever current person I was obsessing over, beads and sequins getting stuck in the cracks in the boards. The house beyond, with its dirt and chaos, may not have felt exactly like home, but my sweet bedroom always did.

Of course, this was an illusion, and regularly the fantasy that I lived alone was dashed by cold, hard, noisy, dirty reality. Our walls were thin and I heard everyone most all the time: Bernadette's cowboy boots clacking on the floor as she nuked herself some grub and brought it back to her room to eat in bed in front of her TV set, curled under the covers with wicked PMS; Christopher blaring an obscure musical on his computer as he sat at the kitchen table eating the Popeyes takeout he grabbed over on Mission Street. The early evening was his break between his day job at a bank and his evening activities as a lascivious drag queen hosting events at gay-boy dive bars. Christopher was a Superman of sorts, changing from mild-mannered Castro banker to glitter-clumped metallic-clad Superqueen in our phone-booth-sized bathroom, leaving a trail of sparkle everywhere he went. I'd always hear him through my bedroom window as he sat outside on the back stairs, gabbing on his cell phone, smoking and ashing into the repulsive ashtray, its butts defying gravity as the accumulation grew upward and outward. Perhaps everyone was just trying to see how long it could go until it tumbled, like a disgusting house of cards. Or perhaps the game was to see which roommate would break and actually empty it. It wasn't going to be me; I felt it should be emptied by one of the more habitual smokers. Plus, I figured it came with the territory of a house of twentysomethings, and I stayed strong in my refusal to take on the Sisyphean task of trying to keep any part of the slovenly house clean.

I never got mad at my roommates for the decrepit state of the house, for their drunken entrances in the middle of the night, loud enough to wake me. I would simply remember my own twenties, and reflect on notions of karma. *You probably deserve this* became my mantra.

Whenever Christopher tromped up the stairs at two a.m., singing show tunes at the top of his lungs, I remembered the Blue House, not so different from this one except it had been worse, in all ways one could judge a home—in its uncleanliness, its disrepair, its odors, its inhabitants' imbibing of drugs and alcohol, its hosting of sordid activities. Listening to Christopher straining to get his voice into territory that is off-limits to anyone but Ethel Merman, I recalled the after-parties I once brought home from the bar, how the telephone would ring and ring and not one of us would answer it, as it could only be one person—Cort, our landlord, whom we were keeping up with our laughter and our music, and the occasional wrestling match that would tumble onto the floor above his head.

When the buzzer rang late at night and Christopher would lead into our home a man he had just met—no, was just meeting now, for the first time, at the foot of our stairway—when he led the man into his bedroom and then left his Chihuahua crated in the kitchen to bark and bark and bark into the night, obscuring the sex sounds streaming from Christopher's boudoir, I would think, *You deserve this,* and remember my old Blue House roommate Elsbeth. She would creep from her room in the dead of night to glare at us, the after-party, all of us high on cocaine and *talking*—talking loudly, talking over one another, talking compulsively, talking as if the words in our mouths were bits of food and we were all starving. "Could you all please shut the fuck up—I'm sleeping!" Elsbeth would bravely share her needs with us and then return to her room, slamming the door. There would be a moment of stunned silence as our addled minds, momentarily derailed, struggled to get back on track. Compared to my coked-out after-parties, Christopher's booty calls and show tunes were really the *least* I deserved.

As if Karma herself recognized I was getting off a little easy in the raucous-roommate department, while I was taking a shower one night, the bathroom door was flung open and Christopher barged in, likewise naked. "Do you mind?" he asked, and proceeded to fumble around in the moldy and overstuffed shelves, ancient beauty products tumbling to the slick linoleum floor. "I got a date and have to wash my ass out." I could tell by his general aura that Christopher was drunk, or maybe very stoned, or perhaps on cocaine, maybe with a bit of Xanax to take the edge off the edge. The faucet turned on and Christopher began to sing a show tune. He did his business in the sink, and left.

I shut off the shower and stood, dripping, among the grime. *You deserve this*, I thought, recalling the many times I'd imposed my sex life on my roommates, either through the vibrato of my cries or by doing it in the living room when I thought no one was home or barging into a roommate's bedroom, half-naked, demanding safe-sex supplies.

I think Christopher was always trying to shock me a little, playfully. As a sober person and an older person whose wild ways were behind her, I could provide the appropriate gasp and "*Chris-to-pher!*" when he performed his wildness for me. I wasn't really shocked by drug-addled twentysomethings cavorting naked through the hallways. But it was beginning to feel a bit shocking that *this was where I lived*. Was I in denial about how screwy and sad it was to live among such youthful disarray? Should I be more concerned? I was, and I wasn't. There was part of me that was entertained, and that part of me was also secure in the knowledge that I was just living here temporarily. Passing through. Taking my mind off my breakup, making sure I didn't lapse into loneliness. But what if I lapsed into something else? What if I just thought I was a visitor, but then I woke up fifty years old still sharing a house with a rotating cast of twenty-three-year-old bartenders?

But I wasn't fifty. Not yet. I was thirty-eight, which felt ancient only in comparison with my roommates. I soothed my nerves with a cigarette out on the back porch, flicking the ashes into the Bloomin' Onion. When in Rome.

About a month later, I turned the corner by the artisanal pork and oyster restaurant and spied an ambulance at the other end of the block. I just *knew* it was at my house. It was possibly there to dig the reclusive alcoholic hoarder out from under a pile of newspaper and succulents, but more likely it was for one of my roommates. I opened the gate and found the door to our apartment swung open, the stairwell lined with EMTs and Christopher at the top, cursing.

"What's going on?" I asked innocently.

"This your roommate?" an EMT asked, thumbing at Christopher.

"Christopher, what's wrong?"

"What's wrong is, I am having a fucking *heart attack*, and these assholes don't fucking *care* that I have to find my house keys before I leave, and I can't find them, and I am having a fucking *heart attack*!"

"We do care," said an EMT in a tone that suggested he had said this many times to Christopher. "But there is a five-alarm fire happening in the city and there are a lot more calls we need to make, so we'd like to get you in the vehicle."

"Just go." Christopher flipped his hands. "Why don't you go rescue important people, then, and just leave me here to *die*!"

"Christopher, don't worry about your keys," I said to him. "I'll be here. I'll let you in when you get home. Just go."

"Don't fucking touch me," he snapped at an EMT attempting to gently help him down the stairs.

The doorbell rang hours later, waking me up. It was Christopher, barefoot on the street, smoking and tranquilized. "I was having a panic attack," he explained. "Once they got me in the ambulance I calmed down and started hitting on them. They loved me."

I unlatched the front gate and let Christopher in. *You deserve this*, I thought, recalling an anxiety attack that a former Blue House roommate had experienced upon realizing just what it meant to live in a home where the residents had sworn off cleaning. Those days were behind me—so why relive them? Why live in a home where you are actually afraid to put your hand into certain cabinets, because there are mouse droppings behind the stove and indeed you have seen mice dash across the kitchen floor and you are scared that there is a huge colony living in one of the cabinets, cabinets no one uses because in this home no one uses the kitchen, for no one cooks? I was haunted by these questions. After living as an extreme dirtbag for so long, the ability to withstand grime was a solid life skill that I possessed. I could imagine many situations in which this skill would be prized—after the apocalypse, for example. On a *Survivor*-type reality show. If I was ever kidnapped and thrown into a dungeon. I'd be quicker to thrive in these situations than, say, someone who'd been consistently mopping their floors their whole life. Right?

As fanciful as such thoughts were, the other side of that coin was that I could withstand living in a dirty place because it was familiar. I'd done it so long, it was something I genuinely understood how to do. Maybe I'd started honing this skill because I was impoverished, and an alcoholic to boot. I'd taken comfort in being able to withstand conditions that many people couldn't. I was *tough*. Where I come from, toughness is prized more than cleanliness, much closer to godliness, if your god was a rough motherfucker. I felt a crooked pride; I was superior to folks whose privileged lives would see to it that they never had to figure out how to cohabit with cockroaches.

But I wasn't that person anymore. Sure, I was proud of who I was in the world and I embraced every single little messed-up circumstance that shaped me. But I didn't think it meant what I used to think it meant—that I was somehow better than anyone, that it built character. The simple fact was, I had moved in with the twentysomethings because I'd needed a cheap place to live in my most desirable neighborhood. And the thought of moving again, so soon, was scary and overwhelming. San Francisco was notoriously expensive, getting more notorious and expensive by the year. Maybe this was the best a single person who made her living writing could hope for.

*Resentment is like drinking poison and expecting your enemy to die*, many a sage former drunkard has said. I tried to avoid situations I knew would just cause me to burn up with gripes and grievances. So I lived as my comrades lived, eating mostly takeout and things I could grab from the disgusting fridge and bring into my room. I never forgot that I had known what I was getting into when I moved in. Unlike my old relationship, which I'd never stopped trying to change, I was under no illusion that my house belonged to me. This house belonged to the young. Every bit of dirt, every empty wine bottle, every booty call was meant to be here. I was the one who didn't belong.

Knowing it wasn't time for me to move just yet, I took more 12-step-program advice and made a gratitude list about it. I scribbled in my notebook: big room, cheerful roommates, local pigeons, cheap rent. And I realized there was something else about living with my PMS-ing, panic-prone roommates that I was grateful for.

I'd changed since my twenties. And though some of these changes had been life altering, enormous enough for me to be *very* aware of them, many were small, subtle, and cumulative. In some ways I still lived like a twentysomething, and I sort of prided myself on my youthfulness. But in most ways, I didn't. My ideologies had changed—no small deal for a person who was once 100 percent ideology fueled. My hobbies, the things I did for enjoyment had changed. What I did and didn't do to my body had changed. My income had changed, and perhaps as a result, so had my style, my taste. What I thought was acceptable or unacceptable behavior had changed. My friends had changed (my lovers, not so much). How I expressed myself had changed. I was not the person I was when I was twenty-five, and living with a bunch of twentysomethings was sometimes-fascinating proof of this.

Which brings me to Christopher's second panic attack. It began as a simple knock on my door during a quiet afternoon at home. I was at work in the office part of my imaginary studio apartment. I'd thought Christopher was at work, too, but there he was, timid at my door.

He had made a major change a month or so prior to this: a pledge to stop drinking and smoking pot and snorting coke. The removal of what really is a structure—a social structure, a coping structure, a structure by which you've come to know yourself—is devastating. Even though it's unarguably a positive change, it's also an apocalypse. All kinds of things lurk under your booze intake—your feelings, for instance. Your hopes and fears, your chronic anxieties, whatever chemical imbalance you might be living with. Your past, and your future. Christopher, prone to panic when he was imbibing, found himself plagued with anxiety attacks when he tried to face life sober. He rapped on my door and called out in a child's voice, "Michelle? Can I talk to you? I'm having a panic attack."

When I first stopped drinking and smoking pot and snorting coke and snorting speed and snorting heroin and snorting ecstasy and chomping hallucinogenic mushrooms, I felt a lot of panic, too. Every morning, panic woke me up, as harsh as an alarm clock, a bolt in my chest where my heart was. My eyes would snap open. Blood would suddenly rush through my veins like a death coaster at Great America. *Oh, great. I'm awake. I'm alive. I'm an alcoholic. How miserable, how humiliating. I'll never drink again. I'll never be happy again. Time to get up.*

I gave Christopher the basics. "You're fine. You're not going to die. Panic makes you feel like you are, but you're really, really not. Just trust it." He refused to lie down because he thought his heart would stop beating. He was afraid to take the calming herbs I offered in case they killed him. He agreed to a cup of tea, which I boiled for him on the greasy stove.

The thing about panic is the more you talk about it, the more you feed it. It's like having a bad trip on acid. You don't want to sit down with a hallucinator and be all, "How you feeling—pretty crazy, huh? Feel like you're losing your mind? Like you'll never come back? What are you looking at over there, a three-headed turtle that looks like your mom, playing a ukulele?" Same goes for panic.

After offering Christopher some reassurances that he didn't believe, I made him the tea and we just talked. I talked about life like life is no big deal, nothing scary, not the void, just this endless stream of moments, some good, some bad, and we are *all* in it together. Here we all are, figuring it out. I talked about the book I was writing, how it was hard. I talked about the flock of pigeons that lived behind our house, how sometimes they all took off with such a *crack* it startled me. How the bunch of them blotted the sun, stippled it like a strobe light with the flap of their wings. I brought it around to my sobriety, how I used to have panic attacks, but they went away.

"That's why I wanted to talk to you," Christopher said. "You're so calm."

Stop everything. "Me?" I asked, incredulous. "You think I'm a calm person?" I didn't want to make his panic attack all about me, but this was wild. An ex of mine once told me she'd avoided being my friend, let alone dating me, for months, because she was sure I was a speed freak. This was during my early, innocent days in San Francisco, before I had even heard of crystal meth. I was not a calm person. I talked fast, and constantly. I was riled up. I had opinions. They were important. They were probably more important than yours, and I would argue with you forever, just to be sure.

"Yes, you are so calm," Christopher insisted, kindly taking a moment from his panic attack to flatter me. In 12-step they tell you that the best thing to do when you are in psychological pain is to focus on something other than yourself, so perhaps I was doing Christopher a favor by directing the conversation toward me.

"Aren't I talking all the time?" I prodded. "Aren't I so loud?"

Christopher thought about it, and shrugged. "No, you're not. You're really calm, and you have your shit together. You're sober, you're a published writer, you're . . . healthy."

Perhaps compared to a newly sober baby drag queen in the grip of a panic attack, I did have all my shit together. Such assessments are relative. But what really struck me was that compared to *myself* at any other point in my life, I really *did* have all my shit together. When it's hard for you to grow up—because you're poor and can't afford the trinkets and milestones of adulthood, or you're gay and the mating rites of passage don't seem to apply to you, or you are sensitive to the world's injustices and decided long ago that if being a grown-up means being an asshole you'll carry out your days in Neverland with the rest of the Lost Children, thank you very much—when adulthood seems somehow off-limits to you, growing up takes time. You have to want it, and then you have to make a lot of changes. Some changes you make consciously and some without knowing it, and some changes get made for you. It's so much work I forgot I was even engaged in it; it just became *life*.

Sometimes you're so caught in old ideas about yourself, it

takes another person to show you who you actually are today. And the person you are today is a lot more grown-up than last time you checked.

About a month after Christopher's panic attack, the day before Thanksgiving, I was preparing two dishes to bring to a dinner. The first dish was sort of a joke, sort of not—broccoli Velveeta casserole. It's a joke because anything with Velveeta in it is a joke. It's not a joke because anything with Velveeta in it is delicious. I call it my heirloom recipe, but the truth is my mom started making it after I was grown and had moved out of her house. Still, it's *emotionally* my heirloom recipe. To make it, you steam a bunch of broccoli, or, if you're really aiming for authenticity, buy it frozen and nuke it in the microwave. Spread it across a casserole dish. Cut thick slabs from your surprisingly expensive loaf of Velveeta, and layer it over the broccoli. When the broccoli is obscured, take a sleeve of Ritz crackers and crumble them in your hands. Scatter them over the Velveeta. Next, melt some butter. How much butter? According to my mother, just enough to wet the crackers. Or, in the accent of our homeland, the North Shore of Boston, "Just anough ta wet tha crackahs." Once you've wet the crackahs, shove the casserole in the oven and bake it till it's an unholy cauldron of cheesy goodness.

If the broccoli Velveeta casserole was a metaphor for who I'd been, butternut squash with goat cheese and hazelnuts was a metaphor for who I was today. The recipe came not from my mom but from Epicurious, and was recommended by a foodie friend of my sister. It called for the roasting of hazelnuts and then the peeling of their skins from their hot little bodies. In my family we called hazelnuts *filberts*. We also called dinner *supper*, the living room the *parlor*, soda *tonic*, a porch a *piazza*, and compost *swill*. The North Shore of Boston in the 1970s and perhaps still today contains pockets of curious old-world language and customs.

I was excited to bring my bipolar, high-low side dishes to the Thanksgiving I'd be celebrating with my friends, the lot of them like me, people from low-income families who'd made it out of our depressing hometowns into lives as artists, teachers, non-profit workers. None of us were quite sure how we'd done it, and many of us were plagued by guilt at the poor or alcoholic or mentally ill family members we'd left behind, haunted by the puzzle of how we'd figured out how to have such great lives when others, people we loved, hadn't. It was luck—no, we worked hard. It was hard work—no, everyone works hard. We were very lucky.

I knew my friends would appreciate and enjoy both dishes. I snuggled the butternut squash with goat cheese and hazelnuts in plastic wrap and took it with the Velveeta masterpiece to the fridge. I opened it up and peered into the graveyard of meals past, realizing I was going to have to toss a lot of leftovers to make room for my casseroles.

As I started throwing things away, I noticed a fly. Gross. I kept working, tossing a half dozen half-drunk Odwallas, all past their sell-by date. Oh look, more flies. Weird. None of them were flying. They looked decrepit, more decrepit than your average fly. The fridge was literally crawling with flies, flies too cold, their wings too shriveled, to fly. Gross. How long had they been in there?

It was a terrible question—*How long has a swarm of flies been living* inside *my refrigerator?* Well, from birth, of course. There was no other way there could have been such numbers, all of them in the same crippled condition. Oh, and what are baby flies called? Maggots.

The fridge had maggots. Or rather, it used to have maggots. The maggots actually were able to gestate and grow up into this marginally functional group of adult flies staring at me from the shelves. Flies healthy enough to have perhaps laid the next generation of flies—maggots—elsewhere in the refrigerator, perhaps behind that produce bag filled with brown, liquefied vegetables, to the right of the gallon of SunnyD that had a sell-by date of 2004.

I shut the door. My heart was racing. I felt like a chick in a horror movie. If I were to open the door again, what would I see this time? If I'd previously been grossed out by the fridge, now I was terrified of it.

I called my two best friends. Conveniently, they were girlfriends and lived in the same place, about a fifteen-minute walk from my maggoty flophouse.

"Hi, can I bring over our Thanksgiving sides and put them in your fridge? Mine has maggots." I didn't sob as I said this, nor was my voice shrill with horror, as would be appropriate. I said it the way my friends and I share all of life's miniature tragedies, the humiliations that pop up right when you think you have it together, to echo your psyche with a wicked cackle: *You'll never be a grown-up! You'll always be a dirtbag! Your ignoble provenance is etched into your very soul, and any attempt to have a normal adult-hood will be punished by a* plague of maggots!

I said it like it was sort of a joke, the dark domestic humor of a satanic Erma Bombeck.

Of course my friends let me come over and store my Thanks-giving dishes in their nice, clean fridge. They appreciated the outlandish gallows humor I had about the situation. But because they are true friends, they could also see how it was *not* funny to find your fridge teeming with flies that were perhaps literally born yesterday. "What are you going to do?" they asked. "Are you go-ing to call the landlord? Is anyone going to clean it? Are you going to get one of those little dorm-room fridges to just keep in your bedroom?"

That I was living in a home where I might be better off with a dorm-style mini-fridge in my bedroom revealed how bad my situation really was. I was by now thirty-nine years old, living with people under the age of twenty-five and a fridge full of mag-gots.

If I turned forty while still living there, I was going to have really low self-esteem. My birthday is in February. I had two months to find a place to live.

That night I hopped into bed and cuddled under my blan-kets. Sometimes my roomy room got so chilly that I piled all the pillows I had on top of me and tried to stay very, very still in my sleep so as not to send the jumble tumbling to the floor. My space heater looked like it was made in 1960, and Bernadette had found it on the street. She had passed it to me after upgrading. It occurred to me that I, too, could upgrade my space heater, buy one I could leave on overnight without fearing it would burst into flames. And I could buy a quilt, some cozier blankets. I know some people are born understanding things like this, or maybe they were raised with a solid quality of life that never wavered as they grew up. They know that the latest-model space heater and a high-quality comforter are their birthright.

I am not one of those people, no matter how many designer purses I manage to swindle into my closet, no matter how many trips to Paris I finagle. I am someone whose path to adulthood is not a clear A to B, a straight line through life. My path is more like A, B, back to A, but it's a different A this time, and now B looks so different from my time back at A—and whoa, here's C, what a trip! I'm a grown-up!

Unable to sleep, kept awake by the cold and the inspiration of my brand-new plan to finally move out, I climbed out of bed and went over to my window. Gazing out that back window at the persimmon tree in full fiery flare, I said a prayer. *Please, I know I can live better than this. Give me a chance, Universe. Hook me up. My time here is done. I'm ready for the next level—someplace clean, someplace adult. I deserve it. You know I do.*

# 2.

# Fashion Victim

Dear stranger, let me explain to you my love for fashion. I love fashion more than *anything*. If I have one regret in my life, it is not that I didn't go to college or live in New York City; it is that I didn't somehow claw my way into the fashion industry. I have loved style ever since I can remember, and I have paid dearly for it. From scream fights with my mom to having debris flung at me on the street, I learned very early that the whimsical dress-up box of childhood slams hard on the fingers of a person who wishes to maintain a sense of theater in her appearance well into her later years.

My childhood memories seem organized around what I was wearing when: the white party dress covered with colorful balloons that I was wearing when I jumped into the hotel pool while on vacation with my grandparents. The pair of denim jeans with "The Best" embroidered on the hip pocket I wore to the library.

The brown polyester and chiffon Easter dress I pitched a crying fit over: Really? *Brown* at Easter? I was *so upset.*

Actually, lots of my fashion memories feature if not *me* being so upset, then some adult in my immediate vicinity feeling provoked by my choices. Around first grade I dressed myself in a colorful combination of clothing (a red skirt, a yellow shirt, some aqua sandals), only to be told by an aunt that I looked like a Puerto Rican—an obvious compliment, yet those in my family seemed to think otherwise. My first experience of high fashion came at first Communion, when I was actually *required* to wear not only a dress with layers and layers of frothy white lace, but an actual *crown* made of shiny fake pearls. From the crown cascaded a motherfucking *veil.* Never again would I be so thrilled to be part of the Catholic Church! I persuaded the powers that be to allow me to visit Benson's Animal Farm, a scrubby petting zoo with attendant low-rent carnival rides, in this outfit, which I told people all day long made me feel like a princess. Nobody liked the scrim of dust I'd kicked up over that once pristinely white lace hem, or the way my veil got mangled on the roller coaster. My family seemed to have an unhealthy fashion philosophy—while it probably *is* the most important thing on earth, the only art form we all participate in every single day of our lives, they thought it should never be taken so seriously.

In sixth grade, the slutty eighties were in full swing, and MTV was beaming images of Missing Persons' Dale Bozzio wearing see-through miniature plastic outfits. I was in love with her, and in love with my boobalicious Barbies, and in love with all the sexy ladies I was stealing glimpses of on cable TV. One day, my godmother took me shopping at the Salvation Army. All the women in my family love the Salvation Army, half because everyone is broke and half because they have antiquing in their blood. They have an eye for snagging the luxury items unrecognized as such by Army management and given a ridiculously low price tag. I was not looking for anything so refined on this particular trip with my godmother, but more something Dale Bozzio would approve of. I quickly became obsessed with a pair of high-heeled clogs that I found in a bin of jumbled shoes. My godmother (who had married a Mormon and converted) squinted at the incredibly high wooden heel.

"Well," she said uneasily, "I guess you can play dress-up in them."

At home, my godmother sat in the kitchen with Mom drinking cups of decaffeinated tea while I assembled my Most Awesome Outfit Ever: my new skyscraper clogs plus a flirty bright-red miniskirt plus my pièce de résistance—a red-and-white-striped tube top. Not the type of tube top that wraps around your ribs, mind you, but a bandeau-style tube top, the smallest tube, which wrapped around my smallest, nonexistent boobs. Any of my Barbies would have looked excellent in this getup, as would any new-wave pop star on MTV, or any sexy hitchhiker on an episode of CHiPs.

"I'm going out!" I yelled casually to my mother and went to slip out the front door.

"Come say good-bye to your godmother," my mother hollered back. Or, Come say good-bye to ya gawdmutha.

I wobbled into the kitchen. I bent down from my new height to give my gawdmutha a kiss. I acted like it was no big whoop that I was dressed like a sluttier version of Jodie Foster in *Taxi Driver*.

"Oh no," my mother said. "You're not goin' out like that. Someone's gonna grab you."

"Virginia, I only bought those for her to play dress-up in," my godmother defended herself.

I *was* playing dress-up. I just wanted to play it outside. On the street. Where a cute boy might see me and be dumbstruck by how *awesome* I looked and fall in love with me so my life could finally start. Even though I looked like a PSA for the exploitation of underage girls, I actually had no idea there was anything inappropriate about my outfit. I just thought I looked really, really cool.

This blind spot would haunt me throughout my life. I always had a difficult time determining what outfits were appropriate for what situations, and this difficulty produced a frustration I could only relieve with rebellion. My petty little life in Chelsea, Massachusetts, was never going to provide me with the opportunity to wear the dramatic, decadent outfits I longed to dress in, and so mundane events would have to do. The occasional no-uniform days my Catholic school offered, for example. To a school-wide Christmas party in sixth grade I wore a striped mini-dress with actual ballet shoes as footwear and a feathered roach clip in my hair. A bean-shaped pleather Jordache cross-body purse cut across me on its ropy strap. The principal phoned my mother and asked her to please deliver a less-totally-awesome outfit for me to change into, and so my pictures on Santa's lap that year featured me wearing a patchwork sack dress straight out of *Little House on the Prairie*. And I loved *Little House*, but word of Valley Girl culture had reached as far as Chelsea, and I was trying to look less prairie, more galleria.

The persecution was just beginning. By seventh grade I was taunted by classmates for my amazing hot-pink-and-black geometric-patterned sweat suit, jeered at for being "punk." I was baffled—they said "punk" like it was a bad thing! A fight with Mom over what I would wear in my class pictures resulted in a photo of me red-faced, eyes swollen from crying, in a pastel sweater decorated with dancing teddy bears, the black-and-white-checked tunic with the spiked belt and asymmetrical-snap collar in a ball of defeat on my bedroom floor.

My fashion sense nearly prevented me from graduating eighth grade, because I had the audacity to wear a strapless dress to the ceremony. The principal—a nun whose own sweaters were suspiciously tight—called the dress "amoral," and declared that I did not look like the product of a Catholic upbringing. I wasn't exactly sure what she was getting at, but I knew I *did* look like Cyndi Lauper, minus the orange hair (not for long!), and the only thing wrong with that outfit was the shapeless gold robe I had to cover it all up with to walk down the aisle. Sister Gertrude and I had spent the final months of my education in a ridiculous stalemate: Each morning, as the class pledged allegiance to the flag, she waited at the glass pane of the classroom door, glaring at me. As our childish voices chorused, "and justice for all," she would swing open the door and march me to the bathroom to oversee the scrubbing away of my navy-blue eyeliner. Every morning I arrived at Our Lady of Assumption School with my eyes smudgily ringed in Wet n Wild, and within an hour I was rubbing it off with a scratchy paper towel. I couldn't give in to Sister Gertrude, and Sister Gertrude couldn't give in to me. When I graduated, she went as far as to create a new dress code handbook for every future student to ponder, complete with crude drawings illustrating what a "punk" haircut looked like (it looked, frankly, like a mullet).

Starting afresh at my next Catholic school—high school this time, and all-girl at that—I dyed my hair black against my mother's wishes. She feared it would make me look like my father, whose existence we as a family were trying to forget. It might have brought out that family resemblance if I hadn't teased it into a sprawling inky mushroom cloud upon my head, with bangs that cascaded into my face, making it hard to see. This fantastic hairdo made my classmates at the all-girl Catholic school furious. I scooted out of class early each day to avoid a pummeling by the beefy Italian girls who were driven to rage at the sight of my tangles. Eventually the principal saw fit to put a stop to this bullying, dealing with it by kicking me out of school so that my classmates' education would not be ruined by the constant distraction of my hair.

I enrolled in the local public school, where I was shoved in the hallway for wearing, out of season, the Elvira-brand black lipstick sold at drugstores each Halloween. I became an acolyte of the darker operas of punk and Goth. The world recognizes these subcultures now, but in the mid-1980s, adopting the look with the dedication I did—black lipstick, hair teased to the point of total destruction—outside the East Village or Camden Row was enough to get you killed. Okay, beat up. I hid in the bathroom or in empty classrooms during lunchtime, and I didn't talk about it at home. My mother would never have understood—she thought I looked crazy, too, and seemed to have more sympathy for the people moved to violence by my appearance than she did for me. After all, I could just dress normal and everyone would leave me alone. But I *couldn't* dress normal. That was the thing.

Though such violent disapproval of one's clothing selections could send many people back to the closet in search of something softer, my instinct was to fight back. I knew that there was nothing wrong with wearing, say, a black lace slip as a dress, with a pair of black Doc Martens. That the sight of me in such a getup could inspire a person to shout horrible, unprintable names at me on the street seemed a bit of an overreaction. Capitulating to the bad vibes the world was aiming at me felt like giving in to bullying, and it would have been.

Getting beat up for the way you look as a teenager is going to force you to make some hard and fast decisions about not just your life, but *life*. It will turn you into a little philosopher, which, by the way, goes very nicely with a high-necked black lace dress and a prim patent-leather purse. Whatever dent to my self-esteem the harassment may have given me, submitting to such meanness seemed far more dangerous. I didn't just like how I looked—I loved it. No amount of negative reactions could convince me that I didn't look totally awesome with my hair crawling off my scalp like a blue-black tarantula, that the oversize crucifix intended to be hung on a wall didn't actually make a fantastic statement necklace. The joy I felt in discovering new looks, in exploring and feeding my burgeoning vanity, outweighed the stress of feeling vulnerable to attack.

I was young, and not so worldly, but somehow I understood that my style triggered not so much a punk hatred as a general xenophobia that included gay people, people of color, and homeless people. Anyone different from my straight, white, mostly male attackers earned their wrath. A larger understanding of oppression began to grow and, hardly knowing a gay person, a homeless person, or a person of color, I aligned myself with them in the world. And in this way my fashion both cast me out of the prevailing culture and signaled to the world my disdain of it. I hadn't started my fashion career angry at the world, but after years of having soda cans flung at your head, you sort of end up there.

My point, and I do hope I've made it, is that I'm a fashion person, down to my bones. As much as I hate when people redeem the needless suffering life has heaped upon them by saying it "made me who I am today," I suppose I could admit the same about the decade or so I spent weathering the punishment our culture sometimes metes out to the differently dressed. Sure, as a sensitive person with strong empathy, I probably would have been drawn to social justice causes no matter what I looked like, but experiencing repressive violence firsthand at such a formative age gave me a political consciousness that has shaped much of my life. It taught me a rugged compassion, and it gave me a longing to take some of the fight I have in me and offer it to those who could use some.

There was one dark fashion era, around age twenty-one, when my interest in social justice actually accomplished what so much bullying had failed to do—it broke my fashion spirit. I became obsessed with second-wave radical lesbian feminism *and* fiercely dedicated to animal rights, which prompted me to shave my head and wear nothing but oversize jeans held to my bony vegan hips with a hemp belt and Tevas on my feet regardless of the season. I got my groove back eventually, but honestly, my political affiliations have remained a constant challenge to my fashion tendencies. It can be hard to care about poverty and economic disparity and also immerse yourself in the fantasy world of fashion magazines, where the garments are often so expensive the price isn't printed. There is a dissonance in being a believer in a new standard of beauty, one that includes all races and body sizes and genders, while developing strange obsessions for particular models and feeling your heart skip absurdly when you recognize them in an editorial—in being a nonconforming, rebellious sort, yet turning hungrily to an industry that instructs you what to cease wearing and what to wear instead; instruction I actually believe.

But, for all the paradoxical mind-fuckery, there was something powerful in my embrace of fashion, something that felt alluring and confusing, yet correct. And that was beauty. *Beauty*. During my conflicted fashion moment, beauty seemed more a tool used to whack women around with than anything else. Looking to subvert if not destroy the concept, I'd cultivated a "beauty" in myself that seemed at odds with the current standards—weird where I could be normal, torn where I could be tailored. I'd set out to widen my scope of beauty to include forms mainstream culture ignored or punished. But what I'd done along the way was demonize the rest of it. In this process, beauty had become my enemy. And suddenly I wanted to be its friend. I think it had something to do with getting sober—how thirsty I was for new things to occupy my psyche, or how the spiritual practice that was helping me stay away from alcohol cautioned against buying into the illusion that *anything* was my enemy. It seemed, after decades of fighting, of reveling in the sharp power of *No!* that the most radical thing left for me was a gigantic, all-encompassing *Yes!*

Let me introduce you to my dear friend Annie. Like me, Annie is in recovery from a bout of radical feminism that temporarily destroyed her amazing aesthetic (think cherry-red or platinum-blond untamed corkscrew curls, Vivienne Westwood Melissa jelly stilettos, and body-con micro-minis). Reared in the same sort of low-income urban decay as I'd been, she, too, struggled to balance her desire for nice things with the knowledge that much of the world doesn't have *food*, let alone a pair of Stella McCartney sandals. (Hey, at least they're vegan!)

Annie has great fashion sense, putting together outfits like a dumpster dress with Dior pumps and a leather jacket she had an artist friend paint the back of. Or a pair of leggings made to look like golden peacock feathers paired with giant clompy ankle boots and an actual—or phony—Balenciaga bag dangling from the crook of her arm. It was with Annie that I bought my first fake designer purse, on Canal Street in New York City, a Louis Vuitton Alma knockoff with multicolored monogram, a big "leather" bow, a gleaming little lock that came with an actual key, *and* a dust bag. It looked so convincing, so expensive, that people treated me differently when I carried it. Saleswomen in department stores were nice to me, and salesgirls in cool little boutiques snubbed me. I had mixed feelings about passing as wealthy. On the one hand, I had lived through grunge fashion, when every trust fund baby was decked out in a torn flannel and an ironic trucker cap. It seemed only appropriate that I, a poor person, should appropriate posh style. But when the girls working minimum wage at the movie multiplex started whispering about my bag, I couldn't bear to have them believe I was a richy-rich. As someone long impoverished, I had a strong sense of solidarity with the downtrodden, and I didn't want this illusion of wealth to come between me and my sisters.

"It's fake!" I hissed at them with a wink and a smile. Like, *You could have one, too!* Fake designer fashion is political! It's the great equalizer! No more class hierarchies, not if my thirty-dollar Louis Faux-ton buys me the same class deference as a two-thousand-dollar "real" one! And who is to say what is "real" anymore? I didn't go to college, but I have a feeling that some people have written some papers on this subject.

But the Cineplex girls gave me stink-face when they learned my purse was not legit. Why would I brag about such a thing? Ugh! One even snorted at me. "Fake!" Then they all turned and laughed at me. *Well, at least I'm not making minimum wage at the mall!* I thought, all class solidarity evaporated before you can say *reality television.*

Annie helped me get closer to fashion in other ways as well. Once, on a road trip, we drove straight across the country, anxious to get the rental car back before we got charged extra. This meant nonstop driving, a brutal and dangerous game in which we sort of lost our minds. We drank Red Bull and chewed caffeinated gum and rolled down the windows so the wind could smack us in the face. And we read fashion magazines.

For miles and miles, I held pages of *Vogue* or *Elle* or *Harper's Bazaar* open to Annie, who would take her eyes off the road to gaze at the goods on each page. We played *What is the ugliest thing on this page, Guess how much that purse costs,* and *What on this page is the most "me"?* Also, desperate to get as much mileage as possible from each magazine on our journey, *Who would you have sex with on this page and yes, you absolutely have to pick someone.*

By the end of the trip, I was hooked on fashion magazines. I was hooked on them in the way that a person gets hooked on things when repeatedly exposed to them while being deprived of sleep and nutrition. I remedied this new need by getting fake subscriptions to all of them. A fake subscription, by the way, is when you put a fake name and a real address on a subscription card and check "bill me later." You'll get a handful of magazines before they cut you off. It's stealing, basically, a sort of benevolent scam well known to the broke and fashion obsessed (in the eighties, when I was broke and music obsessed, I ran a similar scam with the long-defunct Columbia Record and Tape Club, getting a bunch of Van Halen and AC/DC tapes for a penny). For the scam, I came up with the pen name Angelica Ford—clearly a rich woman who had been raised right in this world, raised with privilege, who had probably modeled before marrying a shipping heir from a country that still had a monarchy.

My magazines came pouring in, regenerating a love I hadn't indulged since back before the days of radical feminism. In my youth, in high school, and in the early nineties, I had loved high fashion. Madonna had paved the way for me to know Jean Paul Gaultier, and Vivienne Westwood was the perfect bridge between the world of the Sex Pistols and the world of Chanel. I was thrilled to reacquaint myself with both designers, and to learn about a whole bunch more.

My new morning ritual was to read the magazines with a French press of coffee. This was less than a year into my sobriety, and the novelty of mornings had not worn off. Alcoholics don't get mornings. Waking up without nausea, without a splitting headache, without the shakes, sitting in a kitchen that is actually clean, and cute, and paging through fashion magazines while starting the day—it was marvelous. How I loved starting my day with fantasy, with luxury! Even though I was still relegated to shopping at thrift stores, the education the magazines were giving me had sharpened my eye. I couldn't afford that black-and-gold Miu Miu cocktail dress, but when I saw the eighties version of it hanging in Thrift Town, I knew it to be a fantastic approximation.

As my magazines began to dry up from lack of payment, I became sad. Then I looked at what my *Vogue* subscription actually cost. It cost *ten dollars*. A *year*! Ten dollars! Well, I would spend ten dollars this week alone on burritos! I realized that I was making decisions with an old brain, having not yet grown into this new brain—a sober brain, a brain that maybe didn't want to look and act like a giant angry dirtbag for the rest of her life. A brain that was maybe perhaps hesitantly interested in *growing up*—whatever that was.

Despite the training wheels tacked onto its lobes, my new brain recognized that even *I* could afford a ten-dollar annual magazine subscription. And so when the next you-better-pay-or-we're-shutting-you-off-we-*mean-it*-this-time envelope came, I stuffed a check for ten dollars inside it. And I crossed out the name ANGELICA FORD and replaced it with MICHELLE TEA.

Between my cheap rent and the grand trine of a book advance, a literary grant, and a high-paying job at a fancy women's college, I suddenly had enough money to buy something big. Something expensive. Something I wouldn't want anyone around me to know I could afford, lest they all turn against me in hate and envy. It had been a long time since I'd slunk down a city street to cop drugs—skittish about being seen, slightly guilty about what I was doing, yet also experiencing a deep, dark thrill—but walking up to the possibility of spending a bunch of money on a luxury item felt very familiar.

The object I'd been lusting after was a leather hoodie, one I'd first seen in the pages of *Elle*, and then in *Nylon*. Just the word combo—*leather hoodie*—was enough to get me a little high. Since getting sober, I'd found the most interesting things could get my body, desperate for intoxication, a bit high: spectator pumps, Mark Rothko paintings, the color orange, driving under overpasses, and the phrase "leather hoodie." It was leather—how luxurious, how glamorous! It was a hoodie—how tough, how street! It seemed a nice way to slide into the realm of higher fashion—something already common to me, but insanely elevated.

In order to see the leather hoodie, I had to go to Barneys. I'd never been in Barneys before. I assumed there was probably an electric sensor around the door that went off whenever a current or former dirtbag came through it (nope, only if you're black!). I'd been enjoying a better reception from the world since living in San Francisco—a more open-minded landscape than chilly New England—but if there was a place in the Bay Area where one could be judged for how poorly one was dressed, it seemed like it would be Barneys.

Though I wanted to pass as moneyed, I couldn't risk bringing my fake Louis Vuitton—my Faux-ton—into the store. If anyone would be able to spot its ignoble Canal Street birthplace, it would be someone who handles three-thousand-dollar purses on the daily. I'd get more respect wearing something artfully, painstakingly thrifted, an ensemble that hadn't *yet* reached the inside of a magazine, but could possibly arrive on the floor at Barneys in a season or two. With Coco Chanel's command *Elegance is restraint* as a guide, I wore a simple pair of skinny jeans and a boxy oatmeal-colored top with some necklaces. A pair of grungy hiking boots I'd found at Goodwill completed the woodsy ensemble. I've never been a hippie and I've never spent time in the woods, so in punk parlance my outfit rendered me a total poseur. When your first entry into fashion is so subcultural, it's hard not to see every outfit as a uniform, your clothes doing the double duty of keeping you warm while signaling to the world what you're all about. But I wasn't doing that anymore. I was wearing things just because I liked them and thought they were beautiful.

"Love your boots," said the salesboy on the Co-op floor, where the leather hoodies lived. Shitkickers, the boys in my vocational high school used to call the style, popular with the kids in cabinet making and welding. Mine had a strip of to-die-for flannel lining the ankle. The nineties were back! Who said there were no second chances? I'd sat out the decade's fashion in radical lesbian feminist attire, but was now getting a chance to wear the hiking boots and babydoll dresses I'd snubbed in my twenties. The salesboy sucked his teeth in envy and approval. He'd have to wait nine months for the designer versions to appear, and then another nine months for the more affordable knockoffs to crop up.

I was escorted to the rack of leather hoodies. There was an array of them, including the particular one I'd been coveting, a gorgeous brown leather jacket. *Brown!* How daring, how not-black! The sleeves were weirdly long, with cool wrinkles stitched into the wrists. Leather drawstrings dangled from the hood, which was wide and boxy, making you look tough and mysterious, not like a conehead. There were leather side pockets, and a zipper. Some buttons, like butterscotch candy, ornamented the top. It was gorgeous, and it was about to be mine.

Anxiety rose in my chest like water in a Las Vegas show,

shooting this way and that, choreographing itself to the musical timbre of the salesguy's voice: "Okay, will that be all? Is that debit or credit? Would you like to apply for a Barneys card?"

As my heart rose and fell inside my body, I talked myself down: *It's cool. You have a job. You got money coming in. Nothing bad is going to happen.* I sent a tiny prayer of gratitude to the Universe for bringing me the blessed teaching job at the fancy women's college that had made this jacket possible. I thanked it for the grant that was lodged in my bank account, making me feel truly financially secure for the first time in my life. I thanked it for the book deal that had just fallen into my lap, and its attendant payment. It was really true that I could afford this jacket, even though I had to hurl myself over the unusual feeling of doing it, the haunting throb that whether or not I could afford it, spending nine hundred dollars was just inherently unethical, and if I was a better person I would have found a needy family to give that money to. "Thanks, enjoy your purchase!" the salesguy chirped. He rang up thousands of dollars in merchandise all day long. He had no idea how I was wilding out inside.

When I was done with my purchase I called Annie. "Annie. I bought the leather hoodie," I said gravely into my cell. I was running laps around a Barnes & Noble, still filled with crazy energy from my purchase.

"You did? Oh my god! Oh my god, that's amazing! That's so great! I'm so glad you did it!"

When you are a broke person who is suddenly not-broke, it is important to have friends who are also not-broke but once were, and who can coach you, like a therapist, through the intense psychological highs and lows of making an unnecessary and expensive purchase. My anxiety soon dissipated and was replaced by the very real dopamine high that good shopping can bring. I stopped power walking through the bookstore and began to ethereally drift. Maybe I wanted a book, too. I'd spent nine hundred dollars and hadn't been struck by lightning. What was another twenty on top of that? My perception of money, the relativity of it, shifted inside my body like an acid-trip revelation. Whoa. I remembered having twenty dollars to live off for a week. I remembered breaking a twenty to purchase body lotion at the health food store and then crying. I hadn't needed the body lotion; I was just drawn to the luxury of it, how nice it would be to smell like *yuzu*, whatever that was. This jacket I just bought was like a hundred bottles of yuzu body lotion.

"Where are you right now?" I asked Annie, always a fun question. Once a teenage runaway "sandwich artist" at a Subway in Detroit, she now managed a band that was marginally popular in the United States but wickedly successful elsewhere in the entire world. Sometimes Annie was calling from a muddy music festival where she had to shout to hear herself over the backstage cacophony of rock stars and supermodels; sometimes she was in her truck on her way to thrift the Bins, an infamous Portland secondhand warehouse filled with bins stuffed with old clothes. Currently Annie and the band were in the UK, hobnobbing with Grace Jones, who was sharing her room service fried chicken with them. A British fashion editor was starting a new magazine and putting the band on the cover. Soon they would all decamp for Paris, for Fashion Week.

"You should come," Annie said casually. My heart stopped. I ceased to breathe.

"For real?" I asked, gripped with a panic that Annie was just being flip, sharing a passing idea with me, an idea I would cling to desperately and then embarrass myself in the near future trying to make it happen.

"Yeah, totally," she said, excited at the idea but still sort of *no big whoop* about it. After all, this was her life now. "Fendi is paying for me and the band to have our own rooms at the Westin, but the singer doesn't like to sleep alone, so you can have mine."

"Can I actually come to the shows?" I asked, feeling a little bit like a bitch. I mean, many would argue that a free five-star hotel in Paris during Fashion Week would be enough to warrant a trip to Paris. But to be so close to the *shows*—the *shows*! I had to ask.

"Yeah, duh," Annie said. "Not all of them. I can't even go to all of them; only the band can. But I bet we can go to a bunch. Stella McCartney, Vivienne Westwood, Chanel. Alexander McQueen and Jean Paul Gaultier might be hard, but we can do Karl Lagerfeld and Jeremy Scott. And the band is playing the Fendi party, so we can all go to that. Can you come? It's in two weeks."

Gosh, Annie made it sound so simple! *Here, I booked your ultimate dream for you! A vacation you can't actually buy your way into; you have to be invited. Do you think you can make it? It will probably never, ever happen again!*

"Of course," I said, my heart pounding anew. "Of course I'll come to Paris Fashion Week with you!"

The question of coming to Paris Fashion Week on a couple of weeks' notice needed to be evaluated in two ways: whether it was financially feasible and whether it was a responsible decision. Could I afford a last-minute ticket to France, to stay at the Westin on Fendi's dime? Not only could I now afford it, but I even had this cool new leather hoodie to wear to the shows! However, was I able to leave town without recklessly abandoning my responsibilities? I was a single person, no ball and chain holding me back. No dependents, not even a pet to find a sitter for. But I did have a job, a fancy job teaching aspiring female writers at a college that paid me well enough to be able to afford an impromptu trip to Paris. The paradox was maddening.

If I arranged with a magazine to write about my time in Paris, then it would be *work*, and to not go would be to stunt my writing career. It was a question of balancing my teaching career— something wonderful that had come unexpectedly into my life— with my writing career, something vital that I had fought long and hard for, against considerable odds. This was a once-in-a-lifetime experience. Surely my boss would understand I'd have to miss a few weeks. Just in case she didn't, I decided not to tell her.

This wasn't the same as lying, exactly. I arranged for a writer with more teaching experience than I had, a professor who had actually gone to grad school, to fill in for me. To make sure I maintained a presence in their life, I arranged to have the stu-

dents e-mail me their stories while I was in Paris. I was pretty
confident I'd get away with it. I rarely saw any other faculty, be
they my superiors or fellow adjuncts, so if nobody saw my face for
a couple of weeks, no big deal.

"I have to go to Paris to write about Fashion Week for a
magazine," I told my students the week before I left, hoping this
was impressive enough to quell any abandonment issues that
might arise. I reassured them they'd be well cared for in my absence, and that we would talk remotely. And then, there was a
knock at my door. Surprise, I was being observed! By a tenured
faculty member, a woman with wild, dark curly hair who sat at
the back of my class and listened as I coaxed my students away
from the rape, madness, and sci-fi that filled their stories. I did a
hyperquick intake of my teaching style. It tended toward hippie
(maybe I'd earned the right to that oatmeal-colored top after
all!), encouraging them to let their freak flag fly and conducting
group meditations, but then I'd get supercranky schoolmarm on
them, ripping their little freak flags to shreds. Later the observer
reported back to the department head that I was simply wonderful. My department head contacted me and offered me a job the
following semester, teaching at the graduate level. I was thrilled,
and took the job.

"Great, come by my office next week," my boss said. My
heart sunk. Next week. The week I would be in Paris. I could
bump our meeting to the following week, but I'd be in Paris then,
too. With a pit in my stomach, I realized that I was going to have
to tell my boss about my diabolical plan. I grasped at a shabby
hope that maybe she would understand. Maybe she'd always

wanted to write about some beloved world just out of her reach, and had it been granted to her, she, too, would risk security to take advantage of it.

Yeah, right. My boss was as livid as I'd expected. Not only was I abandoning my class, but I'd intended to lie about it. My defense was weak, but passionate. "You invited me to teach here not only because I am a writer, but because of the kind of writer I am. That I offer perspectives outside the academy, class, and gender perspectives. My literary career is completely self-created, and if I don't grab hold of the opportunity to write about Paris Fashion Week, it's like I am undoing all the hard work and personal sacrifices I've made to get such an opportunity."

Of course, the same could be said about the opportunity to be a well-paid teacher at a prestigious college. Even to my own ears my pleading rang a little tawdry—was I really begging off from college to go to *fashion shows*? Once again I could feel the degraded place fashion occupies in the world of serious, intellectual women. It was like I was asking for time off to get hair extensions and a boob job. I was at an important crossroads. If I left for Europe, I would be leaving against her will and the will of the school. Was I going to hold on to a stable job that gave me not only great pay, but *health insurance*? Or was I going to Paris Fashion Week?

This question was one I'd pondered hundreds of times in my life, metaphorically. I was always having to pick between a metaphorical teaching job—stability, the tried-and-true path, the sure bet—and metaphorical Fashion Week: art, writing, the once-in-a-lifetime chance, the irresponsible, reckless, and memorable. One would think that having grown up broke would make one desperate for financial stability, eager to rest in the economic security of a good job. Rather, it gave me the freedom to take chances. I knew how to get by on next to nothing. I wasn't letting anyone down by not being a college professor—my parents hadn't expected me to amount to much. Against a fair amount of odds I'd built my life into something that constantly fed me surprises, and no matter what, I found a way to get by.

For years I'd quit my menial jobs whenever they got in the way of me doing something for my writing—participating in a reading, going on tour. I'd dealt with my persistent fear of poverty not by working my ass off to snag high-paying jobs, but with a Zen-like acceptance of life's impermanence, and a fragile comfort in the *now*. As in, *Right now you're okay. Right now you have some money, have a home, are well fed. And if poverty strikes again, what will happen? You'll have less, and you'll be fine. You'll write, and be with friends, and live cheaply. Just like before.*

Finally, I turned to the ultimate conundrum decider—the old deathbed scenario. When I was on my deathbed, would I want to look back on a life filled with fear-based fidelity to a series of jobs that were not my true passion?

No. I wanted to have lived. To have taken chances. To *not* have settled for the poor person's reduced experience of life, shackled to a job, making ends meet, but to have lived as much like a rich person as I could, with their fuller experience of the world, with travel and art and proximity to things beautiful. I wanted to live like I wasn't afraid, like life was there for my taking.

When I was on my deathbed, surrounded by young, adoring fans, would I regale them with the time I taught a fiction class?

No. I would tell them about the time I went to Paris Fashion Week.

And so I chose Paris, as if there was ever a question. And I gathered purse-loads of glamorous anecdotes to share with whoever might be sitting by my deathbed hoping for a story. I would tell them about how, in the mad rush of people trying to get backstage after the Jeremy Scott show, I nudged up against Kanye West. His then-girlfriend, Amber Rose, was wearing one of the mint-green cropped motorcycle jackets the designer had just sent down the runway, along with a pair of Chanel sunglasses topped in the brand's iconic dripping gold chains. At Vivienne Westwood, staged in what looked like a condemned French bank, I watched Pamela Anderson horse-stomp along the model path, wearing a tutu starched to look permanently blown up by a gust of wind over her bum. A stand of paparazzi on risers held their cameras like a brass section about to play; when she rounded the bend and headed straight for them the clash of flashes was blinding. Backstage at Stella McCartney I recognized a curly-haired woman as my favorite photographer, Nan Goldin. I struck up an awkward conversation with her, and was rescued by a television crew asking her what she thought of Paris Fashion Week. "Yes," she replied enigmatically, referencing the surreal responses Andy Warhol would give to journalists. When Olivier Theyskens's last collection for Nina Ricci came to a close, an army of models in strange shoes with no heels and long whispery gowns and odd hats that dipped into their faces stormed the runway en masse to the thundering sound of the Cure's *Pornography*, and I actually cried from the whirl of emotion the spectacle produced inside me. Backstage at Karl Lagerfeld I watched Sophia Loren sip champagne in a long fur coat. Olivier Zahm, the grizzled, roguish editor of *Purple Fashion* magazine, asked me to lie upon a carpeted floor at a hotel room after-party, so he could best photograph the tattoo on the back of my leg for his blog. I obliged. At the Loewe show—which I learned was pronounced *Low-vay* and not *Low*—I sat directly across from Anna Wintour and her tremendously cool sidekick, Grace Coddington, all of us at tiny, elegant tables heaped with espresso and champagne.

When the band took the stage at the Fendi party, tears sprang to my eyes, and I turned around to see that Annie was crying, too. Like me and like Annie, the band commanding Fashion Week's attention had been raised poor, in broken families, and there we all were, together in Paris. It was weird and amazing, nothing short of a miracle. For a flashing moment I understood and believed in destiny. We were all exactly where we were supposed to be, and an incomprehensible chain of choices and happenstance had brought us here, together. Then, Kate Moss rudely shoved me so that her friend could pass by, breaking me from my reverie. *This* is what I was living for.

The telephone rang as I was taking an afternoon nap in my luxury hotel, exhausted from a late Fashion Week after-party night and an early morning with Karl Lagerfeld, marveling at the maniacal excess of the furred motorcycle helmets he'd sent down the catwalk. It was Annie. "Meet us in the lobby in *literally* five minutes. We're going to the Fendi showroom and I think we'll all be able to get stuff." I've never dressed so fast in my life. I ran down to the Versailles-inspired lobby and found Annie, Jo—the band's lead singer—and an Italian representative of Fendi. We rode in a little car to the Paris showroom, where we were given espressos and trays of sushi, both of which I consumed desperately. I was as food deprived as I was sleep deprived, my schedule of party and fashion not allowing a ton of time for eating.

The nice Fendi man gave us all souvenirs of our brush with luxury—golden combs stamped with FENDI, which lived in embossed leather comb holsters. I would have been satisfied with such swag, even if it *was* the Fashion Week equivalent of a flashlight keychain at an independent film festival.

After giving Jo a detailed tour of the showroom, the man thoughtfully left the celebrity to "shop" in peace. I'm saying "shop" because Jo wasn't paying for anything. Not the leather dresses, not the fur capelets. Not the stilettos or the jewelry or the purse after purse after purse. I remembered being in the van with Annie at the end of our road trip, keeping each other awake with fashion magazines. *What would you have from this page, if you could have anything you want?*

"Grab a purse," Jo hissed at us, "and throw it in my pile." Had we cast some crazy spell over ourselves during that maniacal sleep-deprived drive? A spell that took some years to manifest, but here we were, in the Fendi showroom, and what would I have from this page, being able to have anything I want?

There was not a moment of hesitation about which purse I desired. It consisted of the slashed, long-haired pelt of some poor animal I hoped had died a natural death, not that I thought too much about it. There was no time for thinking, not when the Fendi man could return at any minute. No time to think about the probable pony that had created my purse, or the snake that had provided the handles. No time to wonder if the tiger-eye stones—or, for that matter, the wooden marbles that had been dipped in gold leaf—had been ethically sourced. For this was the most exquisite purse I had ever seen. I flung it at Jo and she flung it onto the pile and the door flung open and in came the Italian.

He browsed through the enormous pile of clothing Jo had helped herself—and me, and Annie—to, murmuring appreciatively about her impeccable good taste. When he got to my purse he clucked his tongue. "So chic," he said, nodding. "Very special. You pair with some jeans and—voilà."

I felt deeply validated. The man packed up Jo's loot and brought us all back to the Westin. Jo passed me the purse in the hallway, with all the intrigue of a drug deal.

"Better not bring it around Paris," she said. "Wait till you get home to wear it."

"I will." I nodded, gazing at Jo. "Thank you. Thank you so much."

"Punk rock!" she hooted, going back to her room. As insane as my life was, hers was unfathomable in its rags-to-riches lunacy.

It had been a dream, a sort of joke dream, to go to Paris Fashion Week, and inexplicably, it had happened. Once I knew I was going, I jokingly told my friends, "I want to see Kanye West and score a purse," never really thinking that I would find myself in multiple closed spaces with Kanye and Pink, and Kate Moss, and the Kills, and Paul McCartney, and those wicked Geldof girls— and find myself cuddling a batshit crazy Fendi purse that I was sure went for no less than five thousand dollars on the open market. Surely it was part sleep deprivation and part protein deficiency, but after I returned from Fendi I wept, there at the desk in my room at the beautiful Westin. I felt like I needed to reach out to someone, so I e-mailed the person who knows me best: my little sister.

I shoved as much of my otherworldly week into my e-mail as I could, and ended on the quasi breakdown I was having with my Fendi purse. *I must be crazy*, I typed. *But it's all making me emotional. I guess I'm overwhelmed.*

My sister's reply was swift.

*Sometimes*, she wrote, *I sit back in the house that I live in in Santa Monica, where I can see the ocean, where I live with my incredible husband and our beautiful baby daughter, where I'm not struggling, where I get to be a stay-at-home mom like I dreamed, and I go back in time and I say to the thirteen-year-old me who felt so out of place and trapped and hopeless, Don't you worry. You're going to grow up and get out of here and have the life that you want.*

*Michelle*, she continued, *you used to get beat up for the way you looked. You and Ma fought every day for four years about how you dressed. You need to go back to teenage you and tell her, Don't worry. You're going to grow up and get out of here and have the life you want. You're going to get to go to Paris and go to the shows and you're going* *to get an incredible $5,000 purse for free because that is just what is going to happen to you. You're not going crazy. It's a big deal.*

Gazing out my window at the Tuileries, the grounds littered with Fashion Week tents, I took her advice and spaced out and talked to thirteen-year-old me. I told her all about Paris and Annie and Jo and the purse in my hands, and I cried even more. Then, I snuck outside my door, grabbed the end of a stranger's baguette from a room service tray left out for pickup, ate it, and passed out.

That's what I'm going to talk about on my deathbed.

# 3.

# My $1,100 Birthday Apartment

There are many head-fucks a person who grows up broke will contend with for most of her life, and one of them is not really understanding what things cost, or what things are worth. My understanding has always been skewed, and I've seen this confusion—often accompanied by fear and a bit of defensiveness—in other broke folks, including my mom.

Once, on a visit with my sister in Santa Monica, we stopped at a Whole Foods to pick up dinner fixings. My mother tried to help with the shopping, but not only were much of the offerings foreign to her (Gluten-free pasta? Kimchi? Coconut kefir?); the prices struck a deep and confounding terror in her heart. Her eyes grew wide as she took in the costs at the meat counter. "If I lived here I'd starve to death!" she gasped, upset. I watched as the world tightened around my mother, grew smaller. An entire region was now out of her reach. She would remain trapped in

Florida, with other poor New Englanders who'd gambled on a better life and found the same poverty in a warmer climate, with worse labor laws.

"Ma, you would not starve. There are other places to shop. This is an expensive place."

What I wanted to say was, *There are poor people in Los Angeles, too*, but I was afraid to refer to my mother as *poor*; it might make her feel ashamed. Plus, maybe she didn't feel poor. Was poor a mutable identity, like gender or sexual identity, or was it essential, based on the facts of your paycheck, your wallet, your response to the price of a pound of organic grass-fed non-GMO-fed beef? When I was young, my mother would send us to the grocer, Goldstein's, and we were to order a half pound of the good meat and a half pound of the bad. She'd crumble it all together and that would be dinner, Hamburger Helper.

I, too, once flinched and cringed at the higher cost of eating well, but after a point, I came to accept it: *That's just what organic food costs.* I learned that I could buy it and nothing would happen. I didn't wind up homeless choosing the organic kale over the conventional.

For me, part of stumbling toward adulthood has included getting real about what things cost, and not getting mad at the world about it. It's also understanding what I can and can't afford. This understanding is often psychedelically clouded by what I lovingly refer to as my "scarcity issues." It's pretty simple: You grow up with money being scarce, and it gives you hella issues. Mine manifest most powerfully in a terror that everything I have will be somehow taken away from me—probably through my own fuckups and carelessness—and I will not only be broke again, but broker than ever. All the worst-case scenarios I've managed to avoid, like outright homelessness, will make themselves clear as my destiny. In order to stave off this horror, my scarcity issues counsel me, I must make sure my cost of living remains low, forever. Sure, I might be able to clamber over my issues to make a onetime purchase of a luxury leather hoodie, but I must never, ever make a decision that raises my monthly bills— say, getting better Internet (hence my getting online via a telephone cable snaking across the apartment for waaaaaaay too long), or acquiring a cell phone (I cracked years after everyone else in my life, and only at the bullying of a friend, who was then required to come and hold my sweaty hand for the duration of the transaction). I can't get cable, because what if that extra monthly expense is the final straw that catapults me into extreme poverty? Same goes for health insurance. I'll just keep using the free clinics, thank you very much. For years, I did my grocery shopping at Food 4 Less, where the other broke folks wheeled their carts around, collecting our gently dented and discounted cans of soup. My scarcity issues were present whenever I spent more than thirty dollars on anything (later, after much personal work, the number was bumped up to fifty), making me dizzy and flooding me with anxiety, but I slowly learned to tangle with them, to make the purchase in spite of feeling like it might literally give me a heart attack.

In my youth it was easy enough to cultivate a low level of taste. A pint of generic vodka (or better yet, an economical forty-ounce of malt liquor) and a free poetry reading were all I needed to be happy. But in getting sober, your tastes change. Literally—you can, like, taste things. After decimating your appetite with stimulants, you suddenly are in love with food. You crave sweets, or complicated savories. (Plus, what do people *do* if they don't drink? They eat. And go to the gym. And become sex addicts.)

And so it was that I became accustomed to shopping in the fancier grocery stores. You'd never expect that a young woman cruising the bulk bins at a health food store could be having such a profound nervous breakdown, but initially I was. I felt like I was betraying my mother, insulting her struggle by buying pricey food like it was no big thing; like I was somehow checking out of my class politics, aligning myself with the bougie mofos who'd spend twelve dollars on a bulbous heirloom tomato; like an outsider, someone infinitely more at ease inside a grocery store stocked with Oreos and Doritos than one peddling flaxseed crackers and purple carrots.

After a couple of years I stopped feeling like a dirtbag impostor, someone more suited to a block of government cheese than a round of *fromage* aged in a French cave and packed in volcanic ash. I stopped writing the price code for the conventional rice on my bag of organic rice. The punk in me could argue that organic food should be free and I *deserved* a discount on my health food after all I'd been through, but the more sober and clear I got, the more these defenses sounded like the self-serving, juvenile attitudes they were. In my 12-step program, there was a lot of emphasis on living free of fear, changing fear-based behavior. Why would I engage in the pettiest of petty theft, passing off my $3 bag of organic rice as its $1.99 cousin? Because I was scared. I was scared that if I became accustomed to a lifestyle of organic rice I would then be ruined.

Ruined? Sure. Or if not ruined, punished somehow, by someone. A terrible finger would point at me, dirt wedged under the nail, and hiss, *Traitor! Class traitor! Think you're too good for Minute Rice? Huh? You'll see. You'll end up back here with the likes of us, eating twenty-five-cent packages of ramen you can't even cook properly. Ramen is a* soup, *but you cook it like a bunch of noodles sprinkled with a crumbly, MSG-laden flavor packet. Why? BECAUSE YOU HAVE NO TASTE.*

You get over it like you get over it, a bit at a time. By the time I was visiting with my mother and sister in L.A., I did not cry out in pain at the two-hundred-dollar Repettos in the shoe boutique we tucked into; well versed in the math of fashion, I understood that was simply what Repettos cost. Of course, they were worth every penny—they were *French*. Strange new politics entered my consciousness. So much of the expensive clothing I coveted was made in Europe, by people paid a living wage, engaged in a crafts tradition that had been passed down through generations, sustaining whole villages. Slowly, the elevated price tags began to seem like a bit of justice. What was the real price of a pair of thirty-dollar shoes? Could it perhaps be more in line with my class politics to purchase a few higher-quality, well-made items than to comfort myself with a piece of fast fashion made by Bangladeshi women who would be assaulted with high-pressure hoses for protesting their working conditions?

I persisted in lusting after luxury items—like Le Labo Rose 31 perfume, which I'd had the good fortune of smelling when I was put up in a hotel that offered the scent in its toiletries. Le Labo Rose 31 smells like you've stumbled into some sort of divine cathedral consecrated to the worship of women—1920s burlesque dancers, sultry Italian mothers of eight, the drag queens found in Jean Genet novels. Hookers. Expensive, successful hookers. It is a dark rose scent made darker with something spicy and churchy. At the hotel I shampooed and conditioned my hair in it, and I scrubbed all my dirty bits with the smooth white cake of soap. I slathered myself in the lotion. Then I took everything and stuffed it into my bag so that housekeeping would leave me a new set. Then I stuffed that new set into my bag, and did it all again a third time.

As a former drug addict, I'm hesitant to claim to be *addicted* to something like a smell, but the truth is, both drugs and smells set off complicated chemical reactions in your brain. And since I'd surely firebombed my brain's dopamine factory for years, impacting its output, and since smell can fire up your pleasure centers and ramp up dopamine—well, who knows exactly what happened in my brain as I huffed and puffed and blew my mind with the smell of this new perfume? Maybe my crisscrossed, beat-up brain waves were surging at the smell of Le Labo Rose 31, eking out another little drip of precious dopamine. All I know for sure is when I ran out of my pilfered hotel toiletries I *missed* that rich scent, and daydreams of walking into Barneys and having the nice perfume guy whip up a bottle with my name on it took over.

While visiting my sister in Los Angeles I realized, as we were wrapping up with brunch, that we weren't that far from Barneys.

I scooted through Beverly Hills, past Porsches parked brightly alongside the curb, past an ice cream truck selling treats to a little girl who had greeted the morning full glitz—lipstick, dangly earrings, designer sunglasses. Beverly Hills is a circus, and I let myself enjoy the spectacle, maybe even become my own side-show as I fell into the store and stumbled toward the Le Labo bar behind the racks of sale shoes. The risk was never that I *would* do this, indulge my lust for a pricey perfume. The risk was that I wouldn't. That the old fear would set in, the *You can't buy nice perfume, other people do that.* The *Buying fancy perfume is a slippery slope, then what will you buy, before you know it you'll be out on the street!* The *Think of what your struggling mother would say if she knew you just spent $150 on something so stupid.* The risk was that I'd let fear and shame and guilt make the decision for me.

When I drank, I was wild. My wildness, of which I was so proud, took the form of risk taking. If a man sexually harassed me on the street I would remove a shoe and come at him menacingly; I would follow him in circles asking, "What did you just say? What did you just say?" Once, on top of a very tall building, I climbed a ladder to vandalize a sexist billboard, a can of spray paint rattling in my hand. I was naked and wet, because in addition to a billboard, the rooftop hosted a swimming pool and I'd been skinny-dipping.

I'm not necessarily *proud* of these moments, and I am very grateful I didn't accidentally get myself killed. But this urge to identify the most outrageous, slightly dangerous possibility and hurl myself into it—both daring the Universe and trusting that it would somehow hold me safe—has always been inside me. I think it's in a lot of addicts. Life can be scary. On some level it's scary for everyone, and those layers of scary can really pile up when you're female, when you're sort of weird, when you're broke, when you're queer. The way life dares and challenges you can just become your day-to-day, invisible. There's something great about staring solid *Jackass*-style hijinks in the eye and consciously diving in. Acting fearless creates an understanding of yourself as sort of a badass, which generates extreme confidence—which is super helpful when your individual battle to find your place in the world feels more than daunting.

How is all of this transformed by sobriety? How do you indulge your daredevil demons? How do you challenge yourself to do things that scare you? Some people jump out of airplanes, but that's not for me. I'm not actually an adrenaline junkie, and I don't feel the need to face a fear of death. I'm fine with being afraid of death. But my fear of spending money, my fear of betraying my working-class roots, my fear that extreme destitution is always right around the corner no matter how much I work or accomplish? Now you're talking.

So I bought the perfume. At home I sprayed a cloud of it into my bedroom and walked through it, letting the mist of it settle on my clothes, my skin, my hair. I fucking love it. It smells like heroin. No, it doesn't—heroin smells like vinegar, like rot; it smells disgusting. This smells like money. Piles and piles of money, made by some goddessy woman who earned it in her garden or her atelier or her boudoir.

I wish these games of psychological truth or dare would cure me of my money issues once and for all, but I still get scared a lot,

still feel the way my mom felt inside Whole Foods—utterly ignorant of what things cost, but certain that the price is too high for
the likes of me. Blind spots loom, always. And a big one was the
ultimate monthly expense, rent.

I was twenty-two years old when I landed in San Francisco,
with only one friend in the whole seven-by-seven-mile city. I was
estranged from most of my family. I'd dropped out of college after
two semesters. Setting out for some sort of new life in San Francisco, I had one priority: cheap rent. It was only through cheap
rent that I would have any life at all, that I would be able to be a
writer and have a writer's life, a life that in my twenties occurred
mainly after sundown, in bars and taverns and saloons, with
shady characters and wanton women. Cheap rent allowed me to
have time to scrawl in my notebooks, time to sleep in after those
late, scribbling nights. I was always willing to make the sacrifices
one had to make in order to have very low overhead—rowdy
roommates, and too many of them. A front hall that smelled
suspiciously like mouse. Maggots in the fridge.

When I returned from Fashion Week it was a rough landing.
For weeks I'd been shuttled around on the dime of Annie and the
prosperous musical outfit she managed. And then—back to San
Francisco. The dirt smudges on my bedroom walls seemed to
have grown darker in my absence. The Bloomin' Onion ashtray
installation had swelled, now large enough that I could detect its
dank stink through my windows. The windows, how they shook
and rattled in the wind and rain! And the fridge, oh, the fridge!
I dared not even open it. I began to long for a real kitchen, a
clean one, where I could linger at my table with a magazine, or

cook healthy vegetables at night, never encountering a roommate's mess, never having to clean it in order to proceed or just give up the evening's culinary aspirations and flee to the nearest taqueria.

At night I dreamt of Paris. Oh, the luxury I'd known! How I'd slept in a giant, scrumptious bed, and in the morning picked my way through a buffet that included yogurt in quaint little glass jars and a breakfast cereal that was the French equivalent of Cocoa Krispies, only being French it was perhaps made from Valrhona chocolate. How a maid had cleaned my room. How my shower had always sparkled. How my only duty had been to dress up as much as possible and observe high fashion as it was debuted to the world.

I knew I could not, like Eloise or Lindsay Lohan, live inside a hotel for the rest of my life. But I could certainly hit something a little higher than where I currently shivered. Friends had started to ask me what I would do for my fortieth birthday. People did significant things to mark such an occasion. They went to Tuscany or hiked the Pyrenees. For my fortieth birthday, all I wanted was a home with a clean refrigerator.

I started putting the word out. When you live in a city for a long time—I'd been in San Francisco for almost twenty years—the best housing deals are ones you find through word of mouth. I had a couple of leads, but they were falling short—too expensive, snatched up too quickly, or too far outside the area where I wanted to live.

At a literary event, I ran into a friend who was talking to a photographer who documented the literary scene in town. This photographer was also the building manager of a place in the Lower Haight. My friend told her about my plight. "There's a one-bedroom opening up," she offered. "Eleven hundred dollars."

"Eleven hundred dollars!" My cry was not the cheer of incredulous delight it should have been. My cry was one of shock and horror, the gasp of a person who has been insulted. I had become my mother in Whole Foods, gazing at the meat case. *If I lived here, I'd starve!*

The photographer gazed at me curiously, puzzled by my tone. "That's a really great price for a one-bedroom," she said gently. "It's below market value."

"Maybe so, maybe so." I brushed her off brusquely, and with this *attitude*. Fully triggered, my scarcity issues took over my personality. *These people don't know how* real *people live*, I thought harshly. *They think* eleven hundred dollars *is a reasonable price for a one-bedroom apartment? My people can't pay that kind of money. They must have mistaken me for a* rich *person—and who could blame them, with my Louis* Faux-ton *and organic baby spinach in my teeth, stinking like a $150 rose?*

"Maybe so," I told the building manager icily. "But it's just not for me."

They looked at me like I was insane. It was a look I would become familiar with as I recounted the exchange with others.

"How's the housing search coming?" asked friends who knew all I wanted for my fortieth birthday was a fortysomething lifestyle.

"Okay," I grumbled. "I heard about a one-bedroom, but it's eleven hundred dollars."

"A one-bedroom for eleven hundred dollars?" they would repeat. "Not a studio?"

"Not a studio."

"Where is it? The Outer Sunset? The Avenues, the Richmond?"

"No . . . the Lower Haight. Sort of Hayes Valley."

Hayes Valley was having a moment. Not only was there an artisanal one-cup-at-a-time coffee kiosk tucked away in a cute little alley; there was an artisanal one-scoop-at-a-time ice cream kiosk. The one-scoop-at-a-time place was right where the artisanal meat truck parked each week, selling cuts of meat from animals who had gotten massages the whole of their short lives. It was across the street from a candy store that sold chocolate bars made with basil and rosehips, around the corner from a bar that rimmed its strawberry cocktails with sugar and black pepper and served its very own artisanal potato chips with a crème fraîche onion dip.

All of this could be mine, for eleven hundred dollars a month.

"You do understand," friends gently coaxed, "that is only three hundred dollars more than you are paying right now, to live with twentysomethings and a fridge full of maggots?"

Three hundred dollars. Surely I could wrangle up an extra three hundred each month? That wasn't *that* scary. But then what about everything else—the utilities and Internet bills no longer split. I would have to pay it *all*.

"Yeah," my friends said, nodding. "You will have to pay your $19.99 Internet bill all by yourself."

I'd worked enough with my money issues to get a sense of when my perception was wack, and began to understand that my comprehension of the eleven-hundred-dollar one-bedroom was a little effed up. I e-mailed the photographer who managed the building, and asked if I could come and peek at it. She invited me over the following night.

THE ALEXANDRA, the tiled lobby floor introduced itself. A large, leafy plant sprung exotically from its terra-cotta planter. Inside it was all wood. Little holiday wreaths were hung along the stairs, making the hallway smell like a magical forest. I climbed the carpet to the first floor, and entered the open apartment. The photographer was there, showing the vacant space to a straight couple. We greeted each other in that weird way people who are after the same apartment greet each other—friendly, but sizing each other up as competition. I could imagine their calculations:

*Tattoos. Not a good sign. Maybe she does drugs. Can't have a great credit score. Does she have a good job? Does she have any job— can people get jobs with a tattoo on their neck?*

I made my own calculations:

*Fuck, they're totally normal. They look like they could sell insurance on a TV commercial. This is what people are supposed to look like. Crap. They're even married. But maybe that's a strike against them. I'd just be one person in the apartment—less wear, less tear. I'm not going to have a fight with my spouse the whole floor can hear. I'm not going to have a baby all of a sudden and keep the building up with its crying. There are a lot of perks to having a single lady as opposed to a couple.*

Meanwhile, the couple continued peeking at me, imagining the trail of thuggish lovers my promiscuous, tattooed lifestyle would lure into the building.

As it happened, there were not one, not two, but *three* apartments open in the building. The tension broke with a near-audible crack. Our phony smiles relaxed into genuine grins and we strolled around the apartment.

The place was lovely. A giant front room with tall decorative windows overhung the busy street below. A walk-in closet poked off the side, which could also be converted to a teeny office or meditation room. French doors slid open to reveal a middle room with a giant built-in shelving unit shuttered in leaded glass. The bathroom sported a claw-foot tub and charming archaic details. There were hardwood floors, and checkerboard linoleum in the kitchen; a sparkling clean fridge and a laundry room downstairs; a freaking *backyard*, a wilderness with a plum tree and vines of jasmine and a bottlebrush tree and wrought iron furniture and a fire pit and pots of tomatoes and artichokes.

Before I had set out to view the apartment, I'd done what I'd long done at one of life's crossroads—I'd picked some tarot cards. "You're so California!" people always say when they learn of my love of astrology and tarot cards, but I was like this long before I left New England. I got my first deck at fifteen and went about studying in earnest, doing readings for my family.

A good tarot reading tells you what you already know, only maybe you're a bit too clouded with fear or confusion to see it. A good tarot reading brings clarity and perspective. It shows you where you're headed, but it can also show you how to head it off.

"What would it look like if I moved into this apartment?" I asked the tarot while I shuffled, and then flipped over a single card: Wealth.

The last time I selected a single card and got Wealth, I'd been in Vegas, on a breakup road trip with my ex-girlfriend Katy. We'd fought and cried from Chicago through the Midwest, chugging along in her white Ford Falcon, driving from airbrushed sunrise to fiery sunset, through lightning storms that cracked and crashed above our heads, a mirror of our own storm. Electric-blue mascara ran down my cheeks as I drank cans of beer in the front seat, while Katy gripped the wide steering wheel with white knuckles. We both had a kitschy love of Vegas and its ridiculous, gluttonous existence in a scabby desert. Katy liked to play slots and I liked to play bingo; she liked the roller coaster spinning off the side of New York–New York, and I liked the round-the-clock free cocktails. We hoped the glitzy town would operate as a distraction and a DMZ, where we could put the unraveling of our relationship on hold and have some mindless fun, like all the other vacationing hedonists.

Pulling the Wealth card while in Las Vegas could only mean one thing, but I dared not even hope it was true. "Look what I got." I flashed the card at Katy.

"You're gonna win money!" she crowed. I appreciated her wild optimism, even though it was the same trait that kept her hanging on to our rotted relationship. We headed over to the New Frontier, a Western-themed, old-Vegas establishment with regular bingo games.

I *love* bingo. When I turned eighteen in my lousy town, join-

ing the ladies in my family for a round in a smoky church basement was a rite of passage. I was finally an adult, trading in
crumpled bills for a stack of paper cards and my very own dauber,
producing globs of bright ink on the numbered squares in time to
the bingo caller's numerical hollers. I loved everything about
bingo—the smoking, the greasy treats, the adrenaline that built
as my cards got more and more inked up. I loved the lingo—"I'm
waitin'!" hissed a player just one number away from winning. I
loved the winning—unlike in other gambling games, in bingo
*someone* was going to win. Why not me? In the hazy, subterranean
spaces, the aging women of working-class New England became
something more than specters of worst-case scenarios, or bitches
who clucked and sneered at my hair; engrossed in their urgent
hope, chain-smoking, cussing out people who talked during the
game, scowling "Shit!" when they lost, they became somehow
comedic and iconic, both human and cinematic. Sweating my
own urgent, chain-smoking sweat, it was one of the few times,
growing up, that I felt like I belonged to my city and its people.
The way they made superstitious piles of "lucky objects" before
their cards—tiny religious statues and troll dolls, rabbits' feet and
photos of grandchildren, of husbands, of deceased loved ones. For
a bingo player, heaven is a place you go after you die to help your
living relations win a bingo game. The first game I played, I won
fifty dollars. "You're lucky," my grandmother told me, and because
she'd said so, I was.

It looked like the luck had followed me again, because there
in the New Frontier, I promptly won seventy-five dollars.

I was, at that moment, someone for whom seventy-five dollars was a significant pile of money. I had just come off a literary tour, reading my zines around the country, selling them at a whopping three bucks a pop, which was promptly spent on booze, cigarettes, and electric-blue mascara. We went straight to World's Largest Gift Shop, where I considered buying a sixty-dollar taxidermy jackalope—that mythical half-jackrabbit, half-antelope found nowhere but in kitschy souvenir shops—but instead splurged on other useless items for the both of us, and treated us to yet another bingo game, this time at the Showboat casino, a doomed old-timer located off the Strip.

The Showboat bingo hall was way bigger than the New Frontier's, and the prizes were bigger and more creative: A glass box stood in the center of the room, filled with money. If you were lucky enough to win a certain type of bingo, you got to stand in the box while powerful fans were switched on, and you kept all the money blown onto your body.

There was another special winning that evening, the Powerball. For the first number called at the start of the night, any person who called a bingo on it in a subsequent game got an additional thousand dollars.

The room was humming with excitement and filling with smoke. Placed before my cards was a strawberry daiquiri topped with whipped cream, from the bar outside the hall. Katy and I had befriended the bartender, who had insisted I was going to win.

"I already won today," I said shyly. But I had a feeling, a physical feeling inside my body. I don't think I'd ever felt it before. It felt like *luck*. Was this what people meant when they said, "I feel lucky"? I thought it was simply a turn of phrase, but apparently, luck was a real state, one of electric grace.

Next to my lucky daiquiri was a pack of lucky cigarettes and whatever mojo items I could scavenge from my bag—a chunk of cloudy quartz I'd found while peeing on the side of the road, a vintage rhinestone brooch, a penny flattened with an image of Niagara Falls. The caller announced the first number of the night, I19, and the game was on. I loved smoking while playing Bingo, the toxins from the cigarettes merging with the anxiety of the game, producing a slight mania tempered by my daiquiri. The hall was full of serious gamblers, Vegas people, a more varied bunch than the crabby, catty women of Chelsea church basements. A few games in, I won.

"Bingo!" I shouted, but it wasn't the happy, smiling relief of a bingo, because the game was continuing—I could very well get another bingo on this same card, so while one hand was held in the air for an attendant to come check my card, my other hand was still inking out numbers, as my cigarette grew into one long ash on the silver cardboard ashtray.

The attendant had hair that was a million shades of yellow, held up with a purple velvet scrunchie. "You don't even know what you won, do you?" she teased me. I believe I actually felt annoyed with her, this woman who was delivering my winnings. *Couldn't she see I was still playing my card?* "You called Bingo on I19. You won the Powerball jackpot!"

When the game was over, I walked out with fifteen hundred

dollars. I was trembling. "What if we get mugged?" Katy whispered as I shoved a giant roll of cash in my tiny beat-up thrift store purse. We threw a tip at the bartender on our way out, and ran to the Ford Falcon. Once we slammed the heavy doors and punched down the locks, we let loose in a roar of screams. I won the jackpot! I immediately gave half of it to Katy, filled with relief at being able to pay her back for all the gas and meals and hotel rooms she'd bought us. We found a bingo supply store in a strip mall on the edge of town, and I tricked myself out with a special bingo bag, replete with outside pockets to carry your daubers, and a pair of earrings made of teeny-tiny bingo cards. We bought an extra day at New York–New York and hit the bingo hall at the Showboat a couple more times, but my luck had apparently run out. Both of ours had. We drove back to San Francisco and completed our whirlwind breakup.

Ever since that Vegas trip, the idea of pulling the Wealth card from the stack of tarot filled me with a magical feeling of possibility. I didn't think that I was likely to find a pile of cash hidden in the floorboards of the eleven-hundred-dollar apartment, but I did take it to mean that moving in wouldn't land me in the poorhouse; I had sufficient wealth to be able to afford it.

As I strolled through the apartment, I imagined waking up each morning in that bright front room with the crisscrossed window frames. I would feel like Snow White, like a bird was apt to land upon my sleepy shoulders, and maybe if I stood out in that blooming backyard, one would. I thought about the blazing persimmon tree I would be leaving behind. I still appreciated its noble, persistent beauty, but it was nothing next to an actual *backyard* stinking of jasmine vines and exploding with azalea, sweet plums dropping from the plum tree each fall.

In this apartment, every day would be a new day. I would shuffle into the kitchen, open the fridge I shared with no one, pull out some food unmolested by vermin. I would sit at my table and drink coffee and read *Vogue*. All of this was easily worth an extra three hundred dollars. If I had to mug old ladies in the street to get that money, I'd do it. But I figured I probably wouldn't have to resort to that. I put the trust in the tarot, and in myself.

On the night of my fortieth birthday, my new apartment was filled with people. My sister came up from Los Angeles to celebrate. Friends came from Portland and Brooklyn. I requested only crystals, plants, and mix CDs for gifts, and I received a terrarium and a potted vine and succulents and hunks of amethyst and the complete works of Bruce Springsteen. In my kitchen, people drank whiskey around my yellow kitchen table. They snacked on sweet-potato-and-prosciutto pizza at the antique library table I'd found at a thrift store. They lounged on my bed (a French antique carved with flowers and ribbons) and sat on the new white leather club chairs I'd arranged beneath those charming windows with the crisscrossed window frames. My purse collection was housed in the built-in, as was my collection of European fashion magazines. I'd made my writing desk into a vanity and did my writing anywhere I wanted, because the entire apartment was mine. I'd gotten everything I wanted for my fortieth birthday. I got to maybe, just a little bit, grow up.

# 4.

# I Have a Trust Fund from God—and So Do You!

"Magical thinking"—a tendency to believe you can just *wish* goodness into your life and hope the bad things away—is native to alcoholics. Maybe it's how the booze addled our brains; maybe it's because drunks are such dreamers; maybe it's a side effect of the denial it takes to sustain a career of heavy drinking. Whatever the cause, if you get sober and go to those culty little meetings, you hear the term a lot. Oddly, much of the 12-step guide to right living includes a regular indulgence in new-agey practices: believing that the Universe will take care of you, that the god of your choosing (mine is Stevie Nicks) has a plan for you, that you can do the right thing and have faith and it's all going to work out. At first glance it may look a little hypocritical— especially if you're newly sober, incredibly cranky, and looking to disprove these theories so you can get back to drinking.

But after a decade of continuous sobriety I've come to be-

lieve it's just about getting yourself in good enough shape—
mentally, physically, dare I say *spiritually*—so that your desperate
old magical thinking is transformed into straight-up *magic*. I often feel a bit bummed for my nonalcoholic friends, that they
don't find themselves in random church basements practicing
this odd, effective spell casting. Alcoholics aren't the only ones
who need help; we're just the loudest and messiest. So please—
allow me to introduce you to the weird world of intentional af-
firmational nondenominational prayer-ish magical-thinking
*magic!*

As a witchy woman, I am comfortable with the word *magic*,
but if it conjures up images of dweeby guys pulling bouquets of
fake flowers out of collapsible top hats, call it something else.
Call it connectivity—your connection to yourself and the world
around you. Call it intuition, your sixth sense. Call it the power
of positive thinking, like the business world does. At its simplest,
it can be the humble *It's all good* of a friendly hippie. To me,
they're all the same—one person's pagan spell is another's Christian prayer; it's about setting intention. Personally, I like to cover
my bases, casting spells *and* saying my prayers. Even after discard-
ing Catholicism I held on to the saints; I loved their stories of
martyrdom and perseverance, how supernatural their tales were.
Like me, many of them were persecuted by their contemporaries.
Like me, most of them were girls. In my early twenties I became
interested in Santeria, an Afro-Caribbean religion that was created when slaves were forced to hide indigenous spirituality behind a devotion to saints; today, practitioners still use the
Catholic imagery interchangeably with African gods and god-

desses. I've always thought we're just simple humans calling out to energies and forces too big for us to understand. The face we put on it—be it the Catholic Saint Barbara or the cross-dressing Santeria deity Chango—is mutable, and can be determined by what best captures our imagination.

Prayer gets a bad rap in our culture, because there are a lot of nutty people abusing it, trying to push it into classrooms or use it to punish people. Not shockingly, my own prayers avoid such negativity, tending toward the more floaty, nondenominational spiritual utterance—a request for help, guidance, or strength from the Big Unknown—a thank-you to no one in particular for the beauty of a sunset or the love of a smart-aleck friend or a scrumptious meal. Most days I have at least one moment when I cast a glance around my life and see the cozy adorable house that I live in, my foxy adorable love that I live with, my bathroom shelves full of smelly beauty products, my closet full of thrifted finery, and I think, *Holy shit! I can't believe this is my life! Thank you.* My most common prayer is probably *Holy shit—thank you!* And there are always a million things to say *Holy shit—thank you!* for. I have all my limbs. I wasn't born in a war-torn country. My house has indoor plumbing. I'm not hungover and puking right now. I'm not trapped in a small town somewhere. I'm safe. I'm not in jail. My family wasn't murdered by the government. Not to get all grim, but the darker edge of human experience has no dropping-off point. Who knows what random maneuver of luck and fate saved me from unknowable disaster? *Holy shit—thank you!*

Some people are into affirmations—repeating high-self-esteem phrases to yourself in the mirror or leaving them jotted on Post-its stuck all over your boudoir as a reminder of how excellent you are. These, too, are sort of nondenominational prayers, prayers that you'll wake up and realize how awesome you are. I like affirmations. Some years ago, inspired by a writer I heard talking on a panel, I began saying the Money Magnet chant. Someone had asked the writer how she supported herself, and she admitted that whenever she started feeling worried about cash she'd stop and say this affirmation/prayer/spell/wishful thought:

> I am a Money Magnet
> Money comes to me
> Money loves me
> Money is sexually attracted to me
> Money wants to be near me

After a few chants, something would happen—her mom would send her a check; a freelance gig would come through. A writer friend from a working-poor background similar to my own scoffed when he heard this: Perhaps one needs to have check-writing parents for such affirmations to work. I decided to do my own research, adding to the end of the chant:

> I love Money
> I am Money

Did a pile of cash land on my doorstep? Well, it did seem like opportunity knocked a little harder when I was in the Money

Magnet groove, for sure. The sudden offers to do a paid reading or write an article kept me chanting away each day in my favorite prayer spot, the shower. Standing beneath the spray, I'd close my eyes and recite the chant. And like magic, the next day, I'd learn that a grant came through.

Would I have gotten the grant anyway? Was the granting based on my actual application and the quality of my work, not how melodiously I intoned a few phrases in the bathroom? Probably. And, as I do make my living on the haphazard accumulation of speaking gigs and freelance writing, perhaps those shouldn't be surprising either. But there was another, unexpected magic the Money Magic chant worked on me: It transformed my relationship to cold, hard cash.

When a system is oppressing you, it's easy to take the most glaring physical representation of that system and demonize it. The system itself tends to be invisible, an infinite string of transactions and reactions stretching into antiquity. As a poor person sensitive to the stings of classism, I decided early on that I hated money. Money was evil; money was the problem. I avoided financial exchanges when possible, putting on free events, doing free tarot readings, giving away my little books of poetry sometimes. When money was inevitably involved in one of my projects, I shuddered and pushed the responsibility onto someone else: *You deal with this; I hate money.*

Once I got sober, I lost a lot of the booze-fueled bravado that had helped me cope with the harsh realities of being poor. With alcohol, I achieved a persona of tough-assed bitch who didn't give a shit about cash and thought you were a damn fool if you did. Stripped of inebriants, I was just myself—smaller, more vulnerable, broke, and a bit lost. Plus, the practices I was learning in 12-step programs were about compassion—not judging people, not hating. Suddenly, I was thrust into these small rooms filled with people I used to love to rail against when drunk—men, people with more money than I had. But now we were all the same, gathered to discuss how fallible we were, how we had fucked up, how we were trying to be better people, for ourselves and for our worlds. Whatever delusions we'd used as coping mechanisms had withered in the stark light of sobriety. After about a decade of demonizing and avoiding money I realized the disadvantage I'd set myself up for. I was underpaid, if paid at all. People handling the cash at my events sometimes helped themselves to it, probably figuring if I hated the stuff so much, what would I care? And, perhaps worst of all, I had no power. Not believing in a system doesn't make it go away. After working my butt off organizing a huge literary event only to watch, again and again, the person handling the money being treated like the mastermind while I was little more than ignored, I faced the hard fact: Whoever has the money has the power. When I exiled myself from the financial aspects of my work, I cut myself off from avenues of respect, control, and autonomy as well.

The thought of facing the rest of my life as a broke person, without alcohol to lessen the sting, filled me with despair. I had to figure out a way to make this part of life less painful. One of the most powerful things I'd learned since getting sober is to love and accept life on life's terms. Alcoholics have a hard time doing this; we're little id-driven crybabies, guzzling and complaining about how nothing in this life goes the way we think it should. Accepting and even embracing the world as it is can be radical, and it can have powerful, positive results.

I decided to apply some of this sobriety dogma to my money problems. *Money loves me* was a really good start—that money could be benevolent and loving was a revolutionary notion. I imagined the spirit of money as a tenderhearted fairy who longed to share herself with everyone but kept getting kidnapped by dastardly villains. A sort of less cranky Tinker Bell, this money loved me and loved *all* the downtrodden!

Okay, money loves me. But for me to love money? That was preposterous. Yet I knew that in order to heal my abusive relationship with prosperity, I was going to have to start approaching this part of life not with fear or anger or hurt, but with love. Couldn't I love a fairy-esque money with a generous spirit, too easily captured by brutes? Embedded in this fairy tale, my desire for cash began to feel like a righteous conspiracy to break money out of the prison the 1 percent had locked her up in. *Free money!*

What about *I am money?* What was that about? It was partly an impulse to get as *close* to money, this thing I'd avoided, as possible. But it was something else, too: an acknowledgment that, like it or not, I was part of the money system. I did work and get paid. I took my money and spent it, on stupid shit as well as on necessary objects. Acting like I was somehow outside—or above—the money system was ridiculous. It was time to join the human race. *I am money.* Money kept me fed today. Money kept me under this roof. Money bought me this computer, the clothes on my back. Letting go of value judgments, dropping the idea of myself as poor or rich or whatever, I saw myself in the center of a web of prosperity. I had all these things, this life, and I was grateful. *I am money.*

*Money comes to me, money loves me, money is sexually attracted to me, money wants to be near me.* Slowly, the subconscious notion of money as a giant war machine, as the dreadful Moloch of Allen Ginsberg's *Howl,* faded. Money became something silly, something flirtatious. Images flashed as I spoke the chant in the shower: The little money man from Monopoly! Me, naked, on a bed of cold, hard cash, throwing it into the air with abandon! The money pixie, freed from her dungeon! After a lifetime of making money antimatter, I needed to make it something light. It did the trick. Less and less did it seem like money was an evil force with unlimited power over my life. Increasingly it felt like something I was in conversation with—no longer something that wanted to destroy me, but something that wanted to build me up.

The chant didn't "fix" me, of course; it was just one more tool I had to use in the lifelong task of dismantling my scarcity issues. There were others. In my support group I started meeting with a woman who had more time sober than I had. In her I was able to catch a glimpse of the sort of person I might someday become if I managed to keep dodging the lures of booze and coke—she seemed healthy, in body and in spirit. Having established her sobriety, she was able to deal with other issues that had been festering beneath her drinking. Alcoholics don't emotionally grow when they're using; once we get it together, we realize that there's a whole banged-up psyche that needs our loving care. And one thing we were both dealing with was money issues. It's something a lot of alcoholics have to face up to once they're sober, even people with middle- or upper-class backgrounds. Nobody makes good financial choices when they're blitzed all the time. Chances are you can't hold a good job, and you're spending all your cash on booze and drugs. You wake up in the morning vaguely remembering a trip to the ATM, even though your wallet shows no sign of such activity. You do absolutely nothing to plan for any sort of future, because the only future that matters is when you can have your next drink. My friend's basic alcoholic money issues were compounded by the fact that in her own early sobriety she fell prey to a secondary shopping addiction. In the wake of this mess, paying bills became terrifying, a morass of self-loathing, disappointment, and frustration. But a year or so of wrestling with her alcoholism had taught her all sorts of magical tricks. At bill time, she started pulling an empty chair beside her at the table and asking her idea of God to sit down and keep her company while she faced her fears.

I know some of you are throwing up in your mouth right now. These methods may be a bit too deep in woo-woo fairyland for the more logical hard-asses out there, the word *God* too triggering. I respect that. But the idea that she wasn't alone while staring down the barrel of her checking account gave my friend a glimmer of relief. Enough to lick the damn envelopes and get the checks in the mail.

At this point I had enough time in 12-step programs, and had followed their advice with enough dogged desperation, that I could see that they were working. I just felt better. I wasn't as freaked out or stressed out. There is this phrase about people who come into 12-step culture and get super blissed out when they find it working for them: the pink cloud. I was super duper on a big pink cloud. At heart I'm really a hedonist—I just want to feel awesome, all the time. For a while, drugs and alcohol helped me achieve that. Now that using had stopped working, it looked like this new world of self-investigation and higher-power communication was doing the trick. I thought about how my friend invited her HP to bill time, and wondered how I could come up with a similar trick to help me with my own money issues.

For me, the money terrors came when I was purchasing something I didn't need, which in my austere mind was anything outside rent, electricity, and Internet, plus maybe a few cans of beans and a sack of rice. Chills ran up my spine as I brought a seven-dollar bar of Fresh soap that smelled like the armpits of tree sprites to the register. My stomach would plummet as I walked the frock I'd found on the Urban Outfitters sale rack to the counter. I'd break out in a sweat as a cashier rang up a stack of books. *They're books*, I'd scold myself. *You can* always *buy books!* Once, in the bathroom of a soul food restaurant in Tacoma, Washington, I sat on the toilet and read a poster taped to the back of the stall door. It was a cheesy thing listing ways to have a happy life, the sort commonly illustrated with folksy roses and birds and decorative, beribboned straw hats. *Never regret money spent on books or flowers* was one of the commandments. Ever desperate for something permitting me not to have financial regret, I cosigned the sentiment before I could flush the toilet. *Yeah! Books and flowers make life worth living! I'm never going to regret buying them ever again! The books are even tax write-offs!* This ridiculous poster actually had a lasting impact. But like most tools, it wasn't enough on its own. My money issues are so unruly, I need an arsenal. My friend sat at the table with her higher power, so what could my own Stevie Nicks spiritual guide do for me? *Well, she could start by giving me a trust fund*, I thought cynically. And then I realized she already had.

What if the money in my bank account wasn't *my* money, but God's? What if the cosmos *was* taking care of me, and I didn't have to worry about it all the time? My life as a freelancer, like my life as a sober person, was still new enough to be unfamiliar and scary. I was always doing stressful calculation—*I've got enough for this month, but what about next month?* When next month turned out to be fine, it was, *Sure, I've got enough for the next few months, but what about in half a year?* When I asked myself how much money in the bank would make me feel secure, I honestly couldn't come up with a reasonable number. The thought of something else taking responsibility for my finances filled me with crazy relief. I'd learned to turn my cravings for alcohol over to this Stevie Nicksian deity—why not turn my money panic over as well?

So I decided I had a trust fund from God. I didn't have to sweat it. Maybe sometimes the balance would be lower than I wanted it to be, but I was going to trust that I would always have enough to do the things I was meant to do in this life. What if I wanted to spend three months lolling on a beach somewhere, daydreaming? Sorry, not in the cards. Not part of Stevie-Goddess's plan for me. What if I suddenly needed to go to New York City to do something writing related? Apparently, my higher power approved. The funds were available.

Like all of these fanciful tricks, they don't stay lodged in your mind in a constant way. Again and again I would totally forget that I had a trust fund from God. But frequently, in the throes of minor panic, I would remember, and start to calm down. This shit *works*. Of course, for it to make any sort of nonsensical sense, you not only have to believe in some sort of god, but it has to be the kind of god that actually wants you to have money and happiness and an all-around excellent life, including the occasional luxury. This can be hard for some people to wrap their heads around, as many of us were raised with the notion of a punishing god who is sort of like a demonic Santa—seeing you when you're sleeping, knowing when you're awake, always waiting to bust you for some sort of totally human infraction. "Oh—God's punishing me!" How many times have I heard someone say that? It's always after they've shared a relatively harmless piece of gossip and then stubbed their toe or something. Really? Your god is that petty? In my own Catholic upbringing I was taught never to say a prayer for myself, or for material things, but only for other people to be okay, and also for God to pick up my soul if I happened to croak in the middle of the night. I do believe that praying for other people is mandatory, and that following a directive I learned in 12-step—to pray to know God's will for you—is ideal. But I don't see the harm in throwing in a few prayers for things like money, or a robust sex life, or a pair of really great shoes or a vacation. If you are unfortunately saddled with a petty, Mean Girlsy, or otherwise grumpy god, I suggest you get rid of him. One thing people don't understand about gods is you can always trade yours in for a new one, a DIY god created in your own image.

My favorite poet, Eileen Myles, has a poem called "A Blue Jay," with these lines:

> *I begin*
> *to believe*
> *in a God*
> *I could*
> *build like*
> *a porch.*
> *I began*
> *to have*
> *a need*
> *like that.*
> *She shall*
> *be fat &*
> *wrap her*
> *arms around*
> *me.*

If you're going to fool around with all these airy-fairy new-agey ideas, you're going to have to find something to pray to. I call this thing "God," because it's an easy shorthand, but I understand that the G-word conjures an image of a rageaholic lightning-bolt-wielding dad for some people, so I intersperse it with "Higher Power," "The Universe," and "Stevie Nicks." My Stevie Nicks god wants me to have everything I want. Like a quality therapist, she has unconditional positive regard for me. She understands why I would like to have that Creatures of

Comfort dress with the eyeballs and hearts on it. Stevie Nicks god knows that when I look good, I feel good, and Stevie Nicks god *always* wants me to feel good. She wishes she had an extra $575 she could pop into my trust fund right now so I could snag that cute frock, but she just doesn't. Don't ask why—Stevie Nicks god is benevolent as all get-out, but she's still a *god*, after all, and it's her prerogative to work in mysterious ways. I don't get to know or even understand her whole plan for me. But I can trust that she's not going to punish me for wishing for a high-waisted felted wool Chanel skirt or a pair of Stella McCartney eyeglasses or a monogrammed Goyard bag. Stevie Nicks god wants all these things, too!

Do I think people experiencing extreme hard luck just haven't chanted in the shower enough? No way. There is lots of bullshit plonked in the path of people who'd like to improve their lot. But I think it *is* possible to cast a spell on yourself, hold lightly to expectations, and see what happens. Fire your judgmental, old-guard god and let your awesome new HP hook you up a trust fund, or let her be your matchmaker, or your literary agent; use her to get whatever you're after. Figure out what your own weird-ass, shaky, earnest, doubtful praying sounds like and do it in your own shower or at the gym or on the bus or while you do the dishes. The worst it's going to do is make you feel a little dumb and maybe give you some additional insight into yourself. But at its best, it just might help you make some legitimate magic.

# 5.

# Beware of Sex and Other Rules for Love

When I emerged from my eight-year monogamous relationship, ready to date, I was insane—like, feral. I was like a child who had been locked in a closet for ten years and then unleashed upon a world of toys and goodies. I was tripping over my feet and drooling foam from the corners of my mouth at the prospect of new partners. The possibility of fresh romantic adventures was a terrific distraction from my breakup heartache. Plus, my ex had hooked up with someone immediately, and the only way to engage with that seemed to be (A) never date again, as if I was now completely above such landscapes of sordid trysts and disappointments, and also *so* satisfied with my own company that I wished not to compromise my independence even the slightest; or (B) get totally competitive about it.

Everyone told me to give it a minute. *Don't hurl yourself into the dating pool just because your ex has shacked up with the local DJ who tromps around town in Daisy Dukes and thigh-high stockings. Don't jump in bed with the nearest stranger because the two of them start showing up at your favorite brunch spots and 12-step meetings and—horror of horrors—acting* friendly *toward you.* Even though I was being urged by concerned friends to take some time off—a month, six months, a year—I knew I was not that girl. You know—the girl who does a cleanse instead of hitting a club looking for a hookup. Or, like, *knits.* My life as a sober person had calmed down *a lot*, but I clung to the thrill of sex like the addict I was: *You're not going to take* this *away from me, too!*

After I sent my ex on a couch tour of his closest acquaintances, I did what all females recently released from a long monogamous relationship should do: I called my best, sluttiest gay boyfriend and asked him how to get my game back. Unlike my other friends, Lee would never tell me to take a break from dating. He was part of a gay-boy world that contained steamy bathhouses and department store men's rooms, roadside truck stops and vertiginous city parks—places for gay men to find one another and, in complete anonymity and flagrant disregard of the law, get it on. He understood that the thrill of sex was a natural high, as important to the body as a bowl full of kale and a jog on the beach. Lee believes that in submitting to our animal instincts, we encounter a sort of pagan holiness. He was the perfect enabler.

I phoned him from the front stoop of my North Beach apartment. I was smoking, and the skin above my heart was burning. Not with love—I'd just gotten a tattoo. It was of a pair of elegant female hands holding branches of lush blue roses. It was really pretty.

So was my tattoo artist. After sitting beneath him for hours, watching flowers bloom around my collarbone, I had developed a crush on him. I thought maybe he had a little bit of a crush on me, too. I didn't mind making the first move, but every motion I thought of felt clumsy and awkward, too tacky or too buttoned-up. I realized that if I had ever had any game at all, it had surely shriveled up and died during my LTR. Lee would be filled with advice on how to execute my first seduction, and he'd get a gossipy delight from hearing my story. I was filled with anticipation as I pressed my phone to my ear. When he picked up, I overwhelmed him with a deluge of chatter and questions and details. The tattoo artist was so cute, with his pixie-boy rocker shag and the crappy tattoos that crawled up his neck like those of a Russian jailbird! Should I proposition him boldly, or would he think I was too trampy? Should I act demure? Demure takes so long, and I wasn't confident I could pull it off anyway. I didn't want to marry the gent; I just wanted to fornicate with him on the tattoo table after the shop was closed. What if he turned me down? I'd be humiliated! Help me, Lee, help me!

"You gotta be ready to get rejected," Lee said to me, a simple piece of advice, but also profound enough that it stuck with me through the next four years of falling in and out of love like the dumbest baby bird who just *cannot* figure out how to fly out of the fucking tree without crashing again and again and again. "The more you put yourself out there, the more rejections you

get. It's just the law of averages. You can't take it personally."
My BGB (best gay boyfriend) knew what he was talking about;
the gay-guy hookup world allows for extremely particular preferences. Dick size, cut or uncut, age, fitness specifications, eth-
nicity, whether you are a pitcher or a catcher in the game of
love—it's like they're buying a house, not sourcing a BJ in the
back corner of a bathhouse. This culture hadn't hardened my
BGB, but it had nurtured a sort of detachment in him. I found
this advice crucial, as was his response when I asked him if you
have to use a condom while giving a BJ: "The only people I ever
see doing that are Renaissance Faire bisexuals at sex clubs, and
they don't look like they're having very much fun."

There was another problem, besides my near-decade out of
the game: I'd never hit on a person sober. I'd never *dated* sober.
Formerly when I wanted to sleep with someone I would get drunk
and sidle up to my lust object with a blunt, "Wanna make out?"
Sometimes they made out with me, sometimes they ran for the
hills. My ex and I got together over margaritas in a Mexican
restaurant, him wooing me with promises of the *best* crystal meth
*ever*, so pure it glowed a faint lavender glow. He never did produce this mythical substance (and wasn't *pure meth* an oxymoron
anyway?), but we did slide down a dark hole of drugs together,
then clambered out together, and then broke up. When I looked
back at the romances I'd struck up before him, I was embarrassed
at how sloppy they'd been, at my inebriated bravado. It had
worked well enough in my twenties, when everyone was stumbling in and out love, but I was hoping to have more dignity in
my sober thirties.

"You're overthinking it," Lee counseled. "If you're not trying to seriously date the guy, just ask him if he wants to hook up."

"How?" I wailed. "It would be so weird for me to call him . . . and I can't do it at the shop, with everyone around."

"Text him," Lee suggested. Duh. Text him. Nobody actually talked on their phones these days; they took pictures and sent messages. Plus, I was a *writer*! I would be in my element with a text, would I not? I glanced at the clock on my phone. It was nine o'clock at night. My neighborhood was bumping. Handsome Italian maître d's beckoned passersby with platters of bruschetta; down the street, strip club barkers solicited similarly, while dancers in kimonos took cigarette breaks by the curb. Actual *sailors*, in their spiffy white uniforms, barhopped around me. The tattoo artist lived in this neighborhood as well. Perhaps he was sitting on his own stoop nearby, watching the lusty commotion, wishing for a way to jump in.

I hung up with Lee, who offered me a bounty of blessing and good luck wishes and you-can-do-it encouragement. I spent twenty minutes experimenting with variations on the sentence: *I think you're really foxy and if you ever want to hook up you should call me.* "I think you're really foxy. Want to hook up?" "You're a fox and I want to hook up with you." "Hey, fox, want to hook up?" The longer I obsessed, the more ridiculous they all seemed. The guy either thought I was a fox and wanted to hook up as well, or he didn't. A slight change of phrase wasn't going to doom me, nor would it suddenly enlighten him to my charms were he oblivious. The tiny green screen of my Nokia glowed up at me. I hit Send. And was immediately rejected. It was a nice rejection, and may have included a compliment and claim of feeling flattered, but it was a rejection. I deleted it so I could pretend it never happened, and sent the news to Lee: *Denied*.

I wasn't devastated, but it stung. I understood that Lee's *prepare to be rejected* advice was good, but I also wanted to minimize the damage. I recognized that I had poor impulse control when it came to sex and romance, and I wanted to temper my nature with some structure. If this was a game, I needed some rules. At first my Rules for Love were formulated to try to minimize heartbreak and embarrassment. Later they helped me not to waste my time. Altogether and unexpectedly they led me toward an understanding of what I did and didn't want in relationships as I assimilated these new experiences and learned more about myself.

What Rule for Love did I learn from the tattoo artist? Well, first of all, don't hit on your tattoo artist. A female hitting on her tattoo artist is the equivalent of a dude hitting on his lap dancer. Just because they periodically back away from your partially naked body and say, "Nice," does not mean that they think *you* are nice. They are not thinking of you at all. They are thinking of the design they are sinking into your flesh—a process, by the way, that is releasing tons of endorphins and other pleasurable chemicals into your brain, chemicals that might make you feel a little bit goofy and possibly in love with your tattoo artist. Especially if he is super-hot, and he wears pegged skintight black jeans and tiny, shrunken denim jackets and has jet-black hair jagging into his face like a painter inked it there. This entire scene might leave you (me) very vulnerable to thinking (wishing) there is a connection, some kind of energy occurring between the two of you. There is not. If you must ignore my advice and proposition the tattoo artist—who I *promise* is looking at you not like a nuanced, intriguing person with a hot bod, but more like the side of a building in a run-down neighborhood that he is tagging with a can of spray paint—at least wait until your tattoo is done. I learned the hard way. After embarrassing myself with my tattoo artist via text message, I then had to go back for two more sittings to complete my tattoo.

Ultimately, being rejected by the hot tattoo artist was the sort of baptism I needed to bravely saunter back into the world of romance. I wish I could say that my subsequent conquests were less bumbling and ridiculous, but as you will soon find out, they were not. The dating blitz I embarked on after ending my LTR was wild, fun, humiliating, exhilarating, and very, very educational. As relationships flared and failed, I began to take note of patterns. I gained some clarity on the choices I was making. By paying attention, I began to realize and refine what I wanted. I found that I didn't like being single—I *loved* it. I didn't cry all the time when I was single! I wasn't always recovering from an emotionally exhausting argument! I didn't have to endure the wack television choices of my significant other! (*The Real World?* Really?) Another big plus of singlehood: I had way more money now that I wasn't partially supporting—get ready—a *rapper* who'd had an equally hard time supporting himself on rhymes as he had holding on to jobs. Being single was super cool. I felt like I was finally living the life of the liberated, bohemian female I truly was.

Eventually, though, the novelty of my bed being a lazy Susan wore thin. I found myself envying the closeness and stability of my two best friends, Tali and Bernadine. They loved each other so hard, they had matching tattoos of each other's initials framed by a love letter held in the beak of a dove. Bernadine happily declared she would rather see Tali dead than leave her for another woman. I wanted something that deep and passionate.

I was also really inspired by my sister's marriage. She'd found a sweet, sensitive man she could be profoundly silly with, and together they had a couple of babies. Babies! I'd never really been around them, and my ex-boyfriend had been so anti-procreation that even wondering aloud if I might someday maybe want to *think* about having kids provoked one of the huge and downward-spiraling arguments that I could only heal from by embarking on a beauty-product shopping spree. Those fights were expensive; I avoided them. But now, free of that stifling relationship and delighting in being a new aunt, I considered it. Kids. Who knows? Maybe someday. I was open to it.

But first, I decided, I wanted a stable relationship with someone who was so crazy into me that they wanted to freaking *marry* me. Yeah. That's what I wanted at the end of my sex vacation. I wanted to get married. I didn't care about its history of female oppression, all that selling women for dowries and vows of obedience. No one I knew practiced such a marriage, and when I dreamt about marriage, it was not a dream about cutting my life away in service of some dude. It was a dream, first, of a *party*, a big, fun celebration of love in which I would finally once again have the opportunity to wear a veil—something I'd not enjoyed since attending a Billy Idol concert dressed as the bride from the "White Wedding" video.

After enough experimentation with the various models of being in relationship—serial monogamy, monogamy with some "gray area," outright polyamory, dating—I loved the idea of a monogamous connection with someone awesome enough that you knew you'd be interested in them forever, hot enough that you'd want to get it on with them forever, loving enough that you wanted to stay all wrapped up in them forever. For so long, my feelings (or fears—is there a difference?) were summed up, as so many feelings are, by a Smiths lyric: *Love is natural and real / But not for you, my love.* I don't know why I thought I'd never get my day at the nondenominational altar—maybe I was trying to protect myself from wanting it in the first place, or maybe my dating track record didn't inspire confidence. But as my standards for the people I dated grew, so did my standards for the kind of relationship I wanted. I wanted someone capable of the big-time forever love affair I always knew I was capable of.

I investigated my love life. I couldn't deny that the choices I was making weren't helping. Into my Rules for Love, a tier system was built: There were Sex Only people, Dating people, and then the elite and somewhat evasive Marriage Material. If I was serious about wanting to build something solid and lasting, I was going to have to spend less time frolicking in the first two camps, no matter how fun and sexy (or darkly psychologically compelling) they may be.

A rule I eventually devised—and it took a while—was Be-

ware of Sex. The warning came first as a whisper, then as a haunting echo, then as an annoying nag, and finally as a blood-curdling
scream. What I'm saying is, though I started to know better, it
took some disasters before respect for this warning was stronger
than the dizzy pull toward romance. And part of the problem was
limerence.

Freshly sprung from my monogamous LTR, I had no idea how
vulnerable I would be to the onslaught of chemicals your brain
releases when you're attracted to someone. These chemicals are
responsible for every single people-in-love-are-crazy-fools song,
movie plot, and Shakespearean drama ever written. They stimu-
late the same area of the brain that lights up when you snort a fat
rail of cocaine. This state of mind, *limerence*, is a biological relative of obsessive-compulsive disorder. If you are an addict, or perhaps have the sort of low-dopamine, low-serotonin brain soup
best served with a side of SSRIs, you are perhaps more sensitive
to the mind-altering power of limerence. And if you are a romantic, you are perhaps more likely to label this heady, overwhelming
sensation *love*. Being a low-serotonin addict with romantic tendencies, I had to experience many crashed-and-burned affairs to
understand that for me, love really *was* a drug.

As someone who hangs out in 12-step circles, I was aware of
support groups for people who find themselves addicted to sex, or
love, or both. Before I dealt with my own addictions, I'd thought
these love-addict people were terrible killjoys, if not flat-out
crazy. Love and sex and the ecstasy that accompanies them were
the best things in the *world*. They made life worth living! They
were worth fighting for—dying for, even! (I told you I was a ro-

mantic.) But as I began to face up to my drinking and my copious drug ingestion, I started to understand that a person really can be addicted to lots of different things, because the highs induced by the dopamine machine in your brain can become addictive. Some people find that activities the rest of humanity is able to indulge in without consequence—dating, food, shopping— trigger in their special chemistry a reaction that spurs increasingly compulsive behavior. From my own experience and the stories of other alcoholics who sober up only to find themselves ruining their lives with a brand-new eating disorder or maxed-out credit card or STD, I've come to the conclusion that some brains are just super addict-y, and can get obsessively focused on whatever triggers a dopamine release. Your friend who can't stop checking her phone for incoming Likes and text messages? Dopamine fiend. The one who gets weirdly manic and sweaty and spaced out while you're browsing at Topshop? Dopamine fiend. The one who falls in love and off the face of the earth every other month? Dopamine fiend. Maybe that friend is actually *you*. It's certainly me.

Because it would take me about a year to learn about sex and love chemicals and that psychedelic state limerence. I mistook my first post-LTR romance for True Love instead of what it was— hot sex with a sociopath. I was so out of my mind with the tsunami of dopamine this Johnny Depp look-alike provoked in my nervous system, I ignored a ton of red flags. First of all, he was unbearably pretentious. Asked a friend of mine in a cynical voice, "Does Fake Johnny Depp *really* begin every morning with a poached egg on a bed of brown rice and miso?" I understood his skepticism, but the answer was yes, Fake Johnny Depp *did* prepare himself a breakfast of poached eggs, brown rice, and miso each morning. Which prompted the next question: "Well, does he have to talk about it *in that voice?*"

I understood the voice my friends were speaking of. Not only did Fake Johnny Depp talk about his breakfast selection as if it were the most precious, even spiritual moment of his day—he talked about everything like that. The fuzzy kangaroo paw he was planting in his garden. The Roland Barthes essay he'd read while eating his poached eggs and miso in said kangaroo paw garden. He was a recent graduate of Oberlin, and he used the word *praxis* in daily conversation. Frequently I had to ask Fake Johnny Depp what he had just said, ask him to repeat it in the language of the common American English speaker. Because I was in limerence, overdosing on crush chemicals, I thought all this shit was adorable. I liked his swingy "mushroom hairdo," as a concerned friend unkindly called it. I was ready to go shack up with him in a yurt in the forests of Maine, so that he could apprentice to an obscure elderly artist whose hand-carved wooden bowls had garnered much praise on the artisanal hand-carved wooden bowl scene. Everything I had worked for—my writing career, the nonprofit literary organization I directed, my home in San Francisco—I would have thrown away for this guy. All because I loved his swingy mushroom hairdo and the way he flung me around in the sack.

Fake Johnny Depp was, according to my best amateur research in the DSM, suffering from borderline personality disorder, so thankfully the relationship was doomed. People with borderline personality disorder—or, as I like to cheerfully call it, the beeps—are dangerously easy to fall into limerence with, because their signature behavior of delusional mania looks a lot like the throes of first love. They're like a parasitical mimic, taking on the characteristics of love but actually burrowing into your psyche and laying eggs there—eggs that will hatch and *drive you mad!* "What has happened to my awesome true love affair?!" I asked myself, sinking deeper and deeper into the sort of psychotic fighting that kept us up until five a.m., forcing me to cancel plans because I was so sleep deprived and dehydrated from sobbing. I'd lie to my friends about my canceled plans, because I didn't want them to know I'd been up all night fighting with Fake Johnny Depp, because they already didn't like him very much (note: when your friends don't like your date, it's a red flag) and I wanted everybody to get along. But lying about my relationship to my friends made me feel ashamed and low-self-esteem-y, like I was in an abusive relationship. And I started to wonder: *Am* I in an abusive relationship? Because even though Fake Johnny Depp's torments were never physical, they made me feel so completely unhinged that I actually hit *myself*. Nothing slams the self-esteem like hitting your own freaking self. This was the cycle of violence I found myself in, due in no small part to the heady effects of limerence upon my delicate system.

When Fake Johnny Depp ended our brief and volatile affair to take up with a trust fund princess who paid his way to Africa, I was startled to find myself *relieved.* As I walked away from his apartment, the thought *He's not my problem anymore* rang through my head, and I actually felt sorry for the girl he'd newly attached himself to. He soon left her for one of his grad school professors, who paid his passage to Iceland, then left her for a host of others, on and on; he's currently swindling a poor sod who is footing the bills while Fake Johnny Depp fake-farms a plot of land out in Red Hook, like Marie Antoinette playing milkmaid at Versailles.

"What was I thinking?" I gasped to Lee. "He's clearly *so crazy.* Nobody liked him. We fought all the time and I can't even tell you one thing we fought about."

"Was the sex good?" Lee inquired.

"Yes."

"Well, there you go. Good sex does something to your brain chemicals." And so my BGB hipped me to the concept of limerence. Prone to making the occasional cameo at support groups for sex and love addicts, Lee, too, was particularly sensitive to the effects of limerence on his common sense. "You gotta watch out, girl," he warned.

"What am I supposed to do, never have sex again?" I wailed dramatically.

"One step at a time."

I wish that Fake Johnny Depp—clearly a Sex Only person, if not an Avoid Completely person— was the first and last time I confused lust with love and allowed an unsuitable paramour to take up space in my heart and my head. But it takes a while to understand what's wrong with you, and even after you've figured it out, it takes a while to *care,* so I continued dating and sleeping with hotties who were less than Marriage Material.

Take, for example, my yearlong intrigue with a recovering heroin addict living on probation and opiate blockers in her mother's sewing room on the other side of the country. It took us a long time to meet in person, as various issues—say, a court case for driving the getaway car for a grocery store holdup with a dirty syringe—got in the way of her coming to visit me. Because of the distance (and the whole sleeping on a twin bed in her mother's house thing), visiting her seemed out of the question. But gosh-darnnit I am plucky and resourceful, and a *romantic* who was apparently experiencing the effects of the infatuation chemical norepinephrine, which makes you do batshit crazy things for "love." Sadly, experiencing obstacles in love actually *increases* dopamine. Cruel world!

When I arrived in upstate New York to visit Internet Girl-friend, her mother was not thrilled to meet me, a thirtysome-thing, heavily tattooed woman from California, but she endured it the way she had endured the traumatizing years of her daugh-ter's drug addiction—years that weren't actually that long ago. However, after she walked in on us having sex to a Dario Argento movie on the twin bed, I decided we had to leave the nest and bought her a bus ticket to stay with me at a friend's house in the city. Internet Girlfriend didn't like taking my money; she even tried to sell her opiate blockers to junkies at the bus station. I sent Tali a text message from the bus station, seated on a plastic chair near a losing pile of scratch tickets while IG was off hustling the hustlers. *Is it nice or not nice that the recovering junkie is trying to sell her opiate blockers to heroin addicts at a bus station?* Tali texted back quickly: *Oh girl. What are you doing?*

I only ever saw Internet Girlfriend in person once after that visit, but the double-whammy dopamine punch of sext messages (text messages + dirty talk = double dopamine!) kept me in and out of limerence for a solid year. At the end of that year, I broke up with her in an epically long text message while simultaneously flipping through *Vogue* and eating Thanksgiving leftovers. The more I reflected on the apocalypse that was the Internet Girlfriend Affair, the more it revealed itself to be a treasure trove of brand new Rules for Love—what not to date. Don't date people who sell pills in bus stations. Don't date people who you know in your gut are lying to you all the time, whose stories are so shady you start to hope they *are* lying to you. Don't date people whose idea of a good tattoo is an evil, fanged carrot eating a bunny. Not to be a snob, but maybe no hooking up with people who live with their parents. No long-distance relationships. (I know there are lots of long-distance love stories out there; I've seen them on TV talk shows and commercials for dating Web sites. But these are *my* Rules for Love, and for me, if I'm not in the same city as someone, I can't experience real-time hangouts, free of the wild dopamine stimulants of travel and deprivation.) Also, Internet Girlfriend was twenty-five years old. There is a saying among recovering addicts that your emotional maturity freezes at the age you start abusing your drug of choice, and that you don't start growing again until you get sober. I've found this to be true, which means at that point, though I was thirty-seven years old, I was emotionally twenty-five years old. And the more I fooled around with and dated young people, the more I found them to be, well, young. In an annoying way. I didn't want to hang around while they figured out the significant life lessons I knew were right around the corner. I didn't want to wait for them to understand—no, *really* understand—that, for better or worse, I was not their mother. And I didn't want them to grow up and out of the dynamics we'd established. They'd still be young and full of life and lust for the wild world of dating, but as I got older, I realized that if I had anything to say about it, this would be my last time on the market. So I turned in my cougar card, as my new Rules for Love stipulated that the younger generations were off-limits for dating.

I was beginning to realize that having off-the-rails sexual chemistry is not only *not* necessary for a stable relationship; the off-the-rails-ness of it is actually detrimental. Dopamine isn't the only chemical in your relationship chemistry kit. There are other, sweeter chemicals that start surging as the dopamine lightens up, chemicals that facilitate attachment and affection and maybe actual true love. So I made another Rule for Love: no more sex addicts. In fact, no addicts who don't have at least three years sober in a reputable recovery program. Just at the beginning stages of staying clean from heroin, Internet Girlfriend couldn't even see how she was out of her brain with all the other ways you can get yourself high. I was only beginning to understand it myself. For a little while, I didn't *want* to understand it. But then I really, really did.

A funny thing happens when you start implementing standards in your romantic life—they grow. As I started to get a handle on my dopamine issues, I got bored with sleeping around with sexy losers. In my Rules for Love, dates do friendly-type things for one another, not leave their dates to walk home after a hot make-out on the roof of a perfectly functioning automobile (true story). I felt a strange new pride in myself for even *recognizing* this. Having standards was so new and exciting, I swear I was getting dopamine off it.

My Rules for Love continued to morph into actual standards. In recovery circles you are encouraged to make a sort of wish list detailing all the qualities you would like your next beloved to possess. They can be serious, crucial, and deep—I want someone who communicates without yelling; someone who has a spiritual practice; someone who doesn't hate their mom. They can also be shallow, or superficial—I want someone smoking hot; I want someone who has their own apartment; I want someone who makes more money than I do. Some parts of the list are deal breakers—no drug addicts. Some aren't—I guess the person doesn't *need* to have a car, as long as they have a driver's license, because I don't. I kept my list in a little notebook, adding to it as I made my way through broken-down love affairs. *No recent breakups*, I wrote after the crappy experience of being someone else's rebound. After one fling left me with a killer sinus infection, I wrote *No smokers*. I'm a codependent smoker. If my date smokes, I'll smoke. Smoking is awesome in your twenties, but frankly, any older than that and you just look slavish and weak willed (or, even worse, like you're desperate to stay in your twenties).

One standard that took me a while to wake up to was no depressed people. It was tricky in many ways, the deepest being that depressed people were my *type*, and for a long time I didn't even know it. Depression is like a haze, a cloud or an aura that surrounds certain people. It prickles my skin—a slight anxiety, an attraction-repulsion combo that drives me sickly toward them. It's in the folds of their faces, no matter how youthful they may still be. It's in the slump of their shoulders. For so long I thought it was emotional depth, a refined sensitivity that had left them wounded. Chalk it up to having a depressed dad who came home from his long nights at the labor union full of bitter cynicism about the world. If he was my default romantic ideal, I was fucked. There was a bit of opposites-attract going on, too; though I also suffered from depression, mine was of the weepy, bleeding-heart variety. The depressives I sought were more hard-hearted, sarcastic. Their humor was a biting sort that kept me on my toes. I didn't know if I liked it or not, but I *wanted* to like it. I also, in my bleeding-heart way, wanted to take care of and ultimately *cure* my depressed lovers. It's all so textbook it grosses me out, but it's real.

For instance, take the boyfriend who took me on a cruise, on a yacht that sailed down the fucking French Riviera. I thought this gentleman was a Dating person, with his advanced age, regular income, and civilized manner. The ship was tipped with a row of stunning sails, and it slunk through the deep blue waters, docking alongside ancient castles whose beaches we were invited to splash upon. I could not *believe* my good fortune; I thought it would be the time of my life. Instead, I spent my days running bow to stern, dashing into bathrooms to cry tears of anxiety and disappointment. My moody boyfriend was no fun to be on a luxury cruise with. He was snippy and mean, a power grouch. Had he been like this before the cruise? Of course he had. Had his moods already raised the red flags of anxiety in my belly countless times? Yep. Did I ignore them always? Of course I did. Did this guy come with a list of prior offenses well known to me, a strand of excellent girls whom he'd treated carelessly, breaking their hearts? Yup. Did I think none of this would happen to me, that I was somehow different? Uh-huh. Can I even believe I fell into such a classic lady relationship trap? At this point, yes. Yes, I can believe it.

By the time the ship docked in Nice I was such a nervous wreck, all I could do was frantically e-mail my friends back in the States, and try to wring some soothing chemicals out of my brain by buying a way-too-expensive Isabel Marant sweater with round shoulder pads, a trend that would pass by the time I returned home. Even after the most miserable experience of my life, I still thought if my date would just *open his heart to me* we could be happy together. But depression is a disease as surely as alcoholism or cirrhosis of the liver. You can't cure it by dating a happy person. All that happens is the happy person gets depressed, too. The week we returned from our miserable vacation he broke up with me, dodging my desperate seduction attempt by claiming to be sick with diarrhea.

Rebels without causes look sexy and romantic when they and you are young, but as you get older and wiser it all just looks like mental health issues. Cruise Dude had me always walking on eggshells, obsessing over what I did and didn't say because I didn't want to sound *stupid*, because I was dating someone mean enough to think I could even *say* something stupid. Relationships like these siphon your self-esteem. I left my time with Cruise Dude rattled by how I'd once again let a lousy romance linger long enough to eat at my sense of self. Freshly single, with that extra time on my hands, I delved into some extreme self-care.

My self-care regimen postcruise looked like this: a sliding-scale therapist to hash it out with; a couple of 12-step traditions to keep me scribbling in notebooks and forging a relationship with that mysterious higher power (aka Stevie Nicks); going to the gym and outrunning my anxiety on the elliptical machine, taking advantage of the free yoga classes when possible; a shabby on-again, off-again relationship with the Zen Center down the street, bingeing on inspiring dharma talks and then not even bothering to attempt a pathetic five-minute meditation from the comfort of my own home. Despite these noble efforts, the hoopla with Cruise Dude left me at a new low. Normally, I'd brush myself off and get back on the mechanical bull, but now the dating world looked über-pathetic and depressing. If the best indicator of the future is the past (yet another 12-step aphorism), then all I had to look forward to was more head-fucking losers. Try as I might—and I had been trying, hadn't I?—I was going to keep trusting my heart to the wrong cad.

If the elliptical machine, the serenity prayer, and the budget therapist weren't cutting it anymore, it was time for the hard stuff. I began a course of psych meds—Lexapro samples from the free clinic to start, a switch to Celexa when I learned the Lexapro was too pricey, and then a final downgrade to a generic Celexa called Citalopram that did what no amount of booze or wild sex or luv-struck limerence (or the lotus position or downward dog) had ever done: It evened me out and calmed me down, helping me feel, for the first time in my life, normal, content. My serotonin factory was working, and I could feel the soothing, organizing effects. I wasn't looking for dopamine in all the wrong places. I felt self-contained—serene, even. The longer the drug was in my system, the more the love affairs in my past looked like what they were—insanity. They were fun, for sure, and I don't wish them away. Part of me likes that I am (or was) the kind of person down for the thrill of chasing a sordid tryst into a New England sewing room against a backdrop of psychedelic sixties Italian horror movies. It's like being the kind of person who would run away with the circus. These dates *were* my circus. But it was time to stop giving my energy to clowns.

The meds were taking effect, brightening my mood. With newfound conviction to pursue *only* Marriage Material, dating didn't seem as scary. I had no idea who was out there, but I felt my optimism return. I'd always believed there was someone out there, someone whose standards for relationships mirrored mine, somebody capable of the same level of love and openness and kindness that I was. No more Sex Only, no more Dating. It would either be this dreamy Marriage Material or nothing at all.

A little less than a year after Cruise Dude I found myself at a fund-raising benefit for a mayoral candidate who, like nearly everyone I vote for, was too liberal to get elected, even in San Francisco. The event was a bust. I had been enlisted as a prize in a date auction, a practice I actually find humiliating and undignified, something I'd been asked to do a million times and always said no to. I don't know what was different this time; maybe because I'd been asked by my favorite drag queen, someone I had a hard time refusing. Maybe because I wanted to help the flailing candidate. Maybe I was bored, or overly caffeinated. Regardless, that was how I found myself in a mostly empty Italian-American club, speckled with the light from the disco ball, seated in a folding chair at the far end of the room like a classic high school wallflower. The friends I had come with were talking to a sparse group of people I didn't know. One of these strangers walked over. She was striking: pale skin and switchblade cheekbones, cheekbones sharp enough to have sliced the part into her perfect 1950s hairdo. Her eyes were the color of a pair of faded blue jeans, though the jeans she wore were actually quite nice, as were her jean jacket and spiffy shoes. She looked like she'd just walked through a hole in the space-time continuum, arriving in contemporary San Francisco from Oklahoma, 1959. In fact, she looked like she'd stepped out of the pages of my favorite book, *The Outsiders*—like Ponyboy and Sodapop's cleaned-up brother. She looked *good*. She asked if the seat beside me was taken, and when I said no she folded her lanky frame into the metal chair and struck up a conversation. The questions she began to ask me were so . . . *wholesome*. How was my day. Was I having a good evening. Where was I from. What was it like there. I was charmed by her sweetness and confidence. She absolutely did *not* have that *thing* that usually drew me to the people I dated, the dark cloud I'd mistaken as deep or sexy for so long. That vibe was nowhere to be felt, and I found myself drawn to what I did feel off her—easy, good vibes. And happiness. She felt—she seemed—happy.

On our first date, Dashiell actually told me how important it was to be happy—that she felt it should be a choice, and it was what she chose. She loved her life so much, I was taken aback.

She'd been reared in the suburbs and was close with her mom (I'd noted a correlation between unresolved mama drama and difficulty giving and receiving l-u-v). She had a great relationship with her ex, which seemed promising. An ex vouching for your good character in spite of a broken relationship seems to me a great vote of confidence. Next, Dashiell told me that she *loved her job*. This was astounding. I can tell you for certain that I had *never* dated anyone who loved their job. I dated artists and musicians, for whom jobs were the necessary evil that paid the bills while keeping them away from their life's true purpose. But Dashiell was not an artist or a musician. She was . . . a *businessperson*. I had seen them on TV! They were mostly dads, or women from the eighties with shoulder pads. I tried not to hold against Dashiell that she loved her businessperson job so much. I'd just see how things went with this strange creature. We sat at this cute seafood restaurant with mermaids painted on the walls for three hours, fascinated by one another, chatting, nervous but working through it, although she did eat the butt end of a mysterious cut of fish and try to play it off like she knew what she was doing. When the glares from the waitstaff were too much to ignore we relinquished our table, and Dashiell walked me home.

Over dinner, I'd found Dashiell sweet and wholesome enough to be positively exotic. Surely I'd never dated someone so pleasant and cheerful, so satisfied and optimistic. That I liked her back seemed not only a romantic boon but a sign that all the work I was doing on myself was paying off. I'd been training myself to be attracted to someone who was happy and sweet and kind and generally well adjusted, and it appeared that this was happening! Now I just needed to make sure we liked kissing each other. We talked a bit outside my house, and then I made the move. Improving on the "Wanna make out?" slurred seduction of my youth, I now simply went in for the kiss. It was awesome. A swoony, dizzy, knee-weakening, dopamine-releasing make-out. I totally wanted to club her over the head and drag her up to my lair, but I didn't. There was now a Rule for Love, applied to those who seemed to fit into the Marriage Material slot, which Dashiell surely did. That rule was: no sex until the third date.

Three dates? Not since I was twenty years old had I waited so long! *You need to know if you're sexually compatible* was the rational, self-help spin I'd put on my past sluttery, but really I'd just wanted to get high. And I didn't want to use Dashiell like a drug, even if I was already reeling from her kiss.

On our second date we went for pizza, and I waited for Dashiell to unzip her face. Now that I had grown accustomed to spotting red flags, I was hungry for one. Say something questionable, do something weird, hurt my feelings, come on! I was ready to walk out and prove to myself that I wasn't going to be suckered into another rendezvous with a handsome sociopath/depressive/opiate addict/whatever. But Dashiell continued to be sweet, and considerate, and interesting. She was rather serious, but I'd stalked her on Facebook and saw many pictures of her laughing wide-mouthed with her friends, and couldn't wait to see that side of her, too. I sort of invited myself over to her house, met her small, barky dog, Rodney, and made out with her on her couch. When she suggested we move it into the bedroom I said, "Fine, but I'm not taking my pants off." And I didn't. My red pants left pink marks all over her white comforter.

I'd never thought about pacing in a relationship before. I was always so spun out on chemical cravings, I wanted everything to happen all at once. It was sort of delightful to be stretching out our dates—no crazy texting, no seeing each other every single day, spacing it out. Having a proper courtship. Getting to know each other. We both thought our pacing—so relaxed, so gentle, as if we had all the time in the world to get to know one another and fall in love—was magical. We respected one another's independence. We'd both been in relationships with mean and/or unstable people, and wanted to take our time making sure we really were the people we were saying we were.

A little less than a year after we'd started dating, Dashiell and Rodney moved into my apartment. Six months after that, Dashiell surprised me on New Year's Day with a jewelry box. I had been looking forever for a jewelry box that was big enough to hold my cache of thrifted jewelry and that didn't have, like, a twirling ballerina or something similarly froufrou going on. This jewelry box looked like a miniature suitcase, a deep brick red etched in gold. It was perfect. We sat on the couch in our PJs as I discovered drawer after drawer-within-a-drawer.

"There's one more at the bottom," she urged. When I slid it open, I found a fucking diamond ring sitting there. I blinked at it, as if it were a hallucination. "What?" I think I yelped. I was suddenly hot and cold and underwater, in my body and out of my body, dizzy and giddy, laughing and crying. Dashiell asking me to marry her was the biggest natural high I'd ever experienced. I didn't even realize I hadn't said *yes* (though I had thought it went without saying) until she was like, "Well? Well?" And I said yes.

"It's not a blood diamond, is it?" I asked nervously between tears. Dashiell said that she had asked the salesperson and the salesperson had said no and then her friend who had gone with her for moral support had said, "Don't ask again."

I never thought I would give a crap about a diamond. I'm actually certain that I've gone on tears about why people make such a big deal about them, when lots of rocks—take, for example, amethyst, my birthstone—are cool and beautiful and have mystic-crystal properties. But once I had it on my finger I was like, *Holy shit. It's pretty. It sparkles.* And the experience of being proposed to with a ring is sort of a famous experience. I'd seen it happen to people on TV and in movies my whole life, and now it was happening to me. There was something surreal about that, about my weird life suddenly syncing up with the lives of countless normal people everywhere, that I couldn't help but love. In wanting marriage I wanted to find someone I could pledge myself to who could pledge herself back to me, and I found that with Dashiell. But I hadn't expected to be given so grand a token, and it knocked the breath right out of me. It was like that whole otherworldly moment of love and surprise and fantasy and reality all became crystallized in that sparkling mineral, and I think about it all the time—when I'm holding out my hand and gazing at it, overcome with love and gratitude and looking like a crazy lady from some 1950s poster of womanhood.

The years I'd spent trudging through my love swamp of Internet Girlfriends, Fake Johnny Depps, and depressive Cruise

Dudes had taught me every stupid lesson I needed to learn in order to get my romantic shit together. Without those ridiculous relationships, I wouldn't have formulated my rules. And without my rules and the work they forced me to do, I don't think I would have even *noticed* Dashiell. A happy businessperson? How would I have spotted her through the throngs of miserable ne'er-do-wells I was swooning over? And Dashiell wouldn't have fallen for me, either, that spazzed-out, love-drugged, hypomanic chemical mess. Doing things differently brought out a different side of myself, made me a whole different person. And the only person who loves her more than Dashiell does is me.

# 6.

# How to Break Up

Okay, I've broken down the details of the trifling fools I've dated, and maybe you're like, *Ohmigod I am so dating someone just like that right now! How do I break up with them? And what do I do when I'm all broken up?* Well, you go to Paris. But first let's dump these chumps!

I've always found relationships very hard to get out of. Not everyone is like this. Some people are wild heartbreakers, terrified of commitment, quick to bolt the minute you up the intimacy level by, say, making them breakfast in bed. This just happened to a dear friend of mine. The dude broke it off while they were naked and cuddling, haunted by the grocery bags in the kitchen filled with bacon and eggs and fruit and coffee. Being loved that sweetly was too much for him. You do not want to date a person so threatened by love he can't even allow you to scramble him some eggs, so sometimes getting dumped is a blessing. You want to find someone you can dote on and make crush crafts for and bake late-night brownies for and whatnot. Because *this* is what makes love fun. And you want to make sure your love is fun.

Some will challenge this. There is a loudmouthed demographic who believe that love is *hard*, that it's lots of fighting and struggle. There is no arguing with them, because for these people love *is* lots of fighting and struggle. Fortunately, you're not obligated to date these people. I have always known in my heart that a relationship could be smooth and happy, even though almost every single experience up to dating Dashiell seemed to prove me wrong. I don't know why I let myself hold on to this elusive ideal, but thankfully I did, and now I've finally got myself a fun relationship with a person who squeals at her good fortune when I do sweet things for her, who does sweet things for me in turn. It is true that she is not the norm. But she exists, so others like her must exist, and they are worth holding out for. At the center of such a pledge is self-love: You are worth holding out for a happy relationship. You don't have to take a lot of bullshit, or walk on eggshells, or wait for things to get better. You can break up. Let's get started!

One thing I learned from my many failed relationships is that you always sort of *know* when it's over. That doesn't mean you'll end it right away. It's a little like drinking—you might have a sinking suspicion you're an alcoholic, but that doesn't mean you're going to put down the cocktail. You're going to have to hit a couple of bottoms—peeing yourself, maybe, or getting fired for calling in with a hangover one too many times—before you make a change. If your relationship MO is anything like mine, you're likely to stretch the bad times out as long as possible, hoping that something will suddenly change, even hoping that maybe the suckiness is all your fault—you're not *getting it* properly—and if you just hold out you'll have some sort of revelation and finally understand why your date is such a douche and you'll be *okay* with it, and y'all can love happily ever after.

So, feel free to hang out awhile in that holding pattern, treading dirty water, or cut it off now, get your grieving going, and get over it all that much faster! If you're unsure if your relationship is at the point where you need to murder it, here is a little checklist:

*Your date can't say for sure that they actually want to be with you.* They're, like, confused or something. Maybe they want to be *free*, man! They want to try dating skanks and getting STDs for a while. Or—maybe not. Maybe you are the best thing they will ever know, and they should stay with you forever. They're just not sure.

Fire this punk. They don't *know* whether they want to be with the best, funniest, most interesting, and hottest person in the galaxy? (That would be you.) You *do not* have the time to hang out and wait for them to come to their senses. To wait around for such a thing is a massive drag on your self-esteem. Doubt like this slashes right into your heart, and all your self-love starts leaking away. The only thing to stop this drain of your very own life force is to tell this sucker to take his cat and leave.

As far as I'm concerned, there are only two answers to the question "Do you want to be with me?" One is yes; one is no. "I don't know" gets filed under no. I want someone who not only knows they want to be with me, but knows they are freaking *lucky* to be with someone as totally awesome as I am, and I want you to want that, too. I wasn't born with this confidence—no way. I assumed it (faking it till you make it really works!), and then I fortified it by breaking up with people who were bringing me down.

Before you write me off as some crazy diva who is hanging out on a chaise longue powdering my face with a big fluffy puff and tossing bon mots like, "You are so *lucky* to get to be with me!" let me say that I should be feeling incredibly lucky to be with whomever I'm dating, too. It should be mutual. That's the point. And if it's not, cut and run and find someone you *can* have a Mutual Admiration Society with. Because if your date doesn't know if they want to be with you, it is very likely coward code for *I don't know how to break up with you.* Don't hang around waiting to be broken up with. There is nothing more humiliating.

*Your date is all hung up on another person.* Gross! Dump that chump! This has happened to me on a few different occasions, and it never turned out well. Once I was a rebound for someone who stated very clearly that he was on a rebound and that he had very little to offer me. This was *great* communication on his part. I should have ended it right there. You, reader, should end it right there. I got all tangled up in this person's mixed signals for a month or so, before storming out of his apartment on Valentine's Day after he couldn't stop sadly talking about how much his cats missed his ex. Another date would get so upset by the proximity of a recent lover that full-blown panic attacks would ensue, which she would soothe with red wine and pills that would then sicken her, triggering a brand-new panic attack about her health, as she was a hypochondriac to boot. It was a terrible cycle that I couldn't do anything to help. Know why? *It had nothing to do with me.* If you're looking to create a deep and meaningful bond with someone, and they are so obsessed with their ex that they become nonfunctional in that ex's presence, it's time to break up. It's fair to expect a date's enthusiasm and infatuation for you to outweigh whatever grief they might still have over those in their past. If they don't, then you shouldn't be dating them, and maybe they shouldn't be dating at all.

*You've opened up your relationship.* Just break up. Unless you are a free-spirited Polyamorous Polly at heart and you've always wanted to live in a nonmonogamous manner, flinging the bedroom doors open on your LTR is just procrastinating its demise, and guaranteeing that it will be much more painful and dramatic. If you're at the point where you're willing to endanger the relationship by sleeping with other people, just end it. I don't know of a single couple this plan has worked out for in the long run. When I tried it there was a month or so when I was blown away by the new amour possibilities available to me and was giddy, nearly high, with it all. It was a strangely sweet pleasure to share this with my LTR, but the novelty wore off as reality and its attendant feelings set in. Because it ultimately sucks to watch your person get all head-over-heels over someone who grosses you out a little. How can you make out with him knowing he just made out with *her?* Yuck. Plus, I found it a creepy, lonely feeling to be handed so much freedom. I'd like to be held a little closer; would like for the thought of me frolicking elsewhere to inspire at least a *little* jealousy. Or, even better, a lot of jealousy. Do what you should have done a month ago and end that shit.

*You fight all the time.* Your life is better than this. Fighting all the time is bad for your health, raising stress hormones that make you crave Doritos and leave you vulnerable to heart attacks. Listen—there is never any reason to fight. Any conflict can be worked out by just, like, talking. Talking sweetly, even. Being on one another's teams. Constant fighting results in you seeing your partner, on some level, as your enemy. Don't be sleeping with the enemy. Go find someone who is nicer, and sleep with that person instead. And if you're the one starting fights all the time, go to therapy. You don't have to live like that.

*You're not actually dating.* You're intriguing—a flirting that feels like it's building toward something. You're sexting. Maybe the person lives on the other side of the country. Maybe they have a partner so they can't go all the way with you; they can only engage you on the dopamine level and fuck with your mind all day by sending you naked photos or something. Maybe they have commitment issues, or maybe are working the long con and in a couple of weeks you'll find yourself buying them an iPhone or something. Even though you're not actually dating, this person is taking all your emotional and mental energy. You keep waiting for something to happen. Guess what? Nothing is going to happen. How long has it been? Count the days. If something was going to happen, don't you think it would have happened by now? You are being played. Cut off all contact with this person, and get mourning. Your friends might not understand what you're going through—after all, it's true you weren't dating. But this player engaged your heart, your hopes, your dopamine. The crash you are feeling is legit. Cry into your pillow and then get back into the real world.

*You're walking on eggshells.* You're dating someone with intense negative sensitivities. Saying the wrong word sets her off. So does mentioning a person she doesn't like (and she doesn't like most people). Listening to a song she detests makes her spittle in disgust. You've become scared to profess enjoyment of anything because you don't want to be told that you're wrong, that your taste is bad. You hold much of yourself in, trying to talk only about the things she likes. Which means there is not that much to talk about, because you're dating a hater. You become obsessed with doing things to make her happy, so that the two of you might enjoy a pleasant moment and you can relax. *Ugh.* Does this sound like a living hell to you, or what? If you find yourself biting your tongue, not being honest or natural because you fear it will set off your date, stop hanging out with her. It's doomed anyway—believe me. At some point, this negative, moody monster will decide that you are just like the rest of humanity—not good enough. You probably already know this is likely—isn't that why you feel so stressed and nervous all the time? Waiting for that other loafer to drop? *You* drop the other loafer, damn it! Chuck it at her head and get the f *out of there*! Happier people await you.

There are endless combinations of bad dynamics that should send you scurrying for the safety of singleness, but what they all have in common is making you feel like crap, not prioritized, unappreciated. If you have done your own emotional homework and gone to therapy and worked through all the ways your parents ruined you, then you are ready to be present and love another person, to be on their team and make them feel awesome. If your person is not returning the favor, kick them to the curb. Life is too short.

Now, how to break up with this fool? Quickly, and decisively. In person tends to be best, but so much relationship communication is conducted via gadgetry nowadays, I don't think it's the worst sin if your relationship resignation letter comes over the phone or computer. Other people disagree with this, and if you do choose to end the love affair with a text message, be prepared to field some self-righteous outrage. But I believe that a remote breakup often spares both people from those downward-spiraling, endless-processing conversations that so often accompany endings. Those conversations are useless. If you *do* do your breakup in person, try not to indulge them. My easiest kills were ones where I was pulling on my jean jacket and tossing my bag over my shoulder as I delivered the final words. Keep it brief ("It's over." "I can't do this anymore." "We're breaking up." "Fuck you.") and get the hell out of there. Oh, it's happening in your house? "I need you to leave." Boom. But remember, breakup text messages are the Dear John letters of yesteryear. As nothing good has *ever* come out of an in-person breakup, I heartily endorse an electronic resignation.

Once the breakup is in effect, don't try to be friends. Maybe that will happen organically later on, but right away it's a pretty lousy idea. One or both of you are bound to be a bundle of raw nerves, lingering desire, seething resentment—emotional suicide bombers. Passive-aggressive commentary, if not outright scream fighting, is to be expected. Keep your distance. If you have a texting problem, delete your ex's number from your phone. Make a pact with a close friend that you will text or call *them* before you text or call your ex. Texting can be painfully hard to resist—like, your ex has *got* to hear what you have to say, or you think you will feel *so much better* if you just get this one barbed comment off your chest, but really. You won't feel that much better. It will not get you what you think you want, which might not be what you really want, anyway. Don't reach out to your ex—not to hurt them and not to be friends. Get a breakover instead!

Hail the breakover, a breakup-inspired makeover. We have all sorts of falling-in-love rituals, weddings being the most extravagant. But what about coming-apart rituals? I guess getting totally shitfaced is a common contemporary breakup ritual, but I'm thinking of something a bit more positive. That last thing you need when you're feeling rejected is booze bloat and a shame spiral.

Breakups make me feel old and haggard, all used up. Getting a new hairdo or a shot of Botox lifts me out of dumps. Even a mani-pedi and an eyebrow wax remind me to take care of myself—an outward manifestation of all the inner self-care breakups require of you, and a continuation of the declaration of self-love that you made when you dumped that fool. Oh, wait— that fool dumped you? As we say in 12-step, rejection is God's protection! The Universe was looking out for you by taking away someone who was bringing you down. Give thanks by getting a facial. You are made in the Universe's image, and she likes to see you looking your best! Plus, there is a real satisfaction in looking different the next time you run into your ex—*You think you know me? You don't know me. You never even got to see the best of me. Here's a glimpse; eat your heart out, loser.*

Breakovers are good for your self-esteem, and they pay respect to how a breakup leaves you changed. You're never the same after a heartache. That doesn't mean you're degraded, or ruined—you're smarter, sharper. You're a little older. You're going to see the world differently now, and the world should see you differently, too. Get a haircut, or dye your hair some wild shade. Buy a new outfit; thrift it if you must. Pierce your tongue. No— don't do that. I did that after a breakup and it was a disaster. I bit it all the time by mistake, and it became infected. Get a tattoo (just don't hit on your artist). Go on a health kick and detox from the bad vibes. Have a friend teach you how to master cat-eye eyeliner once and for all, and make it your new thing for a while. There is no end to how you can change up your appearance, and it's always a great idea. It's better you're focused and obsessing on yourself than on whatever clueless bozo got the ax.

The second most amazing thing I did to help get over a painful breakup was to get contact lenses. After living my whole life with a strip of plastic cutting across my face—a.k.a. glasses—I could suddenly *see* myself! I became unrecognizable to people, even those who'd known me for ages but had gotten used to clocking my specs to identify me. It was so gratifying to have friends marvel, "You look *so different!*" because I *was* different. I wasn't going to put up with the mad bullshit my latest relationship had put me through ever again. I was a *new woman!* And I was glad it showed. It was hard to learn how to yank apart my lids and poke myself in the eye like some *Clockwork Orange* torture scene, but I mastered it through practice. Plus, it really widened my eye shadow possibilities to no longer have a plastic contraption blocking the mirrors of my soul.

However life changing it was to shuck my glasses, the number one best most amazing thing I did to help get over a painful breakup was to go to Paris. I was lucky to have the spare dough for a plane ticket, but the experience was so thoroughly healing, I would encourage anyone to put it on a credit card or bum the funds off someone who loves you. Have a breakup party and ask everyone to make a contribution to your Paris Breakup Vacation Fund. Do whatever you need to do to get your ass out of whatever non-French country you happen to be in and into Paris. I suppose you could go somewhere else—to Mexico to snorkel with all the other fish in the sea; to Rome to lose yourself in history and catcalls; to Tibet to hunker down in a cave. But I really recommend Paris.

Why Paris? For starters, it's beautiful, and its beauty is of a melancholy variety that jibes quite nicely with post-breakup downer energy. When I brought my own broken heart to Paris, doing a house swap with a French friend (Don't have a French friend? Make one, quick! One should always have a French friend!), I spent my first non-jet-lagged day walking along the Seine in the rain. The weather sucked, which was great. It was overcast and pigeon-colored, like my heart. I took the elevator to the top of the Eiffel Tower and saw exactly nothing through the thick cloud cover. It was a metaphor for my own sorry state—

unable to see the loveliness of the larger world, what with all this sadness fogging my vision.

Travel is perfect for a broken heart, liberating and addictive. The exotic new surroundings can augment your angst and make it seem pretty, somehow. You are the mopey heroine of your own French film. It transforms your days from a frantic scheme to avoid bumping into your ex to a luxuriously lonely experience of solitude. Everything you do, from feeding yourself breakfast to grabbing a coffee, feels like a wonderful treat, because of the novelty. You couldn't send a cutting text if you *wanted* to, because your cell phone is shut off. Yeah, do not get a travel plan—you are going off the grid. To truly immerse yourself in your heart and in the world, you can't be fielding endless cell phone distractions. The temptation to shoot a shitty text to your ex will vanish, as will that lingering psychic tension you get from wondering if *he's* ever going to text *you*. You can't post sexy selfies by the Seine in hopes that it will make him regret everything he's ever done. You can't pull up a map and find your way from point A to point B. Get lost. That is what you are in Paris to do—to lose yourself to something bigger and more beautiful than your petty romantic scuffle, to become one with the city until its elegant mystique becomes part of your own spirit. To excavate your dreamy id from beneath the superego of social media. You won't miss the piddly dopamine blips that a text message brings. Paris will take care of your dopamine.

Parisians are famous for their moodiness and their love affairs, and this is another reason why I believe it makes for an ideal breakation destination. No one will bat an eye if you walk weeping though its ancient streets. Has this heartbreak prompted you to take up smoking? Guess what? Everyone in Paris smokes. Enjoy yourself. Buy a pack of Gauloises, lean under a bridge to escape the drizzle, and hasten your own demise while pondering existentially the temporary nature of it all. This is what Paris is for.

It is also for love. Or if not love, love affairs. People make out all over the place in Paris—in the grocery store before the refrigerated shelves of yogurt, on the street before a metro station, on the speeding underground trains, on one of the ubiquitous carousels, before a crepe stand, by the Seine, in bars, on the paths that encircle Notre-Dame. You would get the impression that Parisians, in spite of their scowling appearance, are DTF, and you would be correct. Take the experience of a friend who came to stay with me for a week during my Parisian retreat. We'd found an English-speaking 12-step meeting helmed by a heavily tattooed French punk who took us out for food after.

"Why don't you go to French meetings?" I asked our new friend.

"They are so annoying," he said in his smoking-hot French accent. "It is all—but *why* am I an alcoholic? *Why? Why?* Who cares why you are alcoholic? Shut up!" The punk had no patience for his countrymen's existential angst, but I was charmed by it. Why had my relationship gone south? Why had I stayed in it so long when it had made me so unhappy? And if it had made me so unhappy, why was I so bummed out that it was over? Such questions were welcomed by Paris. Paris was wondering the same thing.

My friend left us to debate this as she went downstairs to use the bathroom, and along the way crossed paths with a different smoking-hot young gentleman (there are many in Paris). They quickly cruised one another, and the Gallic gentleman swooped in for a kiss. My friend was shocked, and kissed him back. When he attempted to lead her into the bathroom to continue their amour, she said no, and he backed off. That was that. She returned to the table shaken, though not unpleasantly so. She then went on to have a torrid affair with the tattooed French punk, whose heart she broke by not allowing him to whisk her away to his beach home in Normandy.

France's relationship with feminists and feminism is strange and interesting. On the one hand, Simone de Beauvoir is a national treasure. On the other, a French friend routinely endures having her rump grabbed by her boss like some 1960s American nightmare. They have a different relationship with casual sex and love affairs, viewing situations that in America would be inappropriate as simply human. While I am far too American (and American feminist) to live with an acceptance of extramarital affairs and workplace groping, the ease with which sexual encounters can be fallen into in French culture is a bit of a fantasy. I had expected to spend my time in Paris alone and sulking, but when my French friend informed her countrywomen that a lonely American was staying at her apartment, invitations to parties began rolling in. Well, to me they were parties—to the Parisians they were just, you know, life. This is how you live, gathering at one another's homes each night with loaves of bread and hunks of cheese, with bottles of wine and packs of cigarettes. This group was younger than I was by at least a decade, but I never felt like a grody old-lady interloper. In France, as in much of Europe, older women are still recognized as human, oftentimes sexy humans. I did not drink the wine but I smoked their cigarettes as if I had the lungs of an eighteen-year-old, with a "when in Rome" attitude. Indeed, the French seemed not even to recognize their vice as such. When, concerned about my smoking, I said, "I'm going to have to get a facial when I return to America!" I was met with a series of glares.

"Do you think we have ugly faces from smoking?" my new French friends demanded. No! Of course not! But they were French. Things were different for them.

I began a little affair with one boy, only to recognize him as perhaps the wrong boy and then switch my affair to another, who was the right boy. Of course, he was in a relationship already, but being French, his girlfriend gave us the green light to indulge in a petite tryst on my visit—she was conducting quite a few trysts of her own. This conjured in me such gratitude and admiration for the pretty French *fille* that I got somewhat of a crush on her as well. I imagined I was Anaïs Nin, in love with both Henry and June. Such things can only happen in Paris, of course, and there was a moment I thought about living there for a spell, being their *trois*. She was a young model and intellectual, going to the Sorbonne and taking sexy pictures on the side. She spoke perfect English and we engaged in all sorts of conversations. He was older, though still younger than I was, and worked some sort of bureaucratic job that gave him existential conflict. He spoke very poor English and I spoke no French at all, so our communications were blissfully physical.

On New Year's Eve I threw a party at the house I was staying at, and all my new French friends spent the night. The pretty French *fille* claimed her boyfriend for herself, which I thought fair, and I gave them my bed for the evening. I slept on a little mattress in a crawlspace above the kitchen. It was like a tree house inside the attic apartment, and through the window across the room I could spot the cold, pale dome of the Sacré Cœur cathedral against the dark sky, glowing like the moon. I fell asleep and had a terrible dream. In it I had something to say to my ex. He had treated me so badly, and I was going to tell him what I thought about it once and for all. The pain I felt was rushing and urgent; the need to deliver this message was agonizing. I rushed through the streets of San Francisco, looking everywhere. I burst into his house and found him in bed with his new girlfriend, cowering beneath the covers. In the dream I felt a leaden disappointment settle over me. *I was so carefree in Paris*, I thought. *But now I am home, and I have to feel* this *again*. And then I woke up.

When I did, I was so relieved to be not in San Francisco, but in a Parisian attic crawl space. I could hear one of my new friends puttering around the tiny galley kitchen, making espresso in the giant Italian espresso maker. I lay on the thin mattress and considered my dream. I acknowledged how obsessed with my ex I had been, a fact made starker by how little I'd thought of him since being swept away by Paris. Paris had made the world bigger for me, and my ex had become smaller. Even though I knew in San Francisco I would resume my routines—which would include running into my ex at events and recovery meetings—I felt that Paris had gotten under my skin, had perhaps caused me to change, to shift into a new direction. What was my ex next to Paris? What was his girlfriend next to the Seine? No one was anything in the face of the dark river and the ancient bridges that spanned it. I took my New Year's dream as a gift, reminding me of how I didn't need to be anymore. And when I returned home I did run into my ex, and it annoyed me, but that annoyance didn't take up residence in my heart. There wasn't any room, with so much of Paris in there.

So, go to Paris. If you can't do that, go somewhere. Take a road trip, a train trip, a bus trip if you must. Find a place that reminds you that the world is so much bigger than your heart and whoever broke it this time around. Go hang out by the ocean and trip out on its mammoth ancientness. Offer it your heartache— it's big enough to hold it, to dilute it with all that salt and water, melt it away to nothing. Salt purifies. Take a dunk if you can stand it. You're alive. That relationship was but one chapter in your long, long story, one little scene in your epic.

# 7.

# Too Cool for School

Can we go back to talking about money? I'm sort of obsessed with it. Money, and class—who has money, who doesn't, and what it means for all of us. On a recent road trip I was doing my regular road trip duties as the person who doesn't drive. In the past, such tasks once included paging through cumbersome road atlases, squinting at the skinny colored lines that crisscrossed the page, poking it with my finger and saying, "I think we're *here*." Now that GPS exists, my job has become much more enjoyable— reading out loud to keep the driver entertained. On this road trip, I had the Sunday *New York Times* on my lap and was reading aloud a long piece that tracked three girls from working-poor families as they tried to go to college. It was a depressing article; they mostly failed. No one in their families had gone to college, so no one understood how to help them jump through the hoops and suss out the loopholes that could bring them financial aid and overall success. Their parents were bewildered and felt inept.

Their boyfriends, coming from the same backgrounds, just wanted them to stick around and get married. In spite of all this, the girls managed to go to college for a single year, something that looks like a failure but is its own triumph. At the end of that year the lack of support and the feeling of alienation at school, compounded by the unforgiving financial situation, were too much, and each one called it quits. These were Latino girls figuring this out in Texas, 2012. As a New England white girl who tried to figure it out back in 1989, I related to their story completely.

As I approached my would-be college years increasingly confused about how a person goes about continuing her education, a phrase my mother often sounded was "There's gotta be room in the world for the ditchdigger." As a lifelong broke person—her father had dropped out of school to join the war and later worked as a machinist, while her mom had operated a cash register at a department store—my mother had cultivated a sort of defensive pride about her membership in what was once the working class and is now too often the working poor. Frequently this pride veered into bitterness—"Money goes to money," she'd say, meaning that people who start out with money are generally pretty good at sucking up more of it. She was scornful of wealthy people, an attitude I eagerly adopted and then attributed to my punk rock ethos—*Eat the rich! Die Yuppie scum!* I, too, had decided that anyone with more money than we had (i.e. most people) was somehow immoral. And if you believe that people with money suck, it can put you off wanting to accumulate some, even if your lack of dollars is making your life hard.

In my downtrodden hometown, a VA hospital sat high on a hill, a warren of brick buildings beside a red-and-white-checkered water tower so tall it could be seen all over the city. My uncle Rocky, a ne'er-do-well, had drunkenly scaled the thing as a teenager, plummeted, and lived to brag about it. The VA hospital offered a free nursing school, largely attended by working-class mothers on the verge of divorce, women who had to come up with a career quick, to support their brood once their man split. That was how my mother got there—by the end of her schooling, she was both a licensed practical nurse and a divorcée. In exchange for the free education, you agreed to work at the VA after graduation, which propelled my mother into a specialty of taking care of the elderly, though she'd have much rather worked with children. Why didn't she switch her focus once she'd worked off her debt to the vets, then? Or continue her studies to get her RN? Registered nurses command way more bucks than LPNs, after all. "I don't want to be like them," my mom said dismissively when I made the suggestion. "They think they're better than everyone." RN wasn't a job to aspire to; it was a class of people better off than she was— the enemy. You can become obsessed with class, being from a lower one in a culture that insists such divides don't exist. You see shades of have and have-not everywhere you go.

In a way, my mother was right: There's gotta be room in the world for the ditchdigger, and the dishwasher, and the barista and the stripper and yes, the LPN. After all, the world the haves occupy runs on the efforts of the have-nots. Someone has to haul goods to the stores they shop in, provide T and A for courted clients to gaze upon, deliver their mail, care for their parents when the elders start peeing themselves. These are my people. My truck driver uncle and his stripper wife. My postal worker father and LPN stepfather. My grandfather, whose hands were never not blackened from the machines he grappled with all day; not even those abrasive industrial soap granules could scrub it away. My grandmother at her cash register. The older I got, the harder it was for me to see where I would fit in this world, how I would make my own living. What ditch would I dig? I longed for something better, but I didn't know what better was.

When you grow up in a blue-collar world, you don't even know what other jobs are out there. An engineer? A sommelier? A film editor, art therapist, *financier*? Even if one knew these positions existed, one still might not understand what they were, let alone how to get in on it. Gazing out at this stunted landscape of occupations, I was haunted by the question *What do you want to be when you grow up?* I never wanted to be a nurse, or a truck driver. There was only one job in the whole world that I had ever heard of that sounded good to me: I wanted to be a librarian. Who became librarians? Old maids. It was something women *wound up as*, not aspired toward. My aunt Shirley would shush me when I shared my dream of being paid to hang out with books all day. "You don't want to do *that*," she said with a sour face. "You want to be *Miss America*!" And then she'd start singing the theme song to *Miss America* at me.

I was always a rabidly bookish kid. My mother likes to tell the story of how as a toddler, I'd try to make friends with passersby by standing against the chain-link fence in our front yard and begging, "Play with me! I got toys! I got *books*!" (Probably I am still doing this.) By grade school I was reading so far above my age group, the librarian made my mother write a note allowing me to take out big-kid books like *Are You There God? It's Me, Margaret*, reading it before I even understood what a period was. I founded a second-grade newspaper, *The Schoolyard Gazette*, and tried my hand at journalism, crafting hard-hitting articles about chicken pox and penning a comics and jokes page as well. I had enough material for my first chapbook of poetry by third grade. Had my family hailed from a different class, I would have been shoved into a prep school, tested for prodigy potential, encouraged to work my interests into an impressive extracurricular CV. Instead, my father complained to my mother that he thought I was reading too much and demanded she talk to me about it. My mom was a reader herself, and was proud of my reading, but she was also susceptible to her husband's suspicion that there might be something wrong with a girl so obsessed with books. She asked me hesitant questions about fantasy and reality—Did I understand the difference? Did I know that my books weren't real; they were made up? That life, the world around me, was real? I nodded. *Yeah, of course. I'm not stupid!*

But the questions made me a little nervous. I'd been secretly selecting a different fictional heroine each day and then walking through the world as if I *were* her! What would Harriet the Spy do? Or Leslie, from *Bridge to Terabithia*? Or strange Meg Murry from *A Wrinkle in Time*? Girls in books were so passionate and deep, so smart. They navigated their own hard worlds with a grace I envied. What if these fictions *could* become my reality? Well, clearly that would mean I was a crazy person! I scrapped my experiment and returned to the world as Michelle, lonely in my intelligence, a future social outcast.

The idea of becoming a librarian stuck around as a vague, lingering thing, like a song you heard a long time ago that occasionally gets stuck in your head. It felt further away each time it popped up. No one ever told me what a person has to do to become a librarian. Maybe everyone around me thought, as I did, that you just filled out an application at the library and got hired, the way I was hired at DeMoulas Market Basket when I was fifteen, my first cash register of many. Of course, one must go to college if one wants to become a librarian. One goes to library school. And if one is planning to advance one's education thusly, one should put a little thought into where one goes to high school. My dream school was Newman Prep, a pricey Boston institution where the artsy students dyed their hair the color of Coke cans and no one called them "faggot" or threw food at them. But such a school was out of the question. It was too expensive, and it was in *Boston*, where I would get raped and mugged! As if our downtrodden city wasn't teeming with rapists and muggers and everything else.

And so my first high school was St. Rose, a Catholic high school for girls. By the time I was fourteen my freak flag was waving high enough to catch the negative attention of my burly Italian classmates. New England is an interesting place. It's Pilgrim-y and puritanical. People still have an eye out for witches and they are ready to burn others for looking or acting different. I scooted out of class early each day, to avoid pummelings by the brawny girls who were driven to rage at the sight of my chemical-black hair, teased into a sprawling, inky tarantula upon my head.

"What, are you a satanist or somethin'?" they'd ask me regularly. Who could blame the dears—I penned upside-down crosses into the plaid of my uniform skirt and listened to a band called Lords of the New Church, whose lyrics had inspired in me an atheism that thrilled, after nine consecutive years of oppressive Catholic school. I felt like I was learning more about the world from the songs of the obscure bands I was discovering than from the nuns. I didn't believe in religion anymore, so the religion classes felt bizarre. In composition the teacher had us write essays for or against abortion; I wrote a pro-choice screed and was called before the class to explain how in the world I was okay with the murder of innocent babies. "Satan worshipper!" a classmate hissed as I sulked back to my seat.

"If there's no God, there's no Satan, either," I'd snap at my tormentors. *Duh!* Who were these idiots? Rather than argue with my classmates, I eventually began responding to the accusation with devil horns and a smile. By the end of ninth grade the head nun had had it with the community outrage my satanic appearance provoked, and told me I would not be able to return for my sophomore year unless I untangled my hair and returned it to its native mousy brown. It didn't matter. My family couldn't come up with the last installment of my tuition, so it was on to the city's public high school for me.

Throughout my whole life, my mom made sacrifices so that I would be kept out of public school, with its threat of ass kickings and teenage pregnancies. Sure enough, within a week of being there, gangs of cackling females were shoving me in the hallway, sneaking up behind me, and knocking me into walls. Or worse, knocking me into other students, who would then spin around angrily and knock me again. Maybe I could have removed the black rubber bat that I had pinned to my shirt as jewelry, or wiped off the black lipstick I'd found at the drugstore the previous Halloween. I could have allowed myself to be bullied into a plainer outfit and less ghoulish makeup, but not without tremendous cost to myself, something I recognized early on, with wordless instinct. Plus, one thing a decade of Catholic schooling gave me was the understanding that good people are regularly martyred by jerks who don't get it. Eventually I decided to transfer to a third high school, Northeast Metropolitan Regional Vocational High School—the Voke. At least I had some metalhead friends to hang out with there. People thought they were satanists, too.

When I registered at the Voke I was asked if I planned to go to college. "No," I replied. It was a quick answer, born of fear. What college would I even go to? How did you find out about them? How would I get there? Who would pay for it? Because of this shortsighted answer, the better English and literature classes became off-limits to me, and I was forced into strange, pulpy courses: Mysteries and Westerns; Sci-Fi and Fantasy. My piece for an assignment in which we were to continue writing *The Pit and the Pendulum* past Poe's ending so impressed the teacher that he hung it on the wall and made my classmates read it. "This," he said, "is what I'm talking about." Another English teacher commented admiringly on the way I became so engrossed in my reading, tuning the whole world out. It was a practice I'd developed at home, a small place often aurally cramped with a blaring television, chatty phone calls, and neighbors who dropped by to smoke cigarettes and drink tea and gossip loudly. Snug in my book, I found that the whole world fell away; as I grew older and recognized my world to be often cruel and unfair, depressing and ugly, books became a preferable alternative to reality.

After graduation I did try, in my own clueless way, to go to college. After learning about the School of Visual Arts in New York City, I was suddenly overwhelmed with the desire to make movies. My weirdo Goth friends and I occasionally made horror movies with someone's parents' video camera, and I loved all of it—brainstorming the story, choosing which angle to shoot, casting my friends, becoming an evil clown or a spurned lover or a juvenile delinquent. Imagine if doing that could be my life. I sat down at the table with my typewriter and filled out my application, wrote my essay. Nobody helped. When I was done I asked my mother for fifty dollars, the application fee. She turned white as a ghost, but she gave it to me. Next I applied to Tulane. I had romantic feelings about New Orleans from reading *Interview with the Vampire*. Maybe I would live there and write my *own* vampire story among its voodoo priestesses and antebellum ghosts. I'd already written a screenplay about a bunch of teenage vampires living in mausoleums in an abandoned New England cemetery (soundtracked to Bauhaus, of course). I thought my script was pretty great, but I didn't know what to do with it. Maybe at college I'd find out. When I finished that application, I asked my mother for the fee.

"I can't keep doing this," she said, stressed out. "It's too expensive."

I didn't get into SVA or Tulane. A hundred dollars down the

drain; spending it all on scratch tickets would have made more sense. I was disappointed, and plagued by a new feeling that would soon become old—the feeling of not knowing how to be in this world. There was a way to get into college, and I didn't know it. I was probably supposed to call someone. Make an appointment, have a meeting. A person who had gone to college would have known the drill, could have told me how the game is played, but I didn't know anyone who went to college. Plus, smart as I might have been, my grades sucked. I hated reading Zane Grey novels in my Mysteries and Westerns class. I was completely lost in trigonometry. I'd failed gym because I refused to go in the pool and get my giant ratted hairdo wet. The only class I excelled at was philosophy, where I was able to study existentialism. Finally, something I could relate to!

After graduation I watched as friends scattered to various schools. I knew that I was smart, and creative, and it seemed like if I went to college, I might be in the company of other smart and creative people. Maybe there I would find a place for myself. So I took a year off to work to save enough money to pay for tuition at a state school. I knew my state school couldn't compare with the big-city art schools I had originally applied to, but I hoped that I would somehow find a path into a life that was a step up from ditchdigging.

For one semester I slept in a dorm room at a school on the North Shore of Boston. It seemed that the terrible people I'd gone to high school with had followed me here—classmates who spotted my tarot cards asked if I worshipped the devil, and boys who called me "faggot" in the hallways. (Faggot? But I'm a . . .

girl. Oh, forget it.) Wasn't college supposed to be a place of "higher learning" where students' minds were cracked wide open and thinking superdeep thoughts? Not this place. I'd opted to stay in the dorms because the college was an hour from home *and* because I'd read way too many young adult books about girls expanding their consciousness at college and having love affairs and best friendships on the rolling lawns of campus. But my experience was not like that. I had nothing in common with my roommate, who snuck her boyfriend in and had sex with him *right there*, with me a foot away, pretending to be asleep in spite of the noisy grunting and fog of sweat that bloomed off the boy's back, turning our cement-block room into a hothouse. Once a week some jerk pulled the fire alarm in the middle of the night, sending us all out into the parking lot in our pajamas. I'd be too tired for class, and was happy to skip anyway.

And while it was awful from a social standpoint, college wasn't the intellectually fulfilling experience I had imagined. My history professor forbid us to use the term *Native American*, and stopped me from doing a study on the lives of women in ancient Egypt, as women weren't rulers so therefore didn't matter. (Um . . . Cleopatra?) My psychology professor showed us a film detailing how gayness in men is "caused by" stress in pregnant women. At the end of the semester, I found I couldn't afford to keep living in the dorms, so I transferred to a commuter university in Boston and moved home. By the end of the year, my cash was spent and my college career was over. Never once had I sat under a tree on a rolling lawn having deep conversations with other students. Never once had I seen anyone else doing this, either. I remembered what my mother had told me so long ago: Books weren't real. I'd based all my expectations of college on novels written by middle-class women who'd gone to pricey learning institutions, and at the end of it all I had nothing: no new, exciting knowledge; no new, intellectual comrades; no deeper purpose in life; and no money.

Even though my decision to quit is decades old—and even though I'm regularly brought in to teach at colleges around the country in spite of it—I still vacillate. Was it awesome that I didn't go to college, or was it stupid? And is it too late to go now?

Mostly I love that I didn't go to college. When my friends are stressing about their student loans, for instance. I've watched people go to college to study writing, then graduate and get a soul-crushing full-time job in order to pay off that debt, no time to write the book they went to school to learn how to write. Plus, I—and many writers—remain dubious about whether something like writing can be taught. Certainly people learn, they get better and more skilled, but must you pay a hundred thousand dollars for it? I set out to learn to write by writing—something I had a lot of time to do with no debt breathing down my neck. I read my work out loud at free open mic events, learning from the cheers and the boos what worked and what didn't. I read a lot, picking up, mostly through osmosis, a wider vocabulary, an understanding of style, the backbeat of rhythm.

When I'm traveling around, reading my work and teaching workshops, people always ask me where I went to school. I love to watch their reaction when I tell them I didn't. Their expression changes abruptly; I can see a paradigm shift occurring before my eyes. Having grown up in a place where it was normal to not go to college, I wouldn't have imagined it would be so shocking, but time and time again, I've witnessed how the fact blows people's minds. And this is a good thing. It makes people recalibrate their idea of what a person who doesn't go to college looks like, sounds like, and acts like. Sadly, a lot of people hold on to stereotypes of people who opted out of higher education as shiftless bums, not to mention *stoopid*. But there are lots of ways to be smart, and to learn. As a reader, I'm constantly hoovering information into my brain. Yes, a bunch of it is arguably meaningless trivia about the lives of fashion designers (Did you know that Tom Ford takes *five baths a day*?), but I love reading science magazines, too.

Not going to college does not mean you've opted out of educating yourself. Traveling, paying attention, asking questions, and always, always reading feed your smarts. And self-directed learning can lead you into random areas you would not have found in college, like the dozens of "underground," small-press writers who have taught me different ways to write and to live. Plus, I feel like a badass telling people I graduated from the School of Hard Knocks. While others were studying the finer points of the Western literary canon, I was teaching myself how to book a national tour, bringing two vanloads of feminist writers across the country to perform their work in bars, art galleries, and, yep, universities. This tour, Sister Spit, still travels the country every fall. After a recent show at the University of California, Santa Cruz, where hundreds of students turned out to listen to us talk about class, the performers sat in a beautiful redwood cabin talking with students about what they'd learned. And I realized: If I had gone to college, none of us would have been there right then. The thought hit me powerfully. There are other ways to create a life built around literature and learning, and mine is living proof.

But like I said, I vacillate. How could I not, in a world that insists that college is the place to be if you value your intellect and want a prosperous life? It's true I would be more eligible for teaching jobs if I had a degree backing me up, and I'd be able to command a higher rate of pay. But even more persuasive is having access to what I've come to believe is college's top benefit: connections. My mother's glum refrain "Money goes to money" is true, and if you don't have any money, one way to get some is by being around people who *do* have money. And those people go to college. I know that for working-poor kids it's not as easy as enrolling, becoming besties with some heiresses, and getting hooked up. Working-poor kids are likely too bewildered and stressed out (and holding jobs in addition to studying) to have a big social life, and friends they make are bound to be others like them, able to offer support and understanding in this scary new world. But I've seen friends who attended university—some on their parents' dime, some at great cost to themselves—make phone calls that produced jobs, internships, literary agents. It's as if there is an inside world and an outside world, and one way inside is through college. I didn't know that then, and I don't know if knowing it would have made a difference—I still wouldn't have had the resources. But as I grew older and my experience of the world broadened, I began to understand how important networks are, how being part of a network can make your life happen. Understanding this, it's hard not to wonder what my life could have been like with some help from the inside. I could have had a great writing professor take me under his or her wing; I could have had a story passed to a magazine, gotten hooked up with an agent. Perhaps I could have sold my first book for more than three hundred dollars, my second for more than a thousand.

In my early thirties, newly sober, I started wondering about college again. Looking back on my path, all I could see right then was the destruction my prioritization of drugs and alcohol had wrought, the many ways I'd stunted myself. Maybe it *had* been foolish not to have tried harder to go to college. I was engaged in making "amends"—reaching out and apologizing to people my drinking had hurt. One person you make amends to is yourself, because often you're the one most harmed by your boozing. These amends often take the shape of living your life the way you would have if you weren't such a mess. By my senior year of high school, my drinking had already been in full swing. Did I owe it to myself to give college a try?

The question led me to a fancy East Coast university, one of the few colleges that has a grad program in literature that's free *and* that will sometimes overlook an absence of undergrad if you have a surfeit of life experience. And did I ever! I'd published three books, memoirs that explored what life had been like for an off-center, working-class girl like me. I'd managed to get them published on small presses that didn't have much to offer me financially, but they got my books into the world—a dream come true, a dream I had barely dared to dream. Those books found readers, and many of them liked what I was writing about. One even got a review—a good one!—in the *New York Times*! This alone seemed more than anyone from my circumstances could hope for, but there was more. In addition to the ongoing Sister Spit tour, I'd also organized long-running literary series, more than a few, the latest one being at the San Francisco Public Library. It meant a lot to me and to the underground writers I worked with to present our writing in such an "official" place. I hadn't gone to college, but I'd done all *this*. Surely it must mean something!

Nervous but excited, I brought copies of my books to my meeting at the creative writing department at the East Coast university. It had taken me more than a decade, but I was finally figuring out how to do what I hadn't been able to do as a teenager: I was visiting a school, observing the campus, meeting with a professor. The man took a look at the small stack of books I'd brought him, then looked at me. "You're actually more accomplished than what we're looking for in our graduate students," he said.

I didn't realize how much hope I'd put into that meeting until it evaporated. "Yeah," I said, possibly desperately, "but I did it all outside of the system—no undergrad, nothing." The professor looked a little stunned at that, a little confused. He didn't respond, except to stammer, "Well, you're certainly welcome to apply."

Apply? *Do you know how much those application fees cost?* I remembered my mother, stress-smoking cigarettes in the kitchen as I typed up applications to colleges we couldn't afford. And I understood, suddenly, how she felt. I wasn't going to put all that effort and money into getting into a program I was told would likely not accept me. Once outside the office I let a few angry tears sneak out before getting myself together. It was hard not to feel like I was being punished for being resourceful, for working hard.

I was at a funny crossroads. Having just sobered up, I'd lost the glow that booze can lend to poverty. I didn't want to be broke for the rest of my life—I wanted security; I wanted a nice thing or two. I had enough money trickling in to make me know I wanted more. It was a time when a lot of writer friends, tired of toiling over poems few people read, had decided to return to school. I looked into a program for late-in-life female students at Smith College. It wasn't free, but they did a lot to support you as you entered this new and overwhelming landscape. A Smith graduate was urging me to apply. At the same time, an offer came in from an art publisher. They wanted to publish a collection of short stories I'd written, accompanied by graphic illustrations. I'd have to get to work tidying the writing up and would need to go on a tour once it came out, to promote it. I knew I couldn't do both. The school application would be its own effort, no time to work on my writing and reach the publisher's deadline. If I got in, there was no way I could tour the book, and if you're publishing books on small presses you've got to tour them. Did I take this crazy risk and apply to a school on the other side of the country, abandoning the life I'd built instead of going to college, getting into the debt I'd studiously avoided? Or did I stay on the path of crazy risk that had become my life, continuing to build the career momentum I'd created?

"Michelle," my friends observed. "People go to college so they can publish books. You're already publishing books. Why do you want to go to college?"

Huh. They were right. (You may have noticed a pattern—my friends are usually right. It pays to have friends who are smarter than you). Why *did* I want to go to college? I wanted to go because I was scared. I was scared I had made a bad decision a long time ago. That I was missing out on some vital experience that could propel me to increased wealth and glory. But a glance at all my struggling college-educated friends stripped me of *that* illusion. A college education hadn't been the magic bullet that shot them into their dream lives. Life is hard for everyone, a chiaroscuro of awesome triumphs and sucky setbacks. Everyone wants more than what they have and they have to hustle toward it best they can. My path might be different than that of so many people around me, but it's also very much the same. In 12-step there's a saying: Do the next right thing. The next right thing was to allow these stories I'd written about my weird-ass beautiful life to be published, and then do what I could to support that work. What did I want to be when I grew up? A librarian, I'd once thought, so that I could be close to books. It hadn't even occurred to me that I could be the person who *wrote* the books. A writer. And now I was one.

So, I didn't go to college. I still haven't, and I can't imagine I ever will. When the old doubt creeps back into my skull and I start worrying that I don't *really* know what the word *postmodern* means, or that when someone accuses me of being an "essentialist" I have no comeback because I don't know what the frig they're talking about, or that I've never read the gender theories of Judith Butler (even though I think I tend to date people who embody them), I do what I've always done when I want to learn. I pick up a book. I haven't made it past the C's in the *Dictionary of Critical Theory*, but entry by entry, I'm sure I'll reach the end (Žižek, Slavoj). Earlier this year I decided it was time to step up my literary education and read Hemingway, a writer I've always avoided because his reputation precedes him too mightily and macho-ly. Much to my surprise, I stuck it out through all five-hundred-plus pages of *For Whom the Bell Tolls*, shocked at how much I was enjoying a war novel (totally not my thing), humbled by how wrong I'd been about this writer. By the end I was crying on public transportation. Next I moved on to *Madame Bovary*, delighted by how like an antique French soap opera it read. I may not have been able to attend college, but the stuff that's taught there can be grabbed by anyone, any day of the week (at our local libraries, staffed by those awesome "old maids," the real Ms. Americas).

Maybe I'll always harbor distant fantasies about going back to school, because I love to learn and read, and I love to live. Maybe when I'm in my eighties I'll be one of those rad old ladies who wind up on the nightly news for being an octogenarian college freshman. But I doubt it. Having graduated from the School of Hard Knocks, I enjoy operating as the institution's development director, PR person, provost, and department head. It's important to know that there are lots of ways to do things, many routes to life and learning, more than one way to be what you want to be. I'd rather college be affordable enough that the decision not to go is one made by choice rather than default, but even if that were to happen, I'd keep my post as dean of the alternative way, that famously less traveled road.

# 8.

# The Baddest Buddhist

Sometime after my epic breakup, when I was still seething with resentment, I visited with my family in sunny Santa Monica. We were among a horde of people wandering toward the promenade, a public space lined with stores and odd, often sad street buskers, like the man playing a violin with an empty soda bottle, or the "psychic cats"—malnourished felines in Ren Faire garb trained to grab a scroll of psychic hoo-ha for a spoonful of wet food. As we pushed forward, I noticed a man in the crowd who was walking funny and spouting fury. Others moved to give him space lest he suddenly become violent; we did the same. As we passed him I caught a glimpse of his face—reddened, tortured, full of rage.

"I did *everything* for you and you did *nothing* for me! I did *everything* for you and you did *nothing* for me!" he chanted. The people moving by him looked scared, or disturbed. Some laughed at him; some looked briefly compassionate and quickly moved on—the various coping mechanisms we develop to deal with the sight of one of our kind losing it in public. Beneath all reactions, even the cruelest, is a bit of *There but for the grace of God go I*.

That afternoon I felt especially close to the freaking-out gentleman. I couldn't shake the feeling that I had put in a lot of time with my rapper ex, taken a lot of shit, worked really hard, and all for nothing. I'd cared for this person emotionally, financially, even physically, and for what? Eight years of my life, gone. *I did everything for you and you did nothing for me!* The only difference between me and the dude in the street was that I kept my grudging fury on the inside, while he had lost that ability. There but for the grace of Stevie Nicks higher power go I.

Remember that 12-step slogan I mentioned, about how resentment is like drinking a glass of poison and expecting the *other* person to die? I had a churning pit of bitterness and anger in my body, but my ex seemed to be having a great time bouncing around town with his new girlfriend. No matter how much I stewed and sunk, he appeared buoyant, remorseless. I knew I had to do something about it, lest I turn into a woman muttering aloud in public shopping centers. Writing lists of everything I was grateful for wasn't soothing my angst; spending an extra twenty minutes on the treadmill didn't exhaust it out of me. My regular stable of self-help tools wasn't cutting it. It was time to get a serious perspective injection, to declare spiritual war on myself. It was time to get Buddhist about it. I'd long sought solace and wisdom from the occasional Buddhist read, but my current state of mind was pushing me toward a deeper interaction with the ancient discipline. I'd thought Buddhism would save me from hating my ex, but instead it helped me grow up a little more.

While the thought of shaving my head is terrifying (I did it once, during a feminist nervous breakdown, and was shocked to learn that I have a very pimply scalp), and vows of silence intimidating (though it would certainly be nice for everyone if I shut up once in a while), and pledging to swear off meat stressful, Buddhism is the spiritual philosophy that has always made the most sense to me. I believe 100 percent in the truthfulness of it. I believe there is a middle path, and that it is the sanest one to trot. I believe in the five precepts, a scaled-down version of those Ten Commandments drilled into me in Catholic school—no killing, no stealing, no sexual misconduct, avoid "false speech," and abstain from "fermented drink that causes heedlessness."

I find these five rules that Buddhists live by basic, totally fair, and much, much harder to abide by than they look. Even the first one, no killing, is more complicated than it appears. At first you're like, *Duh, I would never kill anybody*. Then you realize that it doesn't say no killing *people*; it says, simply, no killing. Now, unlike Christianity, Buddhism is very much figure-it-out-for-yourself, which is one of the reasons I dig it. For me, no killing means, simply, no killing, and includes the nation of ants I annihilated on my countertop this morning, not to mention the mouse beneath my sink. If I believe that "no killing" is the righteous way to go, why do I find it so hard to commit to? Because I'm human. If these five precepts came easily to any of us, humans wouldn't have been creating religious disciplines around them since the dawn of time. It's our nature to stray, and our nature to regret it. It's our nature to yearn for a sort of purity, and our nature to fail ourselves. The precepts, like whatever you pledged to take up or quit this past New Year, are tough to stick with.

Though it sounds counterintuitive, I've found the Buddhist precept against stealing easier to master than outright murder, even though I often think a little shoplifting isn't such a big deal. I don't judge any down-on-their-luck person lifting food or toiletries or other human requirements from giant retailers. And I also don't judge the scrappy, broke girls I know who have made an art of ripping off fashion from places like Neiman Marcus and Banana Republic—many a time I wished I had their daring and skill!

My own experiences with thievery are so small-scale it's almost embarrassing (bragging about thievery may be one of the realms where the horrid phrase "Go big or go home" is applicable). When I was thirteen years old and began sneaking into Boston, I gravitated to Faneuil Hall Marketplace, a shopping emporium stocked with carts hawking the sorts of juicy trinkets one went wild for in the 1980s. Plastic heart key chains. Shoelaces stamped with ice cream cones or shooting stars. Rolls of scratch-and-sniff stickers that reeked of pickles or root beer. Dangly purple earrings from a cart that sold only purple things. Erasers shaped like unicorns. Smallish items easy enough to pocket if the urge struck you, and the urge did. I coveted these things so powerfully it made me sweat. To me they were emblems of the world outside my shitty small town, a world where people wore cool clothes and thought cool thoughts and did cool things. If I could bring, say, a purple pencil embossed with metallic gold lightning bolts from Boston back to my real life, it would be like bringing an object back from a dream; it would enchant my everyday hours and infuse them with possibility. So I began to shoplift.

I prized my ability to find creative ways to boost an item. Fingerless gloves, very in at the time, were a great aid; I would simply slip palm-sized objects into the glove and wave the shopkeeper good-bye as I walked away. I was also good at faking a sneeze while tossing the contraband into my mouth. At home I hid my loot in an old cedar box my grandmother had given me. The only problem with stealing such cool stuff is I couldn't actually use any of it. My mother would see it and ask me where it had come from, and I knew my stammer would betray me. So, I started selling it. The girls in my shitty Catholic school in my shitty run-down town also drooled at the sight of hair barrettes braided with silky ribbons and bright earrings and neon rubber bracelets. The loot vanished from my cedar box, replaced by dollars.

I might've gone on forever, slowly building a stolen-goods empire. I could be writing to you from prison right now. Instead, I got caught, and the getting caught made me stop my shoplifting ways—about 95 percent of them. That day, I was wandering the aisles of the Kmart at the crummy Mystic Mall with some friends, up to no good. I wanted watermelon Kissing Potion *so bad*. The desire for the taste of sugary candy makeup on my mouth was so strong, I now wonder if I'd had low blood sugar and maybe just needed a slice of pizza. But no—I needed my lips to look all wet and shiny like the girl in the ad with the perfect frosted-blond feathered hair. When we hit the cosmetics aisle I grabbed a package of the roll-on gloss and casually walked it into the boys' department. I buried it under a stack of pajamas and, while looking (so I thought) like I was digging around for the perfect size jammies for a little brother I did not have, I ripped the package open and shimmied the tube of gloss into the wrist of my jacket.

This jacket was a good one for shoplifting. It belonged to Jen Spicoli, the most popular girl in my class and my own best frenemy. Often I would stay the night at Jen's house, planning the all-pickle "health food" diets we would go on beneath the posters of Sylvester Stallone that lined her bedroom walls. In the morning, I would be told not to tell anyone that I'd spent the night. It was like we were having an affair, Jen Spicoli and I, though I swear nothing ever happened between us. I actually sort of hated staying at her house because she slept with the radio on, which I thought was really cool but which very much impeded sleeping. I'd lie awake next to her in bed, having what I now know to be a panic attack. Still, I always wanted to stay over. Jen was cool: She had an older brother who was into AC/DC, she wore black eyeliner, and she had superstraight blond hair pinned back from her forehead, and the softest, tenderest hairs would straggle out from her hairline—baby bangs, she called them. She wasn't just a member of Chelsea's Pop Warner football cheerleading squad; Jen was *head* cheerleader. And in spite of her ambivalent feelings toward me, she'd let me borrow her cheerleading jacket. It was amazing: bright-red corduroy, with her name in cursive on one arm and a patch of the devil on the other. As much as I hated Chelsea, it *was* cool that the city's mascot was a leering, mustachioed Satan. As a bonus, the wrists of Jen's jacket were tight elastic, meaning that anything stuffed up the sleeve wouldn't fall out.

I would have made it home with my watermelon kissing potion if not for the daring of Elena Rubinski, and my own stupidity. Once safely outside the Kmart, huffing and puffing and glowing with the wild dopamine and adrenaline surges shoplifting released in my hormonal body (for sure, this was my first drug), Elena, who had been too chicken to lift anything, decided she wanted the watermelon-scented eraser that had been packaged with the gloss. I was so excited for my friend, that she would soon know the rush and material gain of shoplifting, and I was proud to be her mentor, showing her the ropes. We walked back into the fluorescent-lit apocalypse of Kmart, the stink of fake-buttered popcorn and tangy blue Icees all around us. We walked back to the pile of pajamas and found the gloss packaging right where I'd left it. Elena snatched the eraser. And then the security guard snatched us.

If only, if only! If only I had taken the stupid lip gloss out of my coat and stashed it in a trash can or something. But I hadn't. When the plainclothes guard brought me and a crying Elena into a back room hung with the Polaroids of fellow shoplifters and ordered me to take off Jen's coat, the gloss fell to the floor. The guard didn't put us in handcuffs or call the cops, though he threatened us with both. I managed to convince him that the eraser belonged to Elena, and that she just had the misfortune of befriending a shoplifter. She was let go, and the guard called my mother. I was banned from the store, and Jen Spicoli was *pissed* that I got Kmart-arrested in her cheerleading jacket. What if they thought she was me next time she went in for an Icee? I looked at her like she was nuts; Jen Spicoli was waaaaaay prettier than I was. I *wished* it took but a cheerleading jacket to make me look like her. Nonetheless, Jen became less *fren*, more *nemy*. And that was pretty much the end of my criminal career, minus a few forays into, you know, drug dealing and prostitution.

As much as I might not care about people lifting a bottle from Sephora or any other megachain, I myself cannot do any of it anymore. Quite simply, I'm too old. Too *grown-up* to get caught. The thought of getting busted, Winona-like, for stealing an unnecessary luxury is totally humiliating. As the late, great comedian Lotus Weinstock said, "I used to want to change the world. Now I just want to leave the room with a little dignity." And leaving a Bloomingdale's in handcuffs for boosting a pair of earrings is just not dignified. (Though, goddammit, try as I might to resist, it *does* have a gritty Courtney Love–type glamour to it, does it not?) Being engaged with Buddhism helps me keep in mind the recovery assertion that every problem is a spiritual problem. If I want to steal something, I must think I don't have everything I need already. And in my case, I do. I do have everything I need. Recognizing that lays bare my thieving desire as the bundle of greed or fear that it is. And then I can deal with *that*.

Precept Three: Avoid sexual misconduct. This is so personal, and so subject to interpretation. I think it comes down to this: Do you think, in your heart, that your sexcapades might be hurting you or others? Are you cheating on someone, or helping someone else break a commitment? Are you a sexual thrill seeker, putting yourself in danger by recklessly hooking up with hoodlums? Do you use sex to manipulate people? (And I don't mean a stripper manipulating a dollar off a gent—that's a job. A job that might include such sexual misconduct, and also might not. Totally a personal call.) As someone with a bit of sex addiction mixed into her addiction Christmas stocking, sometimes I couldn't tell if I was feeding the beast or, you know, just enjoying the privileges of a single lady in my place and time—privileges my foremothers *died* for! It's tricky, these precepts. And yet, I believe that figuring out how to handle your sexuality with respect and dignity is a crucial part of growing up. Sometimes being at the mercy of my libido made me feel powerless, and feeling powerless made me feel like a child. Taking control and building that scaffolding of Rules for Love led me to a place where I was calling my sexual shots from a place of sanity, thinking about the whole big picture of my romantic life as opposed to the instant gratification of a two-bit hookup.

What other Buddhist precepts do I maybe sort of obey, maybe not? False speech is variously interpreted as lying, or gossiping. I am guilty of both. I don't lie to my loved ones, with the exception of my mom, because it is a daughter's job to lie to her mother, and plus it's good for our relationship. I would say I lie rarely. A big part of my 12-step practicing is accepting life on life's terms, and if you feel the need to lie you probably aren't doing that. Was I accepting life on life's terms when I decided to lie by omission to my department head at the fancy college and jet off to Fashion Week? No, I guess not. Knowing that telling the truth would get me fired, I opted for deception. This might be the career equivalent of a hungry person stealing a loaf of bread, and then again, I might be delusional.

As these gray areas of lying may make me a compromised Buddhist, so does gossip. It's not that I enjoy laying a reputation to waste—I truly don't. But I'm a *writer*. I love *story*. And what is gossip if not story? It is the same oral tradition that created the best of our myths and legends, albeit in a super-duper debased form. As someone who has tried to shut my trap and felt, well, *trapped*, I have come up with some guidelines. First and most important is, whom am I talking to? My significant other? My tried-and-true bestie? I think this is fine. Do I run around sharing the business of people I hardly know with other people I hardly know? That looks tacky. It *is* tacky. You're sending out a big message to all that you're not trustworthy. And guess what—you're not!

Also, what's the purpose of the gossip? Although the individual being gossiped about may not appreciate being discussed regardless of the purpose, I think there is a difference between sharing a compelling story and trying to turn people against a person. The former is a minor sin, understandable and human. The latter is just mean. I've indulged in both and the contrast is visceral—when I'm gossiping with an agenda I'm hot and cold, sweaty and clammy, and there's a dark jaw gnawing in the pit of my stomach. (Or maybe I was just on speed. Most of my harmful gossiping happened whilst under the influence of the hot-cold sweaty-clammy substance.) Bad gossip makes me feel bad: I've given in to my desire to control what people think of each other, which is always—always!—none of my business. The conversation sits in my guts for days; I'm hungover from it. Like getting caught shoplifting, the punishment is preventive. I don't want to feel like that. And I don't, in my heart of hearts, want to strew negativity and ugly feelings throughout the land. If someone truly is a lousy person, their behavior will doom them without any help from me. Then I can just sit back and enjoy the schadenfreude.

The final Buddhist precept I actually aced by failing: Avoid fermented beverages. I tried my best to drink like a lady, but heedlessness prevailed, and I had to cut the sauce or watch my life swirl down the toilet. Although many people seem capable of imbibing the occasional cocktail without destroying everything they love, many others cannot, and are oblivious to the fact that it's the cocktails that are ruining everything. It's one of the great and terrible powers fermented beverages possess, this ability to get you hooked, wreck your life, and still have you wondering what the hell the problem might be. It took me forever to figure out I was an alcoholic—fighting every night with my boyfriend, feeling sick every morning, a sense of hopelessness, spontaneous weeping, blaming everything but booze for my eversaddening life.

When I was drinking, my rapper ex and I fought all the time. This was at least partially my fault. That's the thing with being a drunk fighter—you'll never *really* know if you were correct to take offense or if you were just being wasted and irrational. But one thing is certain—you'll be the one apologizing the next day. If you are the drunk person in the fight, you are the one who has to grovel and beg for forgiveness. Sure, maybe your date *did* say something passive-aggressive, but your judgment was so busted, how can you be sure? The only hard fact is that you were wasted. If you consume fermented beverages with your significant other, be ready to spend some mornings humbly soliciting mercy from behind the veil of your dehydration headache.

The best worst drunk fight I ever lost had me hopping out of the car at a red light in Los Angeles and running onto the freeway exit, to hide out on the little slope of bushes and shrubs. He'd never find me there! I eventually left my slightly dangerous hide-out and sulked down to the Frolic Room, a real drunk's bar, where the patron saint of asshole alcoholics, the poet Charles Bukowski, used to drink. I ordered a cocktail and sat there, angrily smoking. The bar phone rang. The bartender walked it over. "There's a person on the phone asking if there's a girl with blue hair here." This was in the days before cell phones, thank God, because if there's one thing an alcoholic loves to lose track of it's her cell phone. My ex picked me up from the bar, then drove to the taco truck where transgender hookers hung around selling crystal meth. I would have preferred some speed but my ex made me buy a couple of tacos. I ate them with bizarre defiance, the cheese spilling down the front of my shirt, making a performance of how pissed I was with each petulant chomp. What were we fighting about? I don't remember, though I'll never forget the fight itself because for years my ex liked to tell the story of when I ran away to the side of the freeway and then angrily ate some tacos. He is likely telling it to someone right now. It's a great story. Drinking fermented beverages really puts you at a disadvantage in an argument.

These five precepts I have more or less struggled with throughout my life, and I expect I will continue to flail and to fail in my efforts to uphold them. And what I like about Buddhism, what has drawn me to its message and kept me there in spite of how fickle I can be with my spiritual practices (remind me to tell you about when I interviewed to join Aleister Crowley's creepy Thelemic temple) is its embrace of failure. Buddhism embraces failure because it embraces humanity, and to fail is human. It is a study of human nature and potential, offering a sort of best practices guide to getting over yourself. When you inevitably fuck up along the way, there is no old man doling out punishment prayers, as there was in the spiritual practices of my youth. There is a larger, transcendent view, and the opportunity to try again. Buddhism is just like life in this way. Buddhism *is* life.

Another famous Buddhist countdown is the four noble truths, a cluster of hard-won understandings about our shared life on earth. The first noble truth is, people suffer—something that in the moments after my breakup I took to heart. People misunderstand it as all life is suffering, which paints Buddhists as a pretty somber lot, and I suppose they can be, but not always. It's more like, in life there is suffering. Suffering is real; it exists. (Bonus—in the Pali language, suffering is called *dukkha*, which sounds a lot like *dookie*, which means "shit." *In life, there is dookie.*)

The second truth is that there is one reason for all suffering: We humans have a hard time adjusting to reality. We often have a desire for life to be different than it is, and that hurts. In my case, I wanted my ex to just admit he was a fucking asshole and that we broke up so he could go and date a DJ. Knee-deep in *dukkha*, I mistakenly believed the cause of my suffering was my ex's inability to give me this simple acknowledgment. The reality of the situation was, I was in pain because I needed my ex to be different. In Buddhism, when you have a problem, *you* have a problem. It's yours. When you get over the tantrum you inevitably throw about the injustice of this, it's actually quite nice. If *you* have the problem, you also have the ability to solve it.

The third noble truth essentially boils down to: If you stopped giving a shit, you'd be happier. Why did I *need* my ex to admit he'd left me for a DJ? Because I wanted us to be on the same page about our breakup. But we'd never been on the same page about our relationship, so why did I think our coming apart would be any different? Okay, maybe I wanted to win. I wanted the simple, time-honored pleasure of being the "good one" in the breakup. After all I'd done for him, couldn't he at least give me *that*? Apparently not. And I couldn't make him do it, but I could stop needing it. And according to the final noble truth, getting into Buddhism and following the eightfold path (damn, do Buddhists like to number things or what?) is the way to stop needing all the things you can't have, and thus be happier.

And so, post-breakup, I made my way to the Zen Center, a large, beautiful, welcoming compound that invites the public inside to learn more about the practice through meditations and those wisdom-sharing monologues called dharma talks. The wide hall is intimidating to enter when you are but a failed and dabbling Buddhist whose "practice" consists of a couple of Pema Chödrön books sitting by your bedside for when you're too angsted-out to sleep. The room exudes a dignified calm, covered with a tatami mat, the Buddha in his many incarnations represented by a row of statues next to what appears to be an altar. The respect I felt as I entered was enormous, creating a fear that I would somehow disrespect it by, like, walking somewhere I wasn't supposed to walk, accidentally and unintentionally sending a *fuck you* to the Buddha. It seemed that when people walked to the far end of the room they did a little bow toward the Buddhas; the thought froze me in terror. I decided to not cross the room. Thus began my practice of grabbing a zafu—a round black meditation pillow—from the shelf by the door, then finding the closest spot on the mat for me to shove it under my butt and wait for further instruction. Eventually, a *real* Buddhist—someone who had taken the vows, who had trudged the long, hard road of true Buddhist practice—would take a seat at the front of the gathering, ring a little bell, and impart some simple meditation instruction: Sit like this, keep your eyes open, bring your thoughts back when they stray. Okay, go. And the room, packed with people, became totally quiet, and together, we strangers, all of us engaging with the miseries that brought us here (few Westerners turn to Buddhism because life is going awesomely), hoped this new way would give us *something*. Peace. Wisdom. A new perspective. Acceptance.

There was no end to the misperceptions about Buddhism I encountered as I told people about my cool new hangout. *Oh, I can't meditate; my mind just jumps all over the place; I really can't do it.* Uh, that's sort of the *point* of meditation. You're not special. Everyone's mind jumps all over the place—that's what a mind *does*. Meditating doesn't make that go away—well, maybe it does for super extra awesome meditators who have stuck with it for a decade, but for the average monkey-brained human who sits down and tries to be silent and still for a moment, the whole experience is about sitting there with your crazy jumping thoughts. You sit and observe your jumbled inner narrative—*Hmm, what word should I get tattooed on my neck? I should write a television show! I wonder how so-and-so is doing in the wake of her failed marriage; I should call her—would that be awkward? Speaking of awkward, I can't believe I said that thing to that man about his artificial eye five years ago; God, that was so shitty of me—should I apologize? Huh, I know who should apologize—my ex! I've done* everything *for him and he's done* nothing *for me!* And as you observe this circus, your perception of your own thoughts begins to change.

We love our minds *so much* in this culture. *I think; therefore, I am! My opinions are super important and also witty and smart—I think I will broadcast them all over the Internet!* Our minds are everything. A good one can get you into a good school, which then gets you a good job and all the good cash and prizes that come with it, right?

More important, we *are* our minds. Our thoughts define us. When we're impressed by someone's intelligence, we say they're smart. We don't say they think smart thoughts or express smart opinions; we say they are smart, as if there is no separation between what we think and who we are. I am Michelle Tea because I think Michelle Tea–esque thoughts. But the more you sit back and experience how little control you have over your mind's ramblings, the more your mind seems to be, like all the other organs in your body, on a sort of autopilot, pumping out thoughts and opinions like your heart pumps blood and your lungs pump air. And, like an immune system that has turned on itself, my mind was pumping out sentiments that were harmful to me. They were harmful because I believed them. If I think it, it must be true—right? But maybe I didn't have to believe in the things my mind insisted upon. Maybe I'd be a little bit happier if I didn't.

Sitting in meditation, you get to understand the nature of the mind in general, and your own in particular. Increasingly I began to relate to my mind not as the highest point of my being, the apex of my essence, but more like a rambunctious toddler who wants everything and likes to pout and throw fits—something that required my firm and gentle guidance. And in discovering this, you acquaint yourself with the mind *behind* your mind, the one that can tame the chatter, take you out of the imaginary fight you were having with your ex and return you to the present—you are sitting on a pillow, your legs cramped into a pretzel, counting your breaths. One, two, three.

After instructed meditation in the public hall of the Zen Center, I was ready to go where the *real* meditators meditated, a dark little room in the basement called the Zendo. Though I had mostly mastered the forms of meditating in the public hall, my descent into the Zendo brought back all my fumbling intimidation in an anxious rush. One does not just sashay into a Zendo and plop down on a zafu. There are ways of doing things down there. Which foot steps into the space first, the right or the left? How are you holding your hands? When do you bow, and in what direction? How do you climb off your pillow when it's over? In what order do you exit, and, again, what do you do with your hands? There are answers to all of these questions. I'd gotten some instructions from friends, but I was still nervous. I knew I'd forget, or fuck up. In my nervousness I felt myself rage against these oppressive constraints. Why couldn't I just walk into the fucking room and throw my ass on a pillow? Because some long-ago monk with OCD developed these repetitive behaviors and we've all been following in his compulsive footsteps for millennia?

The more I did Buddhism, the more I got it. In a practice devoted to teaching us to wake up from the hum of our minds, some nifty tricks have been devised. The special way you walk into the Zendo is like a game meant to keep your mind focused. If you're thinking about what foot is falling over the threshold, you're not thinking about, like, if that's your ex sitting there in the same fucking meditation session as you—goddammit, you *introduced* him to the Zen Center; doesn't he understand it is *your* space; what, now you're going to have to fucking meditate together? I mean, such intrusive thoughts might barge in (it's funny how having "intrusive thoughts" is a symptom of mental illness; Buddhism teaches that *all* thoughts are intrusive, and maybe that means we're *all* a little mentally ill), but thankfully, some monk a bazillion years ago came up with this handy tool for snapping yourself out of it—just think about your next step. Okay, now think about your next step. And now think about your next step. There is always a next step.

When I started going to the Zen Center, I think I thought I'd meditate myself into a state of wild bliss wherein my ex's behavior just wouldn't bother me. I thought the point of meditating was to get yourself into some sort of transcendent zone where you had, I don't know, an *experience*. Maybe I thought it would be a little bit like a really rad acid trip, minus the acid. Alas, these were the hopes of a drug addict looking to get high. One thing I have to keep learning as a sober person is, if you want to feel like you're on drugs, you have to do drugs. Unless I start meditating on a batch of pot cookies (not recommended), I'm probably not going to hallucinate that I'm one with the universe.

What I do get from my practice (and, let me be clear, my "practice" is and always has been shabby enough that any Buddhist worth her rakusu would laugh at me) is ultimately something more lasting than a high, something I can have sober, all day, every day. What I get is the ability to see my mind's chatter for the honkadoodle bullshit it is. Some of my thoughts are good—they are skillful, helpful, positive. I appreciate them. They make me happy and bring brightness into my life. But some of my thoughts have the tone, timbre, and validity of an Internet comment board, and I treat them accordingly—delete; ignore; I'll pray for you, you sad, angry person. The more I meditate, the more likely I am to remember that my mind is a wasteland, my opinions not quite as valuable as my ego would like to think. The more I meditate, the quicker I can disrupt the crazy train of thinking. Ever space out while doing chores and come to in the midst of a wholly imagined argument with someone who isn't there? That's what I'm talking about. A meditation practice can get you out of the imaginary fight before the first imaginary punch is thrown.

I did have *one* sort of psychedelic experience while studying Buddhism. I'd taken a 101 class at the Zen Center, and was delving deeper into the roots of the practice, reading new texts (new to me; actually, they are quite ancient), soaking up my teacher's wise, funny talks. While pondering some teachings about the self and the mind, I had a flash. *I am not Michelle Tea! Not at all! Michelle Tea is this life I am living right now, but she's not me. What is "me"?* According to the Buddhists, there's no such thing. In that moment, I finally understood what they meant. It was a complete disassociation with my "self" that was brief and deeply inspiring. I remember it often, especially when having an FML moment. *Fuck my life? This isn't my life—it's Michelle Tea's life! What a cool, weird, amazing, wild life she has had! How excellent that I get to ride along with it!* It makes "my" life seem like a movie, which makes the harder parts, when I'm knee-deep in *dukkha*, much easier to get through. Somewhere behind "Michelle Tea" is a presence that is a little smarter, a little more caring. It's rooting for Michelle Tea and it's rooting for everyone. It's not taking any of it seriously, because it knows that Michelle, like everyone else, is just a little speck in a universe too vast for her lumpy human mind to comprehend. Just a little flash of this, every now and then, is the best we can hope for.

So Buddhism didn't get me high, and it didn't make me stop hating my ex. What it did do is show me exactly where the problem was located: in my mind. Which was great, because my mind, unlike my ex, was something I had some control over. I guess I got what I came for, in the long run. My ex and I still disagree about the end of our relationship; he still denies that his overlapping affair had anything to do with our demise. As for me, I know that we broke up so he could pursue other people. But I also know we broke up so I could get out of a terrible relationship I might have codependently stuck with for another eight years. We broke up so I could meet my true love, and get married, and experience the sort of intimacy I always knew was possible. We broke up so that my ex could also eventually find his own true love, a person who seemingly embraces all the personality quirks that made me want to kill him. The Buddhists are right—in life, there is suffering. But there is also relief, and joy and humor, and occasional psychedelic moments of oneness. And when I start forgetting that, all I need to do is put a pillow under my ass and start counting my breaths.

# 9.

# Getting Pregnant with Michelle Tea

**B**ack when I was dating a lot of scrubs and then got super bored and put the brakes on, something else happened, too. I realized that if I was ever going to have a baby in this life I was going to have to have one *now*. Not only was it difficult to nail down a decent date, but the likelihood of meeting someone competent enough to raise a rugrat with felt slimmer than ever. Nothing in my dating history led me to believe my dream co-parent was lurking nearby with a love note and a bouquet of ovulation predictors. Plus, even if I was wrong and Mx. Right was in my imminent future, you can't start having the kids conversation for, what, a year or two, right? I was forty years old. I realized that if I was going to do this thing, I was going to have to do it alone, and fast.

How fast? I jumped on the Interweb to find out. After googling my fertility analytics, I cried. The stats were grim. My tears surprised me; I wasn't one of those women who desperately want kids. For much of my childbearing life, the thought of a creature growing inside me called to mind that scene from *Alien* when the monster eats its way through its host-mommy's chest. I know it's supposed to be the most natural thing in the world, but childbirth always struck me as parasitic, invasive, the stuff of horror movies. Then, around the age of twenty-seven, my body began to crave the physical experience of being pregnant. This freaked me out on many levels. How can you crave an experience you never have had? It made no sense to me, but I longed for the sensation of a life inside me, a growing roundness, transformation.

My date at the time was a sporty lesbian who was very good to me—too good. She was an alcoholic's dream: an enabler. Not much of a drinker herself, she loved to ply me with fancy jugs of beer I couldn't afford, pitchers of margaritas at our favorite Mexican hole-in-the-wall, recreational downers pawned off her coworkers at the AIDS hospice she cooked at. She also prepared me amazing food and, when I was broker than broke, brought me along on her food bank rounds, letting me grab a few cans of beans. She was ethically comfortable with this—the food bank was for poor people, and I was living way below the poverty line, selling old books and clothes to get by, counting change I'd kept in a jar for just this—a worst-case scenario. But in spite of how bad off I was, she was delighted by the thought of me getting pregnant.

"Are you crazy?" I snapped. Although I could no longer deny that biological clocks were *real* (I'd hoped they were antifeminist propaganda) and mine was ringing pretty shrilly, my body was clearly insane. I didn't want a kid! I hadn't identified myself as an alcoholic yet, but I knew that drinking and partying were my first priority, with writing about my drunk, partying escapades a close second, and trying to be a marginally decent girlfriend a *very* distant third. Making a living was fourth priority. This was no environment to bring a child into. Thankfully, my date was physically incapable of knocking me up, though in my drunker moments (most moments after seven p.m.) I found myself sharing my envy of straight girls and their ever-present risk of accidental pregnancy. If I just—*whoops!*—got pregnant, then I'd have to keep it!

"I could find a sperm donor and inseminate you while you're sleeping," my enabler helpfully/creepily suggested.

"I'd kill you," I said, meaning it literally. "Like, actual murder."

That moment of strange pregnancy craving faded away, but it had left my perception of pregnancy changed. Babies no longer seemed like malevolent creatures that sucked the nutrients from your blood, destroyed your vagina, and killed any dreams you might have harbored for a life of fun and adventure. They just seemed like, well, babies. Some people have them; some people don't.

At forty, I finally started seriously asking myself how I felt about having children. I realized that the only thing really holding me back was money. If I had scads of cash I'd love to have a brood dashing around my spacious loft, playing on swing sets installed in the ceiling and creating avant-garde finger-paint murals on the walls. But my scarcity issues said *No fucking way are we supporting another mouth in this house*. I was afraid to pay the extra dollars to upgrade my Internet service; what would a kid cost? But I rebelled against this as well. Poor and low-income people all over the world have children. This experience cannot be the privilege of rich people alone. Surely I have more resources than lots of the women out there doing a great job single-mothering. If they could do it, so could I.

Except I couldn't. According to the Internet, my chances of getting knocked up at forty were dismal, and if a miracle occurred, the likelihood of carrying to term was also abysmal. I cried at my kitchen table, recalling that kitschy Roy Lichtenstein print of the 1960s lady sobbing into her manicure, *I forgot to have kids!*

After I wiped my snot away and shut my computer, my optimism returned, as it tends to. The Internet didn't say there was *no* chance, just a low chance! Like everyone, I knew some ladies who had popped one out in their fourth decade. Maybe I could, too. In order to find out, I would have to get some sperm.

I know a ton of foxy gay men, and I figured I could persuade one of them to donate their sperm to my pregnancy project. I started by asking only men of color. White people famously wreak so much havoc everywhere all the time, I wanted to do my part to not propagate the race, for the good of the planet. But gentleman after gentleman of all ethnicities turned me down. Maybe some of them wanted to have a baby themselves at some point; others feared that knowing they had offspring out in the world would freak them out. I made it clear I wanted nothing to do with them—no financial support, no parenting assistance, nothing except a willingness to be known by the kid when they got older. But some men feared that they would feel responsible for the child regardless, and didn't want the angst. I understand that this is a really monumental thing to consider—essentially fathering a child and leaving it for someone else to raise—but for me at the time it felt infuriatingly simple: You've got *tons* of sperm; I have none—can't you give a lady a break? Be a feminist, for goddess's sake!

Eventually I learned of a gay boy who'd told friends he'd totally be into sharing his sperm with a needy, baby-mad lady. I knew him casually but had big affection for him— he was a drag queen whose acts were especially brainy and creative. He worked at nonprofits despite a sensitivity to injustice that made even a job in the nonprofit industrial complex too Orwellian for him to handle. Though he was a nightlife habitant, he had seemingly none of the drug and alcohol issues that sometimes accessorize the lifestyle. He was sort of wholesome, and political, and creative and glamorous. And when I asked him if he would be willing to come to my home and ejaculate into a warm bowl for me to somehow inject semen into my uterus, he e-mailed back, *You had me at "warm bowl."*

I had sperm! But I still wasn't 100 percent certain how a person got herself pregnant in this independent fashion. My inquiries led me to a whole subset of my larger community: women who have knocked themselves up, and were excited to share how they did it. I learned that those needle-less syringes used to give babies their medicine also made great sperm shooters, *and* you could get them for free at your local corporate pharmacy. I didn't feel too bad about scamming all the freebies, as I was buying the place out of their ovulation predictor pee sticks. When my ovulation line got really pink Quentin would come over, along with my friend Rhonda, a hardy skateboarding Scorpio with no fear. Quentin would go into my kitchen and, um, pleasure himself. I left my laptop in there for his enjoyment, but I don't know if he ever used it beyond watching Cyndi Lauper videos on it after the deed was done.

When the deed *was* done, Quentin would holler out to Rhonda, who would slide across my apartment in her socks and retrieve the vintage Pyrex bowl of sperm. Together we would suck the goo up into the syringe, then I would lie back on some pillows, spread my legs, and my dear friend would insert the thing and pull the trigger. How is that for sisterhood! What would you do for *your* bestie?

We did this a lot, Quentin, Rhonda, and I. Somewhere in the midst of it I met Dashiell. Though I have already documented her considerable charm in these pages, when we first began to date I really didn't think it would go very far. I assumed that she, like everyone else I tended to be attracted to, was something of a jerk. I waited for her to drop her charade of gentle chivalry and go mental on me. I was too mature now to put up with any more drama—it had finally become so boring, not even hot sex could justify it. And now that I was trying to have a child, anyone hanging around would have to be of a high-enough caliber to expose a baby to. My hopes were low. But date after date, Dashiell stayed constant. Her kindness was authentic, not manipulative. Her moods were steady, not unpredictable. She was the real thing, the kind of person I'd probably always wanted but was now finally healthy enough to attract. And once she found out I was in the midst of trying to impregnate myself, she would surely bolt. A young, hot, mannish woman with not only a *job* but an actual *career*, who understood how to take care of herself? Who had impeccable style and disposable income? Her own apartment and a very cute, if barky, small dog? Why would she want to date an older woman with a bun in the oven?

The more I fell for Dashiell, the longer I waited to tell her about my main activity, the more it felt like it was too late to tell her, the more it felt like I had really fucked up. I was a constant flutter around her, but my secret ate at me. I asked friends for advice.

"It's your business; you don't need to tell her anything right now," some 12-step friends sagely counseled.

*You should have told her on THE FIRST DATE*, texted another friend, a single, mannish woman herself, no doubt horrified at the thought that one of her very own dates could be inseminating herself on their off nights. This time, my friends' advice wasn't really helping.

One night Dashiell and I sat side by side at the bar of a fancy French restaurant. I was wearing a tiny strapless Jean Paul Gaultier for Target dress, and got delicious shivers every time Dashiell touched my waist. Like all women, even homosexual ones, we were talking about Ryan Gosling.

"I wouldn't want to have sex with him," Dashiell clarified. "But I would love his sperm." I coughed and a tiny stream of whatever lovely lavender-infused mocktail the bartender had sent my way slid out of my nose. Dashiell patted me on the back, giving me more shivers, and looked alarmed.

"I'm sorry!" she said earnestly. "Was that a weird thing to say?"

"Ah, no," I sputtered. "Just went down the wrong pipe." Goddammit, now was the time! She had opened the door so nicely with that comment. I could just say, *Absolutely—I, too, would have loved Ryan Gosling's sperm, though I must say I couldn't be happier with the intelligent drag queen sperm I found!* But I didn't. The bar was so public, so crowded! What if Dashiell had a feeling? She'd have to feel it here in this chaotic, trendy restaurant—how awkward. I closed my mouth down around my straw and sipped at my mocktail.

Since the restaurant was near my house, we went there after dinner. We messed around on my bed for what seemed like hours. Still, my secret nagged at the back of my skull, keeping me from fully letting go to the moment. I excused myself to the bathroom, and splashed some water on my face. *Just tell her; just tell her.*

I didn't walk back into my bedroom so much as run. Then I jumped onto the bed, landing on my knees beside Dashiell, who looked alarmed at the sudden commotion. "I'm trying to get pregnant," I blurted. "I've been trying since before I met you, and I didn't know how to tell you, and at first it wasn't appropriate but then I didn't know how to say it and then so much time passed and then—well, I just didn't know how to say it. But I am. I am trying to get pregnant right now."

The biggest, slowest smile spilled across Dashiell's face. She stared at me, taking her own moment to collect herself. "That . . . is awesome," she said. "That is so awesome."

*But*, I waited for her to say, *I'm not hooking up with some preggo lady, so, this has been fun, thanks for the coq au vin, I gotta motor.*

"You think?" I asked timidly. "You're not mad, or freaked out?"

"No, no!" She scrambled up from the bed so we were eye-to-eye. "My friends made me promise not to tell you, because they were afraid I'd scare you off, but I want to have kids more than anything. Like, that's what I want in life. To have a family."

I stared at this person, apparently the magical result of every new-agey "manifestation" practice I had ever indulged. She was the epitome of all my hopes and desires, the one I prayed to Stevie Nicks higher power to deliver: a healthy, sweet person whom I was hot for and who wanted a family.

"So . . ." I said hesitantly. "You still want to keep dating me?" And she did.

"I know it's your thing; it's not my thing," Dashiell clarified, lest I think she was trying to be my baby daddy-mommy. "But I just think it is so cool you're doing this." Even though it went against my new take-it-slow ethos, I knew that soon it would be *our* thing. I felt it in my heart—Dashiell was the one. The real one, the real deal, true love. And somehow, we would have a child together.

After a lot of failed home-insemination attempts, I bundled up all my scarcity issues and went to a fertility clinic, where I learned that I have even fewer healthy eggs than the average fortysomething woman—and that average lady doesn't have very much. The doctor brightened when he learned my significant other had some ovaries of her own, and that they were a good eight years younger than mine. After a million ultrasound wands probed my vagina, after some terrible procedures in which dye got painfully squirted into my fallopian tubes, after two surgeries to deal with grapefruit-sized fibroids that were lodged in my uterus, after two million billion thousand shots of chemicals and hormones, after pills and patches and a procedure that palpitated all the eggs from Dashiell's overgrown ovaries, after a few transfers, in which eggs fertilized with Quentin's sperm (on Gay Pride Day, heeeeeey!) were shot into my uterus, we are still not pregnant.

Somewhere along the way I began blogging about our attempts to get pregnant, with Dashiell's blessing. I was a little scared to ask. The people I've dated all hate turning up in my stories—but then, I always write about them after the whole romance has crashed and burned. It's easy, sort of, to write about love gone wrong, but more challenging to write about the happy times in a way that doesn't bore the shit out of *you*, let alone your readers. I'd never written about a happy relationship before. I'd never had one! I didn't want Dashiell to feel like I was using her for writing material. She is also a much more private person than I am; I didn't think she'd take kindly to having these most intimate details of her life exposed. But to my surprise, she said yes.

"I'm proud of us," she said simply, and proudly. And so I began blogging about our fertility misadventures, and the sisterhood of self-impregnated women swelled to include all sorts of women who had tried, failed, and tried again to have a baby. Some were doing it themselves; some had husbands, or female partners. Some were on fertility diets, drinking fertility shakes and popping fertility supplements; others were downing Clomid in a clinic, getting IUIs at home from a midwife or on a table from a doctor. Some did IVF. Normally, when I wrote for the Internet I avoided the Comments sections, as they were inevitably filled with anonymous, mean character assassinations and the like, and even though you know they are written by sad people with serious emotional problems, it still feels shitty. But these comments were *wonderful*. A chorus of strangers cheering me and Dashiell on, plus sharing their own stories for perspective and comfort, *plus* offering the tips and wisdom they'd gleaned on the way. Most of my friends found children grotesque, so to suddenly have access to a community of women with so much experience, information, and support was incredible.

Because of these women and their stories, I know it is not unusual to have to try and try and try to get pregnant, and I know that regardless of how many disappointments there are, for many women there is a healthy baby at the end of the journey. Dashiell and I have so many options—more of her eggs on ice, and when we run out of those she can perhaps get pregnant (though she'd really, really, *really* rather not). Or we can adopt, or we can say fuck it to the whole thing and go live in Paris for a year. We can start hoarding animals, an alternative to parenthood many of my friends have opted for. It's really hard to say what the future will hold, but even if I never wind up anybody's mother, I will never regret all the years I've spent trying. It's introduced me to this whole other part of the world, the world of babies and the people

who have them. My community has widened, and includes people I wouldn't have gotten to know otherwise. I've learned about
how resilient I am—okay, I probably didn't need *more* proof of
that, but there is something about struggle and perseverance that
makes me feel close to myself. And close to Dashiell. Throughout
it all we don't fight or squabble, or let dark moods infect us. We
keep it together for one another, and always show love. All I
know about our future is that it will be the two of us together, and
there will be love—stable, healthy, grown-up love.

# 10.

# Ask Not for Whom the Wedding Bell Tolls

In 2006, my little sister shared some exciting news with me: The handsome, gentle, intelligent man she'd been dating had finally popped the question. I barely had a moment to experience pure, unadulterated happiness for my sister's dream coming true, because swiftly after she made her announcement she issued me the sweetest, most terrifying invitation: "Will you be my maid of honor?" Of course! I shrieked. I am accustomed to shrieking, "Of course!" to anything my sister asks me, because I love her to the core of my heart and there is nothing I would not do for her. I think I even felt a tingle of joy, joy that I, too, would get to wear a special dress (you *know* that I was ill acquainted with weddings if I thought a bridesmaid dress was exciting) and share in my sister's big moment. But then the terror set in. I had *no fucking clue* what a maid of honor does. Surely there would be duties, and I was totally ignorant as to what they were. I knew that I would be in some sort of service to my sister, and this set my nerves buzzing. My sister, you see, has always managed, somehow, to be an adult.

As the big sister, I should have been paving the way through life for Madeline, but it's always been the opposite. As a teenager, the most I could have helped her with was how to not get busted drinking in public, and even at that I failed: The first time Madeline ever sipped an underage beer, she was nabbed by the cops on a beach. I felt terrible for her. I had been successfully dodging the police for years, once even hiding in a stranger's unlocked van while a couple of officers swept their flashlights across the night streets in search of yours truly. It was a point of pride that despite my many youthful indiscretions I *never* got caught by the cops— not drinking, not doing LSD or mescaline. Not vandalizing, not trespassing. Maybe if my first beer had been interrupted by a trip to the clink I would have laid my bottle down, like Madeline did, but I doubt it. As similar as we are, the products of identical places and times, we are deeply different. We are like the inverse of those twins separated at birth and reared in dramatically different homes who turn out the same—we were raised in the same home, yet wound up dramatically unalike. Scientists should be studying us.

Madeline seemed to have been born understanding how the world works, and how to fight her way into it. In spite of the lack of support at home, she made it to college, and she graduated. Not a community joint, either—not that there's anything wrong with that!—but a fancy private institution. She may be still paying it off two decades later, but she figured it out. She managed to move to New York City, and nabbed a job in casting, building herself a career that took her to Los Angeles, where she met her soon-to-be husband, a guy with the good looks of a model and the bookshelves of a really hip English professor. She owned a new car, while I had never even managed to learn how to drive. Her home furnishings were purchased in stores, rather than found on the street or scrounged off Craigslist. She got her eyebrows done. The first time I ever got a manicure was with Madeline, following her into her regular Manhattan nail salon, where I paid a stranger to torture my ragged cuticles. I may have a coat of crimson gel polish gleaming on my nails as I type this today, but back then I thought it absurd to pay anyone to do anything you could do for yourself, and I could certainly paint my own fingernails. Sloppily, globbing the varnish onto the skin, dragging the brush over the chunky band of cuticle because I didn't exactly understand what you were supposed to do with it. I looked like perhaps I had just dunked my fingertips into a pot of finger paint, but I had done it myself! I had to admit that my nails post-manicure looked elegant, lovely, chic; like they were someone else's. Still, the experience had left me unsettled. Pay someone to paint my nails? Next thing you know I'd be wanting *servants*!

I needed to figure out how to be a competent maid of honor for my sister. I sussed out my bridesmaid duties with the help of the Internet. I was to be her right-hand man, her fixer, the one she brought glitches and problems and assorted bridal conundrums to. How the fuck was I going to be able to fill this role? My taste level and basic understanding of the modern world was . . . well, I don't want to say it was *below* hers, as that sounds so judgy, but let's just say that when she bought eyeliner she went to Bloomie's and I hit the Wet n Wild rack at my local Walgreens.

Unlike me, my sister had always known she wanted to be married, and she'd never had any qualms about it. I'd always thought there was something funny about *wanting* to be married— don't you just fall in love, and then the love inspires the yearning for marriage? When I was younger it seemed strange to want to be married before you'd even met the person you'd be married to, but I know I'm in the minority with this type of thinking—just look at the bazillions of wedding dream boards on Pinterest, pinned by hopeful singletons. Like my sister, these ladies must have understood something about the concept that I didn't. They clearly trusted in it, believed in it. Surely, dating a mish-mash of men, women, and in-betweeners never made marriage seem like something I could attain fairly easily; it simply wasn't legal for me to marry most of the people I had crushes on. And so the idea of it remained remote, in spite of the stubborn aesthetic attraction I had to the notion of a big white dress and a party for love—and the deeper attraction I had to the notion of a love so sturdy it could last forever.

Maybe my sister knew how ignorant I was—it's not like she didn't know me; we're sisters—but, then again, maybe she took for granted that my social life, like her own, had been peppered with attendance at various friends' nuptials. In fact, the last wedding I'd been at was my uncle Rocky's marriage to Rita when I was seven. I don't know if I explained to Madeline that Uncle Rocky's wedding was the last I'd attended, but perhaps there was another reason why she may have assumed I understood marriage: Madeline knew I was sort of, kind of, not really married myself.

Remember that ex I told you about, the rapper I lived with for eight years? Well, one night after a drunken bingo game at the Blue House, we got fake-married. It wasn't totally spontaneous; we had done perhaps a week's worth of planning. My ex had found a dress being sold by a homeless man on the street. It was pale blue and cut on the bias, velvet on top and silk on the bottom. The man agreed to sell it for five dollars only if he was promised that a beautiful girl would get married in it. Voilà, my wedding dress. I wore a crown of feather butterflies, curling ribbons, and plastic rhinestones, found in the toy aisle at Target about a year prior. I phoned my friend Candy, a witch, and asked her if she'd marry us. She told us to come over and bring a check for $19.99. My roommate spotted me and my ex sneaking out of the house postbingo, me in my crazy outfit, and demanded to know what was going on. She was bummed that I hadn't let her in on the momentous occasion. "We're eloping!" I explained. "No one knows!" I'd planned to tell folks casually as I ran into them, mention it to my mom and sister next time we talked on the phone. Still, I felt bad and let my roommate come along to photograph the ceremony.

Candy resided with her wife, Joey, in a live-work space, subsidizing their rent by throwing occasional sex parties. The place was in slight disarray when we arrived, with a grocery store carrot cake sitting on the counter. Voilà, our wedding cake. Shoved into the frosting was a tiny Barbie figurine, hair colored blue with a Sharpie, meant to represent me, and a squat Batman figure meant to depict my ex. Candy decided that my dress could fulfill the something old *and* the something new requirements as well as something blue. For something borrowed she pinned a thrifted rhinestone brooch onto the velvet bodice, and then took a pot of glitter and sprinkled it into my hair. She didn't really know my ex, so she gave him a quick interview, mainly wanting to make sure he wasn't on drugs. Of course he was, as was I, but we lied. My roommate took some pictures, Joey played the theme from *The Godfather* on her guitar, and we all did tequila shots. She presented us with a marriage license crafted from construction paper and crayons, and voilà, we were fake-married.

It's not that the marriage was a fake because it wasn't legal— lots of gay people are forced to marry one another without legal recognition or protection, and those marriages are real. It wasn't fake because we eloped—elopements are real. It wasn't that we didn't have rings—we'd bought the cheapest ones we could find, from the Joyeria on Mission Street. Mine even had a tiny chip from a tiny diamond wedged into the setting. (At least we *thought* it was probably a diamond.) The wedding wasn't fake because we only paid $19.99 for it—cheap weddings are real. It wasn't real because it just wasn't real. It was a feeble, drug-addled stab at commitment that did not stop us from breaking up eight years later. I know that even the realest of weddings can't keep a couple from splitting up, that most unions end in separation. But trust me, this one had more in common with the backyard play wedding I'd had in first grade, when I'd married Georgie next door with rings from a gumball machine, than it had with my sister's pending nuptials—nuptials I was expected to be a fairly important part of.

Thankfully, by the time my sister got engaged I had sobered up. One thing I'd learned from my 12-step brainwashing was that life wasn't all about me, an important if heartbreaking lesson for any alcoholic. I'd become better at putting other people's needs before my own when appropriate, had gotten good at showing up for the folks around me. I knew I couldn't make my sister's wedding be all about my potential failure as a maid of honor. The wedding was about one thing and one thing only: my sister's happiness. I always find it sort of relieving to have something larger to pledge yourself to. I couldn't think about what a fuckup I was, or how my own marriage was a sham and how maybe that felt lousy.

All in all, I was not the worst maid of honor ever. Madeline was a merciful bride and required very little of me; she's a woman who knows what she wants, and she didn't need a lot of advice. Or maybe, in the words of one of my many 12-step programs, she knew "not to go to the hardware store for a bag of oranges." At DSW I dutifully snapped pictures of various strappy sandals with my phone, sending them to her for approval. I was psyched when she trusted that the chunky silver forties-style heels I preferred looked best with the open-necked forties-style bridesmaid dress she'd selected for me. Unlike the dress, I really *would* wear those shoes again!

The day of the wedding—held in motherfucking Rome, of all places—I was at my sister's beck and call. I accompanied her to the hair salon, where a handsome man named Maurizio whipped her locks into a perfect Audrey Hepburn updo. It went perfectly with Madeline's tea-length wedding dress, very sweet and modern and *Roman Holiday*. I was delighted when Maurizio insisted I, too, sit in the chair and get my hair done. My first time in Europe as an adult, I easily mistook the flamboyance and neat grooming of the men to be signifiers of gayness, and the whole time Maurizio played with my hair I obsessively tried to figure out how to say *I'm bisexual* in Italian; the closest I came was *I'm half-lesbian*. Thankfully I resisted the urge to queer-bond with my hairdresser, because as it happened he was very heterosexual and would have found my comment at best random and at worst a kinky come-on.

At the hotel where the wedding would soon occur, I stood fidgeting by Madeline, who sat fidgeting in her chair. We were waiting for our cues to walk, and she was getting increasingly flustered at how long it was taking. Was there a problem? Had something happened? Of course not; it was just Italy. Things move slower there. I scanned the skirt of Madeline's gorgeous Monique Lhuillier dress, making sure the strips of feathery ruffles that gave it texture and volume had not picked up any hitchhiking lint. She looked perfect. The day, which had threatened rain, had delivered only sunshine. Eventually an Italian person came and signaled it was time for us to proceed.

I went first, clutching my little bouquet of white tulips, down a stone ramp that led to the little landing where Madeline and her beau would say their vows. I stood in my spot and watched Madeline descend, looking crazy beautiful and stylish in her veil.

I felt a surge of pride for her; she had done so much to get here, weeding through the glut of truly assholish boys who were the only option in the city we'd grown up in, contending with commitment-phobes and potheads in her adult dating years. Now she had found this truly excellent guy, and here we were in motherfucking Rome, and she looked like she'd stepped out of the pages of some impossibly chic wedding magazine.

My mom sat in the front row of folding chairs, already crying. When she rose to recite an Irish poem in her shaking, emotional voice, I almost cried, too. But panic dried up my tears when my sister, realizing she had forgotten her vows in the hotel room, turned to me. Because I was the maid of honor. And I should have been carrying a copy of the vows for this exact moment. But I wasn't. I was carrying only flowers. I looked back at Madeline, my face slowly shifting into a bug-eyed expression of *oh shit*. It was the moment of maid-of-honor truth, and I was failing her.

Before getting into casting, my sister had been a dancer. And dancing is showbiz, and in showbiz the number one rule is the show must go on. Madeline, lovely and lighthearted, seized the spirit of the moment and free-styled her vows to her husband, who free-styled them back, the both of them conjuring up heart-felt promises before our teary eyes. I didn't want to let myself off the hook for being a bumbling maid of honor, but perhaps this was one of those moments when a mistake really leads to something more special than the original plan.

I hadn't been to any weddings as an adult, but I couldn't imagine one any more festive and romantic than my sister's. As the sun set, platters of antipasto were brought out, the first in what was an onslaught of food. The wedding cake was topped with sparklers that hissed spouts of glittery fire into the night. I was so enchanted, so happy for Madeline and her new husband, I did not think at all about how my own fake wedding measured up. Well, hardly.

I couldn't help but reflect on it. How after my fake wedding, when I returned to my punk house, my living room was filled with revelers, none of whom actually lived there. Apparently I'd forgotten to lock the door, and when some friends came by looking to party they just let themselves in. A Kenneth Anger movie was playing on the VCR. The partiers thought it was cool that my ex and I had gotten fake-married by Candy the Sexy Witch, and offered us some celebratory cocaine. I stood in the kitchen and flung my bouquet backward into the living room. It was caught by an androgynous individual named Captain, who has not since married. Know why? Because it was a bouquet from a fake wedding.

In spite of wearing a ring on that finger for a string of years, I tend to forget that I was ever "married." I never called my ex my husband, and he never called me his wife. Perhaps the adult formality of the terms really illuminated how *not* husband-and-wife we were. That is how Dashiell got a surprise while looking at an old photo of me on Facebook. "Honey, what's that ring you're wearing in that picture? It looks like a wedding ring." Oh yeah, I got fake-married to someone back before I met you— sorry, did I forget to mention that?

Dashiell was jarred but recovered quickly. Having met each other in our thirties and forties, we each knew the other had a history—periods of long, committed relationships; periods of shameless slutting around. We actually like it about each other. We come together having experienced a variety of romantic connections, and we know exactly what we want. We want each other, and that's it.

Still, I felt haunted by my crappy first marriage. I feared that I could not adequately convince Dashiell of what a drug-addled, shabby pretend wedding it had been. I didn't want *that* to be my first marriage and ours to be my second; everything about Dashiell felt like the first time—the first healthy relationship, the first time I was treated so gently, the first time I could love from a wide-open heart because I wasn't taking pains to protect myself. I wanted my and Dashiell's wedding to be my one and only. Was I being like a born-again schoolgirl trying to reclaim a lost virginity?

Everyone gets to create the wedding that best suits them, but I do believe the betrothed should not be nursing ecstasy hangovers, have miniature heroin habits, and snort a rail after tossing the bouquet. I believe in a community gathered to witness and celebrate, helping to hold the couple accountable to their vows when times get rough. Perhaps my phony first wedding provided me with an anti-template as I set forth to plan my marriage to Dashiell: I didn't want it to be *anything* like that. But how could it be? I wasn't that person anymore, and hadn't been her for more than a decade.

Knowing very little about how anyone gets married, Dashiell and I started planning our wedding, seven years after my sister's Roman affair. It seemed the first order of business was to pick the venue. As someone who has been throwing events all over San

Francisco for the past twenty years, I know a lot of cool spaces, but I really didn't want to get married on a stage where I'd once read my poetry. I wanted a place I didn't already have a history with, so I could always be nostalgic about the place we got married. And so I started booking walk-throughs at a bunch of locations, some very traditional and some unusual.

I decided if I'd only performed in a venue once or twice, and not for a very long time, we could consider it. I remembered a large, nonprofit building that had a handsome brick-walled room with a wooden balcony, and scheduled a visit.

"You're thinking of getting married *there?*" Tali chuckled when I told her. "Good for you. I hear they give you the space for free if you include a needle exchange as part of your ceremony."

"It's not that bad!" I cried, but it didn't take too long after we arrived to realize that it *had* been a while since I'd been in there, and perhaps I remembered it differently. The entryway was papered with fliers for harm-reduction studies and psychotherapists and roommates wanted. The trash, recycling, and compost bins sat dumpily along the wall. The place *did* kind of feel like a free clinic, someplace you'd go for an HIV test, not a wedding. I walked up to the entry to the brick-walled room, and found it occupied by a free Zumba class. Dashiell and I peered in the window at the scowling dancers. "I don't know," Dashiell said uneasily. Fair enough. I decided I would not consider places that hosted AA meetings and Zumba classes as wedding venues.

Our next stop was the Polish-American hall. I sort of love ethnic halls. They remind me of the old-worldy-ness of New England, and inspire rare twinges of homesickness. Like the nonprofit building, the Polish joint was *cheap*, and that was important. Weddings are expensive! Expensive enough to make my breath catch when I heard what other people spent on theirs—twenty thousand was considered cheap. A married couple told me to expect to spend thousands on invitations, thousands more on photography, and another thou for a DJ. My whole body surged *no* at these predictions. We had to find a way to be crafty and still make it classy. I wanted a grown-up wedding, one that was elegant and memorable. I wanted to wear white, my slutty past be damned. Even though many traditions didn't work with Dashiell and me—for instance, neither of us had fathers in our lives to escort us down the aisle, so we decided to walk to the altar together, hand in hand—I wanted to hold on to as many that did. I wanted to experience this classic expression of love and commitment.

I showed Dashiell pictures of the Polish hall on the Internet. She scrunched her face at the images of children in Eastern European folk costume dancing across the wall.

"What about *all that?*" she asked. Plastic tubs of toys were jumbled beneath the skipping peasant children.

"They run a daycare," I explained. "And I bet those decorations can come down."

We arrived at the space after dark, as arranged, waiting for a woman who never showed up. As we waited we observed the trash piled up against the building—plump dirty diapers, fast-food wrappers. Eventually a car pulled into the driveway, letting out a Polish-speaking guy who showed up to take out the trash. My surge of Polish pride—the last name I was born with was

Swankowski, y'all—came about rather recently, and I actually know very little about my heritage, let alone a single Polish word aside from *kielbasa*. I mimed and pantomimed and gesticulated with the Polish man, begging him to let us in.

"Let's just go," Dashiell hissed behind me. Unlike me, Dashiell cares about making scenes and begging strangers. The man grew tired of our strained communications and went into the building. I paused for a moment, then followed him in.

"Don't!" Dashiell cried. "He didn't say you could go in there!" Unlike me, Dashiell cares about trespassing and breaking laws.

"It's fine," I said dismissively. "We're just going to peek."

A swing of the door brought us face-to-face with those garish frolicking Polish folk dancers. They were painted onto the wall of this room that was scattered with toys and smelled vaguely of baby poop. The door to the room was open and I could see into the rest of the hall, smaller and dingier than it looked online.

"No," Dashiell said over my shoulder. "Hard no."

As someone who likes to say yes to lots of things, especially odd clothing and home decor sourced from dusty thrift shops, I have been blessed to be with someone like Dashiell, whose dial is set to no. Dashiell is a Virgo, a sign excellent at editing. I am an Aquarius, a sign that likes to live in a *sure, why not, let's try it out* state of mind. Dashiell's hard nos have actually assisted in my quest to grow up, as she has prevented me from bringing things into our home that would make it resemble a dorm room, or the bedroom of a little girl circa 1965. I respect Dashiell's elegant, streamlined, *adult* aesthetic, and I always respect her hard nos. I shut the door to the Polish hall.

We decided to hit an open house at a pricier venue that looked like a log cabin and was located in a beautiful public park in San Francisco. I didn't think it was affordable, but in the warped world of wedding expenses, it was touted as a cheaper alternative. The drive to the building took us through rows of willowy eucalyptus trees, the clean, sharp fragrance coming right into the car.

"Oh my God," I breathed dreamily. "This would be such a magical way for people to arrive at our wedding!"

Inside, the place was lined in lumber and stone. "I think this is probably amazing," I whispered to Dashiell. "But I also can't tell if it's a little Flinstone-y." Around us walked a thin blond bride-to-be, flanked by her take-charge parents. The mother and father grilled the venue's representative on caterers, tables, insurance—all things that had to be additionally rented. Soon another woman walked in with her parents, and another. I realized that people's parents often pay for their weddings. Right? Wild. I knew we couldn't compete with couples with these extra resources. The log cabin was beyond our means. We slipped out the door as a couple of natty gay men slid inside, oohing and ahing.

I had planned a second viewing for us that day. "It's a long shot," I said, prepping Dashiell. "It probably won't work. But it's *free.*"

The space was an alleyway in the Tenderloin that the city had leased to an art gallery for one dollar, and that the art gallery had transformed from a site of urination and dirty needles to a *forest*, complete with towering redwood trees and stands of bamboo, ferns and flowers, Japanese maples, and scrambling vines of jasmine. Artists had painted murals on the walls, laid down mosaic walkways, and built a koi pond. There was even a working kiln, and the place was strung with romantic lights. But again, it was small, and awkwardly laid out. And it was in the Tenderloin.

The Tenderloin, for those not familiar with San Francisco neighborhoods, is the city's skid row. The prevalence of cheaper housing and single-room-occupancy hotels makes it a great starting-out spot for immigrants and a great ending-up spot for drug addicts with advanced downward spirals. You saw everything in the Tenderloin—people yanking down their pants to take a poop on the curb, people sticking a needle into their skin, people vomiting down their shirts, talking to themselves, talking to you. Driving into the neighborhood was the exact opposite of driving into the eucalyptus-lined parkland we had just visited. I imagined our moms dodging grabby drunks on the way to our wedding; my sister nervously guiding her kids around splashes of puking pukers.

We entered the alley through the back door of a small art gallery, and stood before the tall gates that separated the forest from the wildness of the streets. A festivity like a wedding would attract all the neighborhood lingerers to the fence. I could imagine the schizophrenic barrage of emotions I would feel—annoyance at drugged-out drunkards heckling my wedding; a desire to protect my guests from them; an awareness that this was their neighborhood I was interloping on; anger at the poverty and racism that impacted these lives so miserably; despairing hopelessness at how the problem is so much bigger than I am; self-loathing at my privilege. Ugh. This seemed like a bad idea.

Thankfully, the space just didn't work logistically, so addressing any deeper social questions was moot. We asked to be let back out through the gallery, and the gallerist pushed the glass door against the jumble of people who had congregated in the entryway, politely asking them to move. A woman turned toward us as she shuffled, a cloud of smoke escaping her lips. I held my breath as we walked through the small crowd, but Dashiell didn't.

"That was *crack smoke*," I hissed as we approached the car. "That fog we just walked through? *Crack smoke*."

"Oh my God." Dashiell felt her neck, her throat, her face. She looked nervous. "I think I can feel it!"

I cracked up. "You cannot feel it! Get in the car. Let's get out of here." I slid into my seat and shut the door as a gentleman unfurled his penis from the fly of his pants and began urinating on the building before us. Dashiell clambered in after me, looking distraught.

"It just would not have even occurred to me that that was crack smoke!" she said with a dazed, earnest innocence.

"We cannot risk our mothers inhaling secondhand crack smoke at our wedding. That was a sign from the Universe," I said.

In the end, we found the perfect place, a Swedish-American club on the affordable side, with ye olde wooden walls and beams and thrones, and a low stage for us to say our vows. It felt special and elevated and, most important, on the cheap side.

"You don't have to use our catering," said the venue's manager, who wore a long trench coat and panama hat and looked like he had escaped from a noir film. "Some people just like to bring in barbecue or something."

BBQ? How genius! On one of our first dates, Dashiell and I went dancing at an outdoor soul music party, sweating and swooning as we fell into each other on the dance floor. With her shoulder-shaking, finger-snapping moves, Dashiell looked like she had just jitterbugged from a 1950s dance-off right into contemporary San Francisco. When the party got too crowded and its revelers too drunk, we dashed to the BBQ joint across the street and ate burgers and mac 'n' cheese and banana pudding. I checked to see if the spot catered, and it did. And it was cheap. We'd have BBQ at our wedding, with pies and banana pudding taking the place of a tall white wedding cake, one of the traditions we felt we could live without.

I was haunted by the predictions some married friends had made on what our various wedding expenses would cost us, those thousand-dollar DJs and photographers. Luckily, the arts community I'd been a part of for the past two decades was filled with talented people who *wanted* to work our wedding, and at a reduced rate. I couldn't believe our wild luck! The DJ from the soul party where Dashiell and I had fallen in love offered to spin Motown at our bash, for a kindly rate. A photographer I'd modeled for offered to shoot the event, also for less than average. One of our guests worked for the lighting design company that had just lit up the redwood forest where a boorish tech tycoon had a decadent wedding involving cocaine, environmental crimes, and computers flung into rivers; he offered to light our wedding for free. We opted out of letterpress invites, as pretty as they are, for a cheaper design so classy no one noticed the difference. I got my gown at J.Crew. For a dress, it was expensive, but for a wedding dress it was a steal! My hairdresser surprised me the day of by refusing to take payment for the amazing fishtail side braid she'd magicked my hair into. My bestie Rhonda, a landscape designer, filled the hall with dramatic vases of branches and leaves, lush aubergine flowers on the tables, the most gigantic air plants I'd ever seen accenting corners, fat bouquets of hydrangea and lilies, boutonnieres and corsages wound with exotic ribbon.

To top off this embarrassment of riches, I was pregnant. Our second go-round with IVF had resulted in a positive pregnancy, and by the day of our wedding I would be ten weeks along. Although I lived with the constant fear that my wedding dress wouldn't actually fit by the time our big day rolled around (those IVF hormones make you *bloated*), we were both so thrilled, so tickled that our future son or daughter would be, in this funny way, present at our wedding. We had an appointment with our obstetrician the morning of the rehearsal dinner, and we brought along our moms for a peek at their grandkid-to-be.

It hadn't occurred to us that we might get bad news.

The day before our wedding, Dashiell and I learned that the little blob of life we'd seen on an ultrasound just two weeks ago had shortly thereafter ceased to grow. The obstetrician's wand slid over my stomach, revealing the same amorphous bit of matter we'd seen weeks ago, no larger, and now with no flickering heartbeat.

There is no good time for a miscarriage, but surely the day before your wedding counts among the very worst. I was in shock as I sent out a volley of text messages to all who'd known I was expecting. There were a lot of them. I knew that there was a tradition of waiting until you were out of the first trimester danger zone before sharing the news, but I'd found that hard, if not ridiculous, to adhere to. I am a wildly public person, and all sorts of people knew my business. I'd been blogging about our attempts to get pregnant for two years, and anyone who knew we'd recently had an egg transfer was inquiring about how it went. Plus, there was my body. Although I shouldn't have been showing at all, those IVF hormones had pumped up my belly till the elderly were offering me their seats on the bus. I looked pregnant. I *was* pregnant. So I had shared the good news, and now I would share the bad.

It wasn't until I spoke to Madeline that I broke down. "I feel like our wedding is going to be a sad thing now," I cried into my first cup of coffee in three months. "Everyone will be feeling so bad for us, or they'll be uncomfortable, that way people get uncomfortable around tragedy. It will be tragic, and awkward. It's going to feel horrible."

"Everyone loves you," my sister consoled me. "Everyone is so happy that you and Dashiell found each other, and they are coming to celebrate that. You'll see. It is so awful that this happened, but you're going to have a beautiful wedding."

As I noted before, weddings are showbiz, and the show must go on. There was no time to mourn, to collapse under covers and eat takeout and wallow in sadness. For starters, I needed a mani-pedi. It's true I almost lost it all over again when the woman painting my nails pointed to my protruding stomach and asked, "You have a baby in there?"

"No," I said quickly, and turned my face away, down to the

*People* magazine I wasn't reading, my cheeks burning. Even though this is the question you are *never, ever supposed to ask any woman ever*, I didn't blame her. I looked pregnant. Only hours ago I would have replied to her question with a yes and a smile. I placed my hand under the UV lights that baked the gel polish onto my nails, and the woman slid away quietly.

After the mani-pedi it was home for my progesterone treatment. Part of the IVF procedure is dosing yourself with progesterone from right before the egg transfer deep into your first trimester, first with nightly intramuscular shots that leave your butt both sore and numb, a grotesque combination, and later with little oval suppositories. Normally, when a fetus is found to have stopped developing, a woman would stop her progesterone. But stopping the progesterone increases the possibility of having a natural miscarriage, which can be an epic, painful, blood-soaked experience. I had a D and C—an abortion, basically—scheduled for two days after our wedding. In the meantime, I did not want a natural miscarriage to kick in. And I certainly didn't want it to happen at my wedding, as I glided around in a long white gown. The *Carrie*-esque, pitch-black humor of this did not escape me; the evil, nagging voice inside me, the one that insists that all my efforts to have a nice, normal adult life are bound to dramatically, flamboyantly fail due to some deep internal flaw, cackled wildly. *You would!* it hooted. *You totally would have a miscarriage all over your wedding dress. That is so you.*

The night before our wedding, Dashiell and I lay in bed, too exhausted to cry. In the morning I woke up and inserted my progesterone, this time too excited to cry. Partly I worried about being so distracted from emotions I was bound to feel sooner or later, but I was also grateful for it. There was no time for grief. My hairdresser was on her way to our house, and the photographer would follow, and it was time for me to finally slide into the dress I'd been hiding in my closet, time to step into the satin Lanvin pumps that were possibly the most expensive part of the wedding. It was time for Dashiell and me to marry one another.

With the help of our friends, the venue, beautiful to start, had become otherworldly in its romance. The flowers were exotic, and the space wasn't simply well lit; it was decorated with shadows in the shape of trees, so that it seemed we were gathering in a dark, majestic garden. I had grown deeply fond of our caterer, a French woman who had brought in a team of French-speaking ladies, all of them rushing around, prepping the dessert table with the most decadent lime pies, apple pies, pineapple cakes, and of course the banana pudding. An entire salmon, its scales replaced with rounds of cucumber, had pride of place on the savory table. It looked positively royal. After taking a barrage of photographs with every possible combination of family, it was time for Dashiell and me to hide. The guests were soon to arrive, and to our delight, the little room we'd selected to hide out in had a window that peeked out onto the street. We held hands in excitement, looking out at the parade of friends, all dressed up for our wedding. There was Tali, in a bow tie, ready to be our officiant (she'd clicked a box on a Web site and been instantly ordained a minister!); there was Annie, climbing out of the cab from the airport, her blond curls a wild halo around her head. A limousine pulled up and two cousins from Chelsea poured out, all long legs and wild hair. There was that person and that person, in their sequined jackets and cocktail dresses, their suits and their acid-washed jeans, their ascots and thrifted maxi dresses.

Dashiell had planned with our DJ when the music to cue the procession would begin, and when the melody would change to cue our own walk down the aisle. Ducking behind a wall, we caught little glimpses of my nephew, the ring bearer, stumbling down the aisle clutching a bird's nest I'd carefully tied our rings to. My nephew had only just learned to walk, so it was a little touch-and-go, but he took to his duty so loyally he refused to relinquish the nest, and it had to be pried from his hand. Next came our flower girl, my five-year-old niece. Worried that she would fling all the flower petals onto the floor in one fat handful, I had told her to do it slowly.

"One at a time?" she'd asked.

"Yeah, totally," I'd said. I'm not used to talking to children. I'm used to talking to my sarcastic friends who are always joking and joshing. It did not occur to me that my niece would actually walk down the aisle with the slow concentration of a butoh dancer, meticulously placing one petal at a time onto the floor.

"Oh my God," I whispered to Dashiell from our peeking place. "It's like . . . Yoko Ono. It's performance art." Eventually, Madeline leapt from the stage and helped her daughter along. As the audience was mostly filled with performance artists, it was a highlight of the event.

My highlight of the event was when Dashiell in her custom-made three-piece suit and I in my trailing gown clasped hands and set off together down the aisle. At the sight of us the entire audience rose from their chairs and let loose a thundering cry of joy. They hooted and yelled and screamed and whistled. They cheered and clapped and stamped their feet. Dashiell and I looked at one another in utter shock, before cracking up. My smile was so big I thought it would break my face. I didn't think, then, of my sister's promise that our wedding would be filled with love and joy; I wasn't thinking of anything, so totally in the moment I was. But I would think of it later, how her promise was so true. Our wedding was filled with love, and we were at the gorgeous, beating heart of it.

Tali started crying before she even opened her mouth to speak, delivering a speech about the history of queer love we were a part of, referencing this new ability we have to actually, legally marry one another. Her crying was contagious; soon bunches in the audience were dabbing their faces. Our friends were largely ignorant of weddings, being mostly queer people whose friends hadn't been permitted to wed; many of them had grown to dread weddings as those awkward obligations that force you to hang out with family members you can't stand. It felt magical to be in the midst of this controversial tradition, doing it our way, making it meaningful not only for us but for a community of friends alienated from the rites of love and commitment.

I pulled my vows out of my bouquet of hydrangea and lilies and spoke my promises to Dashiell: I promised to snug and be snugged. I promised to respect her autonomy. She pulled her vows from the pocket of her suit and promised me the same. Unsure of who we would now be to one another—husband? But

Dashiell's a girl! Wife? Fine for me, but Dashiell is way too much of a boy to be anyone's wife!—I didn't know what to tell Tali to "pronounce" us. "Each other's person?" I suggested weakly, knowing how awkward it sounded. But she figured it out herself.

"I now pronounce you married," she crowed, once our rings were safely jammed onto our fingers. We kissed, and bounded from the stage, Dashiell instinctively raising her hand in a fist pump. It's just how she expresses joy. We dashed back to the little room that had been our hideout, to catch our breath while the guests filed into a cocktail room.

"We did it," Dashiell said, wrapping herself around me. "We did it."

"Did you hear everyone cheer? Did you hear that?" I asked, as if she could have missed the entire room rising to their feet and thundering their love at us. We kissed and kissed and kissed some more, and then went out to join our party.

By the end of the night I had heard from many people that our wedding was the first they'd ever felt an actual emotion at. They talked about how Tali had made them cry, how my niece's flower petal placement had been the best piece of durational performance they'd seen in a long time. I hoped that at least some of the couples left feeling inspired—after a year of wedding planning, I now wanted to go to someone else's wedding! So far, none have made any announcements. My bridal bouquet was caught by a particularly slutty fag, but then again, even slutty girls settle down sometimes.

# 11.

# You Can't Fire Me; I Quit

At fourteen years old I was eager to join the workforce. I went to city hall and fetched a card for my mother to sign, granting the government permission to override the final years of protection offered by child labor laws.

"Are you sure you want to do this?" My mother scrunched her face. "Once you start workin' you'll be workin' till you're dead, you know." It was sweet of her to try to stave off lifelong wage slavery for another year or two, but I was desperate to become a career woman. And I knew where to start. My run-down hometown had recently gotten a *mall*!

Our new local hot spot, the Mystic Mall, was built on the weed- and trash-encrusted empty lots where the city had notoriously burned down in the seventies. The humor of its name was lost on me. It wasn't a galleria of new age shops selling cut-rate crystals and swoopy Stevie Nicks shawls; it was simply named after the nearby Mystic River. Still, it's not incorrect to say that the mall became my temple, a place filled with objects of worship that elicited many urgent prayers. Marianne's sold clothes so cool, I'd never seen anything like them—shirts that looked *just like leather*, slashed with zippers! Neon button-up shirts with neon-splattered *neckties*! Deb sold fingerless gloves, the kind worn by Madonna and Sheila E. and Adam Ant in the music videos I'd studied on TV. The Gap of yesteryear was *nothing* like The Gap of today; it hawked heart-covered T-shirts with spaghetti straps that tied into bows. Record Man offered Billy Idol and Van Halen records, some of them collector's-item picture discs, with Billy's bleachy spikes and luscious sneer gazing out at you from the grooved vinyl. At Mr. Tops you could pick out a T-shirt and flip through the gigantic three-ring binders stuffed with glittery decals, and the worker would sear your selection onto the shirt with a giant steaming iron, even laying out your name on the back in fuzzy letters, or sticking a velveteen lightning bolt on the shoulder. It was the eighties, and the opening of the Mystic Mall corresponded almost exactly with the introduction of MTV, which corresponded almost exactly with my puberty. Suddenly, I knew what cool was, and I wanted to be it. Amazingly, this brand-new mall, right here in my uncool hometown, could help me.

To score any of these things—a U2 pin from the revolving pin case at Mr. Tops, a fringed skirt from Marianne's, purple eye shadow from the drugstore—I would need money. Coolness was a luxury in my family; there was very little extra for such frivolity. But I was beginning to understand that this idea of coolness might, in fact, save my life—get me out of my hometown and into the larger world. The need for a J-O-B was serious. My mother signed the card, and I was hired at DeMoulas Market Basket, the gargantuan new supermarket built alongside the mall. There were still some laws governing how many hours I could work, but I worked as much as I could—after school at St. Rose, buttoning my smock on over my Catholic school uniform, and on weekends.

At first it was exciting—picking up my tray, the cash neatly organized in the little slots, and proudly walking it over to my cash register. I loved the *clickety-click* of punching the prices into the machine, loved counting back the change. Girls who'd worked there longer taught me how to steal packs of bubble gum and where to stash them in your drawer, how to space out the bathroom breaks you spent smoking in the ladies' room. And as the novelty of employment wore off and the monotony of the work wore on, these little tips were what the job became about— not so much how to work as how to *un*-work. How to steal little bits of time for yourself, shave something extra off the top. I learned to daydream, especially while bagging groceries. I wrote stories in my head, the story of my life thus far, and realized that with twists of tone and vocabulary I could make my story sound glamorous or triumphant, funny or tragic. *Maybe I'll do this one day*, I thought, sliding cans of baked beans and plastic packages of hot dogs into paper sacks with Tetris-like efficiency. *Maybe I'll write about my life, and make it glamorous and triumphant and funny and tragic.*

I quit DeMoulas right before I got weird, dyeing my hair and drawing upside-down crosses on my uniform. It had begun to feel like too much to do both school and the job, and to have time left over for important bonding with new friends, finding secret places to chain-smoke cigarettes and compare notes on boys and music videos. But after my weirdness was firmly established I realized that I actually needed a job more than ever—for bus fare to sneak into Boston, for pins declaring my favorite bands, and for packs and packs of cigarettes—and tried to get hired back. But DeMoulas would no longer have me. "You've got to wash that pink streak out of your hair," my old boss said, shaking his head at me.

"It doesn't just *wash out*," I said, offended. "It's *permanent*." I'd recently learned what a poseur was—a person whose commitment to rock 'n' roll was not legitimate, someone who was only pretending to be hard-core, who was going through a phase. Rock 'n' roll, I had come to know, was my *life*. From here on, everything about my appearance was calibrated to broadcast this allegiance to the world around me, in hopes that, beacon-like, it would attract to me others whose devotion to the underground was obsessive and true. Thus far, it hadn't. Thus far, it was simply getting in the way of me having a job so that I could continue to afford my rock 'n' roll lifestyle. Manic Panic doesn't grow on trees! Oh, the irony!

There was only a single store in my hometown that would hire a girl with a pink streak in her hair in 1986—Mr. Tops, that make-your-own T-shirt shop with its books of glittery decals and trays of velvety letters. One woman who worked there looked just like Martha Quinn, the MTV VJ with the pixie cut. I shyly commented on her look-alike-ness while browsing through the book of rock decals, and she said she knew that. I told her that

Martha Quinn was one of the women dancing in lingerie in the J. Geils Band "Centerfold" video, and she told me she knew that, too. I told her that the J. Geils Band was from Boston, right across the bridge from us. She was aware of that. Fake Martha Quinn seemed to know as much rock trivia as real Martha Quinn! When I asked if Mr. Tops was hiring, she gave me an application, and a week later I had a new job. One where the boss didn't mind if I came to work wearing white greasepaint meant for actual clowns as foundation makeup. One that didn't mind if I played the Cure's doomy-est album, *Pornography*, over the store's sound system—even if the customers did. It had all the makings of an awesome after-school job, except for one thing: I couldn't do it.

First of all, I couldn't fold the shirts. Folding things in general—shirts, wrapping paper, towels—is something I bumble at to this day. My creases are weak. Bits are sticking out where it should be streamlined. After learning that my best efforts resulted in stubborn imperfection, my frustration overwhelmed me and I stopped trying. I sort of rolled the T-shirts into soft lumps and hoped nobody noticed.

Then there was the giant iron that melted the decals onto the poorly folded (and thus wrinkled) shirts. Customers would choose a simple, sparkly decal that I'd have to iron on smack in the middle of a shirt. I'M A BEAUTICIAN—NOT A MAGICIAN! A TOUCH OF CLASS. MAKIN' BACON! (That one had a cartoon of two pigs having sex. Gross.) There was the little puffy green guy always sticking up his middle finger, sometimes proclaiming, DISCO SUCKS. There was DISCO SUCKS BUT ROCK IS ROLLING. PAYBACK'S

A BITCH had a deer holding a rifle. It took me a while to realize it was a hunting reference. People didn't hunt in my hometown. There wasn't any wilderness, or animals.

The real stress came when somebody wanted their name on the back of their shirt. Or even worse, a proclamation of their love—DONNA LOVES SULLY; DOM'S GIRL 4-EVA. These jobs required exact spacing not only between the letters but then between the words, all of it placed perfectly in the center of the garment—low but not too low, high but not too high. And you had to be sure to depress the iron slowly, lest a slight breeze ruffle your painstaking work and produce a wonky result. My results were often wonky. Sometimes an entire baseball or football or hockey or cheerleading team would place an order and I would be in tears, salty mascara trails cutting through not just my white greasepaint but the dusting of baby power I sprinkled over my face to kill the greasepaint's intense, clowny shine, creating a grayish mud on my face. I looked crazy; I felt crazy.

I liked my bosses, a couple of doctors who lived in a little castle by a beach somewhere and had ties to the Boston music scene. I hated showing them my mistakes, seeing how anxious it made them. So I began hiding my fuckups, balling them up in my army bag and then throwing them away in the dumpster behind the mall. Instead of thinking their new employee was totally inept, they now thought that someone was stealing their T-shirts. They never suspected me of thievery—with my uniform of vintage black dresses purchased from the Salvation Army, they knew I had no interest in baseball tees and sweatshirts. But after coming into the store and finding me so engrossed in a paperback that it took me ten or fifteen minutes to realize they were there, they decided I was unintentionally abetting shoplifters by reading *Portnoy's Complaint* rather than keeping my eye on the goods. I was fired.

This began the chain of firings that defined my teenage employment. Many of these terminations were appearance related, and the rest probably due to alcohol. The hair salon that let me go for missing a busy receptionist shift after staying up all night sleeping out for New Order tickets, drinking so much rum I couldn't make it in. There was the ice cream parlor that dumped me for a similar no-call, no-show on a hectic Sunday morning. You wouldn't imagine Sunday mornings to be a popular time to chow down on a banana split, but this ice cream joint was in Faneuil Hall, and there was often a line of people waiting for their scoop before we opened. I guess being on vacation makes people feel wild and free enough to eat hot fudge sundaes for breakfast.

The night before my ice cream expulsion I had gone to nearby Providence, Rhode Island, to see the Ramones, and then to an all-night after-party at the home of a friend with out-of-town parents. The concert and the after-party involved huge quantities of alcohol—at the tender age of sixteen, my alcoholism was already in full effect. When I woke up for work I'd only been asleep for an hour or so, just long enough to feel completely sickened by what I'd ingested. I decided I would pretend that I hadn't known I was on the schedule that Sunday morning—even though I was on the schedule *every* Sunday morning. When I showed up for my after-school shift on Monday, the manager wouldn't even let me in the back to collect my things. "Employees only," he snapped coldly, slapping my dog-eared copy of *The Basketball Diaries* onto the counter. Fired again.

Not *all* of my jobs ended in such dramatic terminations. Some jobs I just stopped showing up for, like the one at the copy shop. I was the only female employee, working with a bunch of twentysomething dudes who wore vaguely corporate drag to work but played in bands after they punched out. "A tie is an arrow that points at your dick," one said to me glumly, flicking his neckwear. When I asked if I could step outside for a "cigarette break," another replied, "Sure—right after I have my 'heroin break,'" then rolled his eyes. Weeknights were busy, copying reams of court transcripts from nearby law offices, but weekends the financial neighborhood was shut down, so I could usually hang out reading *Rolling Stone*—an article about William Burroughs called him an "antihero" and a "cult writer"! What a cool thing to aspire to!—or Hunter S. Thompson's *Hell's Angels* and *Fear and Loathing in Las Vegas*. But one Sunday morning, after another night of heavy drinking (Bacardi 151—highest proof possible *plus* the bat logo was *so Goth*!), I was simply unable to get out of my sickbed and onto public transportation. I was a no-call, no-show. I now knew better than to pretend I'd confused my schedule and, somewhat embarrassed, just never returned.

I said *somewhat* embarrassed. My work ethic was developing alongside my reading preferences, and the writers I was discovering were total miscreants who would never let a stupid *job* stand in the way of a crazy adventure. And my teenage nights were increasingly filled with crazy adventures. I was brought onto the stage at the local *Rocky Horror Picture Show* to lip-sync "Time

Warp" with the fully costumed cast, resulting in a brief romance with the bisexual witch who played Frank-N-Furter. I snuck onto the tour bus of my favorite Goth band, Christian Death, and begged to run away with them until the pink-haired driver threw me out. I went on a NoDoz-fueled overnight road trip to Pennsylvania to help my gay best friend, Joe, find his lost gay boyfriend, Lizard (my mom thought I'd slept over at a friend's house and spent the following afternoon at a museum). In the summertime my friends and I sprayed whipped cream on the bottom of cardboard boxes and went sledding down a hill. We blew up an inflatable raft and tried to float among the Swan Boats in the Boston Common. We got in fights with jocks who tried to beat us up for our awesome hairdos; we ran from cops who tried to arrest us for public drinking. And so my young life slowly but irrevocably split into two lives: the wild life I wanted and loved, and the straight life I endured to make the wild life possible. Straight life equals school, jobs, lying to Mom about my whereabouts. Wild life equals riding in the trunk of an overstuffed Hyundai, downing a four-pack of wine coolers, and making out with a tangle-haired Goth boy who hadn't figured out he was gay yet. I needed these jobs to keep me in Aqua Net and thrift store finery, and I needed to abandon them when they stood in the way of a mescaline trip at the Museum of Science or a jaunt to Western Massachusetts to see Joan Jett play for free.

The work-life balance plagued me throughout my teen years. As much as work could get in my way, without a job I didn't have the money to take the train into Boston to be with all my new, cool, black-clad friends. I didn't have the funds to purchase my preferred beverage, Smirnoff Blue Label vodka mixed with Very-fine iced tea, or a pack of Marlboro Lights to chain-smoke while blitzed. My life ground to a halt without employment. With no cash to get into the city, I was trapped at home, playing Trivial Pursuit, eating Kraft mac 'n' cheese, and zoning out to MTV. I realized that having a job to fund your life's purpose was every bit as important as being ready to quit your job when it got in the way of your life's purpose. The only life's purpose I could divine at that moment was to hurl myself into hard, wild, reckless living, with the fearless intensity of the (male) writers I was reading, and hope that someday I, too, could put it all down on paper, and maybe some lost, drunk, broke teenage girl could read it and begin to understand her own place in the world. There had to be more than boring, soul-slaughtering high school, a place where boys threw food into my hair in the cafeteria; more than these jobs, equally boring, with checks that felt shockingly low after so many eight-hour shifts.

The summer I graduated high school I got hired to hand out coupon books to passersby in Harvard Square, in full view of the punks who congregated in the area around the subway stop known as "the pit." I was afraid they'd judge me, maybe start a fight with me; though we all looked like interchangeable weirdos to normal people, the Harvard Square punks were a different breed than I and my art-fag, Goth-rock friends. Some of them were runaways, homeless kids; I was intimidated by their authenticity and toughness. But their punk ethics wouldn't let them fuck with a kid broke enough to take such a humiliating job. Instead, they helped me out by sneaking off bundles of coupon books and dumping them in the Charles River. I was paid by how many books I handed out each day, and my paychecks went up thanks to the punks. I had the money I needed to get myself around, but now that I was out of high school it seemed that I should be looking for a more adult job.

What is an "adult job"? Presumably, it is any job an adult works, which means every job is an adult job. Thrust into the grown-up workforce, I searched for jobs the same way I always had—walking around, looking for HELP WANTED signs—and got my first real full-time job at a café on tony Newbury Street. Newbury Street started out ritzy, with the actual Ritz-Carlton, and got punker and rockier as you traveled upward to Mass Ave., where shops sold noisy records and bondage-y clothing imported from the UK. The café, being right in the middle, served rich people and rockers, and sometimes both at once, like Ric Ocasek or Aimee Mann. It wasn't a terrible job—the boss was nice, the food was tasty, and I got to eat all I wanted. But was it an adult job? Was I an adult?

My mom thought I should be looking for employment that utilized the training I'd gotten at the Voke. The problem was, I didn't really get much training. The only shop that had captured my interest was the highly competitive cosmetology department. I didn't make the cut, according to the meanie who ran the joint, because she would not allow students with blue hair in her shop. I was heartbroken; I'd actually thought my amazing indigo dye job was proof of what an excellent, innovative hairdresser I'd be. Instead, I wound up in graphic arts, simply because some metalhead friends were there. Graphic arts was essentially printing, during a time—the late 1980s—when the industry was at the start of an upheaval. Soon everything would be computerized, but not quite yet. The old machines were obsolete and not worth learning; the new ones hadn't trickled into this out-of-the-way vocational school. The male instructors only put females on the fading printing presses if they asked; being lazy and uninspired, I did not. I was left in the "computer typesetting" room, where I was asked to type out the one-sheet school newspaper, published two to six times per year. Otherwise I typed out song lyrics in dramatic fonts, or checked V. C. Andrews books out of the library. Or put my head down on the desk and slept.

As my graphic design shop hovered in some strange technological limbo, so did the industries it purported to prep me for. Eventually I took my mom's advice, quit the café, and got a job at a publishing house in Newton (Mom had found it for me in the want ads). It was in the design department of a company that published industry magazines for industries I'd never heard of. My job was taking shiny sheets of text, running them through a wax machine, and then cutting the type and laying it out on giant boards. As more and more type was set via computer, there was increasingly little for me to do. I wrote stories and practiced reading tarot cards. I saved up enough money to take a vacation to Montreal and to pay, with the help of some basic student loans, for that one year of college.

If you grow up blue collar, you're generally not expected to find a job that you love; *love* and *job* are two words that rarely show up in the same sentence. You *endure* your job. Ideally, you make "enough" money. Not enough to get ahead, or beef your savings up to the recommended safety zone of eight months' living expenses. Not enough to invest in retirement and certainly not enough to invest in stocks, or even learn how people do such things. Ideally, you make enough to cover your bills. Ideally, you have some health insurance. Ideally, your boss isn't a suck-ass and you can slack off a little bit. Ideally you're not working *too* hard, because all you're really doing is making some other guy rich.

After my experiment in the adult workforce and my subsequent experiment in college, my time for experimenting was up. I'd had a single inspiring class during that year, a creative writing workshop taught by an old guy who wore tweedy three-piece suits and climbed up on the desks to recite poetry. Maybe he'd seen *Dead Poets Society* a few times too many, but as literature and Hollywood had set me up for disappointment with my paltry education, this guy's class was the only one that offered the sort of cinematic collegiate experience I'd been expecting. Not only did the teacher excite me by embracing the wild, performative aspects of literature; he liked the things that I wrote. When I read them aloud in class he would stand very close to me, stepping on my foot as if it were a brake when I spoke too fast.

Right around this time I became aware of a revolution in self-publishing, led by girls like me: zines. People were taking their own writing—fiction and rants, poetry and analysis, drawings, letters, clip art, really anything they wanted—and they were pasting them into these singular magazines, running them off at copy shops or after-hours at their workplaces or schools. I found a book for sale at a record store: *Angry Women*, a collection of interviews with writers who were as edgy and wild as Hunter

S. Thompson and Jim Carroll and William Burroughs, but they were *girls*. And they were *into* being girls. They wrote about it and talked about it; they crafted weird performances about it. Some made sex movies and some wrote operas, but what they were all doing was creating culture—weird, underground culture—using their lives as the raw material.

None of this was being taught in my schools. Maybe if you had a bunch of money you could go to some really cool, expensive art school where you'd be encouraged to rewrite classic male literature in the voice of a sexually abused, sexually liberated female protagonist, like one woman in the *Angry Women* book was doing, but I didn't have access to that level of education. *I* was going to be my education. I realized that the most I was going to get from college was what that *Dead Poets* professor had already given me—confidence that I could write. I wasn't suited to be a student in this dull way. I wasn't suited to join the workforce, either. I was suited only to be some sort of an artist, a refinement of my teenage life's purpose to live fast and crazy and risky. To befriend *Rocky Horror* drag queens. To write snarky rants and read them at dive bars. To stage counterprotests to antiabortion protestors; to walk around red light districts offering free condoms to streetwalkers. To paste together zines filled with writings and ravings. To stage my own poetry events, inviting other young people trying to live as writers. To book a cross-country tour, as if we writers were a rock band, and travel through America in a big blue Chevy van. All these things were one for me, and all were my work: creating culture.

These activities require immense skill—people skills, management, marketing, promotion, graphic design, publishing, distribution, writing, editing, talent scouting, analysis, mapping, courage. But it took me more than a decade of doing this work for it to become what our culture recognizes as work—something that pays.

A blessing of my working-class upbringing and its low expectations for career success is that I was able to devote myself wholeheartedly to things that didn't make me a cent. Had I gone to college I'd have been saddled with student loans, and a "good job" would have been more important. As it was, I was disappointing no one in my family by earning my living straightening racks of secondhand clothing at a thrift store, or patching together calls at a phone sex company. Once I was paying my own way in the world, though, I knew that I had to try a little harder. Having no money didn't mean I'd be stuck at my mom's house eating ramen; it meant I'd be stuck on the street eating at food kitchens. I became a more efficient hungover worker; as an adult living in the party city of San Francisco, my drinking went from teenage weekend benders to imbibing every single night of the week. If I called in sick every time I had a hangover, I'd never show up. Still, once a job began to interfere with my *real* work—readings and tours—I would quit it.

This was actually my way of aiming higher, doing better than the people I come from. Sure, I wasn't making much money, and I often didn't care about whatever disposable job I was working at any given moment, but I *had* found something that gave my life purpose and meaning, something that brought me happiness. It just didn't pay. I may have been working a shitty job like everyone back in my hometown, but my shitty job was funding an excellent life.

There is a contemporary, self-help-y wisdom that if you do what you love, the money will follow. I've found that to be true—it just took ten years for that money to track me down. Those ten years living below poverty level would likely be unacceptable to someone reared in a wealthier environment, but I always expected I'd be poor. I hadn't expected to be able to build a life around being creative, and I *really* hadn't expected to ever make a living at it. But after ten years of putting on shows around San Francisco, I caught the attention of a grant writer. I don't think it's a coincidence that this happened about a year after I got sober, either—I've found that when you make a big, positive change in one area of your life, the resulting magic infects everything.

"Do you know," the grant writer asked, "that there are nonprofit organizations that don't produce half as many events as you do, and they get hundreds of thousands of dollars in funding?"

Uh—no, I hadn't known that. Or maybe I had, but I never thought there would be any money for a runt like me putting together events where single moms and lesbians and recovering drug addicts and performance artists and feminists and poets and drag queens and filmmakers and burlesque dancers and bloggers and crafters and witches and politicos and zinesters and academics and club kids and hookers and bikers and students and rappers and cartoonists and strippers and astrologers and trapeze artists and graffiti artists and photographers and vegans and fat activists and hasbians and fags and teachers and foodies and comedians and nerds and ex-cons and hippies and punks and porn stars and philosophers and homeless people got together and told their stories and shared their work. But I was wrong.

I didn't get the first few grants my fairy grant-father wrote for me. No big deal, he assured me—most people don't. You have to keep trying. So we kept at it, and as predicted, we began to get funded. I named my organization RADAR Productions, because I thought that this work I was doing spanned wide cultural distances, yet seemed invisible. Also, Radar encompasses everything, and there was a lot I wanted to do. First I began a regular reading series, a free one. Like my fairy grant-father, some people at the San Francisco Public Library had noticed all the literary work I'd been doing, and began paying me to bring writers in for a once-a-month reading. I would spend those afternoons baking cookies, and after the authors had read from their work, I encouraged the audience members to ask them questions; if they did, they got a homemade cookie. There were always lots of questions.

I professionalized Sister Spit, those national tours I'd started in my twenties when I was drinking all the time and didn't care about sleeping on floors across the USA. Now I worked with a professional tour booker who put us up in hotels and got us on the road in a rental van guaranteed not to break down (unlike past vans, which cracked their engines at midnight in the middle of the Deep South, or burst into flames in Lovelock, Nevada).

I brainstormed ideas for literary events with my fairy grant-father, and the grant people liked them! Soon I was getting paid to put on the fun readings I'd always done for nothing, and the writers I was working with were getting paid, too. With the help of Tali and Bernadine I started a writing retreat in Mexico, in Akumal, on the Caribbean coast of the Yucatán. Fairy grant-father had a condo there, and he rented to us dirt cheap during the off-season, and got some other condo owners to do the same. Soon the building was filled with writers who spent all morning and afternoon completing memoirs and plays and graphic novels, swimming with sea turtles on breaks and gathering together each night for home-cooked meals of ceviche and fried plantains and chilaquiles, with churros and casserole dishes of lemon ice for dessert. In recognition of the economic situations of the low-income writers and artists we worked with, our retreat, the LAB, was always free; the artists only had to get themselves to Mexico (and in the few cases when that wasn't possible, we'd chip in and help). We funded this project by throwing a giant fund-raiser once a year, and begging pieces of art off every artist we knew. The ticket price, art auction, and a raffle where we gave away donated prizes like books from local publishers and rainbow-flag dog blankets sewn by Tali's mother brought in just enough for us to pull it off.

We began a yearly poetry contest, open to everyone, in which the winner—selected by an established poet—would get his or her manuscript printed in a handsome letterpress chap-book. I approached the legendary City Lights Booksellers and Publishers, the nexus of the Beat Generation's long-ago literary happenings, and asked if they would allow me to helm my own imprint. An imprint is sort of a press within a press; I would se-lect and edit a series of books that would go out with both the

Sister Spit and the City Lights names attached to it. It was my hope that City Lights would see that the bedraggled, upstart, underground literary voices I'd been championing for so long were in many ways the next wave of Beat literature—radical, experimental, written by people living uncompromisingly at the fringe of our culture. To my absurd delight, they agreed! And so a dream I didn't even know to have as a child—You love books so much? Why not publish them?—came true. There is a belief in recovery circles that what your higher power has in store for you is so much more wicked awesome than anything you could ever think up yourself, and more and more I was finding this to be true. An unexpected surge of outside help and community support had elevated the work I'd been doing for so long, elevating my life in the process.

Around this same time, I sold a novel for a bit of money, then got paid to write a celebrity's memoir for a bit of money, and then got a grant to write a whole new novel—all at the same time. I was being paid a living wage in an expensive city to do the only things I really had any aptitude for: creating culture for misfits and writing about my own topsy-turvy life. It felt like nothing short of a miracle. It still does! And if I had put any of my day jobs first—at any point in my life, stretching all the way back to when I was a juvenile delinquent—it wouldn't have happened. Stacking low-wage job atop literary pursuit atop low-wage job resulted in me running an actual 501(c)(3) nonprofit, one of the most adult jobs I can imagine. I don't always *feel* like an adult in this role—especially when faced with incomprehensible budgets, or when I have to meet with funders and explain to them why it's worth their while to give money to an organization that prioritizes the perspectives of feminists, sex workers, and other cultural outsiders. If I have to try to bum money off rich people, it makes me feel like a twelve-year-old asking my mom to buy me an overpriced accessory: desperate, shaky, and defeated. Figuring out the appropriate thing to wear at any moment can give me hives, but I rise to the occasion as best I can, because it's the adult thing to do. I have found Kelly Cutrone's titular workplace advice, "If you have to cry, go outside," to be valuable, though sometimes I haven't made it out before the tears start splashing down.

But as discouraging as these tiny failures can feel, it's not too hard to pull myself out of the funk of it—all it takes is one hard look at the big-picture triumph: *I'm running a freaking nonprofit! I never even went to college! I should be back in my hometown with three kids I can hardly feed and a good-for-nothing man stealing dollars from my purse!* If that doesn't put things in perspective, there's always: *I'm an alcoholic! I should be wasted right now! Who cares if I accidentally wore a see-through blouse to meet with a funder, and then said the F-word twice? At least I'm not drunk!* (Truly, one of the best reasons to sober up is how it makes the most basic accomplishments feel like major wins. The all-purpose *At least I'm not drunk* brings relief to any situation.)

My path to making an adult living has been a weird one, but I suspect a lot of people's are, especially during an era of transitional industries, a dragging recession, and a vanishing middle class. It takes wiles and wits and weirdness to perfect the balance of love and money; it takes perseverance and patience and long-haul thinking. Often you have to walk away from the sure thing to stay true to your heart's desire, and sometimes that desire needs to be put on hold to get the bills paid. At any point, wherever I am on that seesaw is where I'm supposed to be—smack in the heart of all-grown-up, without-a-net living.

# 12.

# WWYMD: What Would Young Michelle Do?

hat would young Michelle think of today's Michelle? Who cares? That Michelle was a jerk.

Okay, that is sort of a joke. I don't mean to sell my younger self out so easily, especially when what ailed me was not so much a bratty phase as a full-on nervous breakdown. When I look back at the things I did in my twenties, I can be a little shocked at my behavior, but I also remember that *that* was as well as I could do at that moment. And if it seems baffling to me now, I must have lost touch with how it felt to be me, right then, right there. Take, for instance, the time a waiter at a Chinese restaurant in Cape Cod reached out to rub the fuzz of my velvet bodysuit. (It was the nineties. How I wish I still had that velvet bodysuit today.) I was aghast that this man thought he could just reach out and put his hand on me, and I shrieked, "Don't touch me!" throwing my little carton of soy milk all over him. It's actually even worse than it sounds—my little carton of soy milk was one of those boxes you have to punch a straw into. To "throw" it at someone requires you to sort of aim and squeeze continuously. It lacks the drama of a single drink tossed into a face, *and* it requires you to commit to the act of dousing a stranger with liquid, since you have to keep squeezing. *And* all you get is a sort of weak stream of milk. *Soy* milk.

That I was walking around town sipping at a carton of unflavored soy milk might tell you all you need to know about my state of mind at that time. Many things had happened at once. I'd realized I was bisexual right around the time I realized I couldn't afford college right around the time I realized my stepfather had been spying on me through holes he'd put in my bedroom walls. The political consciousness I'd developed as a teenager surged, brutally. I had a sort of terrible revelation, in which all forms of earthly oppression became very visible to me. I could see their interconnectedness with a horrible clarity that made it difficult to live. For me, in that moment, there was no difference between the urge to kill off a people via genocide and the struggle of an underpaid migrant worker picking my vegetables. If you think I'm demeaning the reality of mass murder by comparing it to unjust labor practices, you're not understanding the almost mystical state I was in. You know how some people, via spiritual training or psychedelic drugs, can have a visceral comprehension of the deep and total *oneness* of everything? From the accounts I've read, this can be a pretty blissful experience— to know that we are not separate from one another, or the ocean or the sky or that frog over there sitting on that lily pad, all things crucially bound to each other. What I was going through was like the bummer version of that—there was no difference between factory farming and the oppression of gay people. There was no difference between laws that made me, as a female, keep my shirt on (while men's bare chests roamed free) and the laws that justified slavery. And so a person who ate meat was to me no different from a fascist dictator, and if I should eat the egg of a factory-farmed chicken—well, I might as well be conducting medical experiments on third-world women. This was my state of mind right then. It was not a relaxing place to be.

I think a lot about this time in my life. It was powerful, intense, and, thankfully, short-lived—life snapped me out of it after a couple of years, though its influences echoed for longer. How did I survive when all around me—from the food on the grocery store shelves to the advertising on billboards to news headlines and casual conversation—seemed to confirm, again and again, that this planet is a terrible place and we humans have made it that way? Well, it was hard. I didn't have many friends, because I couldn't bear to be around people whose opinions differed from mine when everything felt so life-and-death. I could spend time only with people who thought like I did, other edgy, defensive individuals, all of us waiting to bust one another for thought crimes so we could call them out and thus feel like we were doing what we could to make the world a more just place. I couldn't eat a lot of food—all animal products were out, including honey, because who were we to barge into the bees' homes and steal their creations? It was hard to eat even vegetables knowing that underpaid, uninsured people of color had picked them for me. I became frighteningly skinny, and often would feel faint and need to consume half a jar of peanut butter in a single sitting.

My fashion suffered as well. I couldn't handle the way the world sexualized females, and after learning my stepfather, whom I'd admired and trusted, had been peeping on me, I didn't want to wear anything that had been created to sexualize my body. Women's attire, which I had loved so passionately for so long, became suddenly sinister. Why were we wearing skinny stilettos if not to make it harder to run away from an attacker? Why were we wearing short skirts if not to make it easier for malevolent men to sneak a peek, if not a grab?

Not even my sex life was immune to this philosophical virus. I was paired up with a woman at the time, and our available repertoire was fast shrinking. Strap-ons? No way! Why would we want something that resembled a *penis*? While we both had fond memories of tying one another up at the start of our dating, simulating violence was now forbidden. As was most music and literature, and art, and movies. I recall myself at the height of this, sexually frustrated, my hair cropped short, wearing baggy jeans held up with a woven hemp belt and a roomy, gender-neutral T-shirt, eating a bland bean burrito and reading a giant coffee-table book about the grim legacy of aboveground nuclear testing in the 1950s (*American Ground Zero: The Secret Nuclear War*; it's actually fascinating and you should read it yourself if you get the chance). Poor me! I was twenty-one years old. I was supposed to be partying and having lots of dumb sex I'd later regret. And I would, soon enough. But right then and there I felt like I was the emotional receptacle for all the feelings of grief and despair the rest of humanity should have been feeling but wasn't.

I once read that what makes a poet a poet is the ability to see likeness in things that are not immediately similar. I do have the mind—heart? soul?—of a poet, and so the leap between the illegality of prostitution and the fact that people of the same sex couldn't marry was a short trip for me. Every day a new problem revealed itself—ageism, cultural scorn for fat people, the sexism embedded in our very language. My world got smaller and smaller and I got angrier and angrier. I thought, quite seriously, about destroying my neighborhood frat houses, places that harbored what I assumed to be rapists in training, if not fresh offenders. I thought about moving into a forest somewhere, "living off the land" in spite of the fact that the last thing I'd grown was a sprout in an egg carton back in first grade. A sprout that died. Maybe I would settle down on "women's land," one of those rural communes occupied by other women who couldn't handle the world. If I was of a different class or had health insurance, I might've wound up in a hospital of sorts—the kind with a rolling lawn and regular therapy and craft sessions. But I was loose in the world, very much alone in spite of my relationship, which was on the skids. Nothing could survive in such an unforgiving, harsh landscape, certainly not love. I consoled myself with lonely drinks of Mezcal, the relief the alcohol brought to my body astounding and necessary. If this was what the world truly was, who could handle it sober? Not me.

How did I ever climb out of this heap of misery? It was both easy and not easy. Simply put, I could not survive without beauty and pleasure, two things that my nervous breakdown had out-lawed. In that way, my recovery was inevitable. But it was hard, and in some ways I will always be haunted by what I experienced. Because all of it was true. There *is* a continuum between oppression and atrocities. By participating in the world, I *do* become part of numerous problems. Eventually, the answer to my politico-spiritual conundrum was also somewhat spiritual in nature: I ex-ist. As surely as the migrant workers and the frog on the lily pad and the ocean, I exist. So it must be okay to be here. And if this is the time and place I have been born into, then I will be of it, no better or worse than any other of my kind. And slowly I began to open up to the world, and in doing so, to my own imperfect desires, my human nature. My girlfriend and I broke up, and I moved to San Francisco, to move in with an old friend who didn't know what I'd been going through. The sight of me—my hair shorn, my sacklike clothes barely hanging on my emaciated frame—shocked him. I looked like I was dying. But in fact, I was coming back to life.

Really, though, it was a KitKat that did it. I was standing at a bus stop, starving. Hunger was my daily state. Realizing I needed change for the bus, I walked into a corner store to break a bill. There was a goddamn KitKat bar, glowing in its red wrapper, right there at the counter. Oh my God, how I have *loved* a KitKat bar. Its yummy crunch, a cookie and a bit of chocolate, the action of snapping a slender bar from the brick of it, savoring the sweetness. As if on autopilot, I reached for it. Put it by the register. Handed over the bill, damp from my sweaty palm. The man gave me back my change, unaware of the magnitude of the transaction. Some part of me, some selfish, human part that yearned for sweetness, had won out. I ripped open the wrapper and gorged myself on this not-vegan, corporate chocolate whose cacao beans had surely been sourced under terrible circumstances.

"I ate a KitKat bar," I confessed to my roommate. He looked at me, confused. I had simply reported the eating of a candy bar, but I had said it in the voice of a person who had just run someone over with her car, so there was, you know, this dissonance. I retired to my room. How could it be okay for me to have eaten this candy? It was like I'd pushed a button that said *I'm for the torture of animals and corporate domination and child labor in colonized lands.* But could my purchase have only pushed a button that said *I'm for cheap and available sweets whilst having seriously low blood sugar at a bus stop?* Maybe it pushed both. Maybe there *were* no buttons, and whether or not I bought a candy bar at a corner store actually meant very little.

Soon enough I was dating people again. In San Francisco, in the nineties, even the boys I found myself making out with were flirting with all sorts of newfangled perversions. One guy surprised me greatly by confessing that he would like for me to doll him up like a Barbie and smack him around a bit. I loved making out with this person, my hands twirling in his long, curly hair, but I couldn't do it. And it wasn't because Barbie was sexist propaganda that brainwashed girls to aspire to twenty-two unrealistic beauty standards (which I had recently written a slam poem about), and it wasn't because S and M mimicked actual sexual violence (another recent poem topic). It was because *I* wanted to be dolled up like Barbie and get smacked around a bit, and I was only at the start of coming to terms with this, making a strange peace between my deep political beliefs and the irresistible pull of sexual desire. The romance fizzled out, but there were others. I rendezvoused with people who kept all sorts of sex toys under the bed, and when they fished them out, I didn't flinch.

Beauty and pleasure—these things are inside me, but they're outside me, too. They're bigger than me and I am no match for them. My time under the influence of injustice has widened my notion of beauty, so that I see it in people, places, and things that are commonly overlooked. That period when I rejected beauty made it so that I now have *more* beauty available to me than the average person. Things that people get funny about—body sizes and types, hair, feet—don't bother me. A part of me, marked by that dark time, is now called to spot the beauty in everyone, as if it were my job. I must say I'm good at it—perhaps it's my poet's nature again.

I still wonder about my ability to love and empathize with animals and yet eat them. It seems a disconnect must be in place, a kind of denial, but the more I probe, the more I believe it's not denial but acceptance. I am a feeling, loving human who lives off the meat of other feeling, loving beings. Most everywhere I look on our planet this is the case, life consuming life. I am not outside any of it; I am in it—implicated, inevitably guilty, guilty of having desires and the ability to fulfill them. A chicken in the Crock-Pot, a fur coat in the closet (used, but still) hanging alongside clothes made under dubious circumstances in countries I'll never visit. It's not that I don't care. My heart shakes with rage and anxiety when I read about striking garment workers being shot at by police, or impoverished children picking the cacao beans that might have made my KitKat bar. I try to make choices that align with my highest beliefs. Sometimes I do and sometimes I don't and in between I try not to have a panic attack over it.

Once I looked at a photo of an Indian child playing atop a pile of garbage and I thought of my niece and thought—that's her. There's no difference between my niece, whom I love with all my being and who will never play in an international garbage heap, and this child I will never know, his hands grimed with trash. It is still inside me, this ability to experience connectivity, and it still feels as powerfully true. I sometimes pull away from caring too deeply because I fear falling back into that long-ago paralyzing, unhappy state. I've wondered if my caring is like my alcoholism—I lack the ability to do it in moderation. Whereas some people can, say, rescue feral cats and still have a normal life, the saving of a feral cat could lead me to throwing away all my shoes and painting on recycled paper with the juice of berries (true story).

What do I say to this long-ago Michelle who is aghast that I've turned into a materialistic meat eater? How to explain that the same ethics currently keeping her alive today will stunt her tomorrow? Could I get her to understand that change is inevitable and not to be feared, however scary? I doubt it. I know how awful I was to argue with, how harsh and all-or-nothing my stance. I made friends cry, I was so unwavering, and I didn't care. People's feelings were not half as important as the much more abstract issues I was obsessed with. Now I think people *are* the issues. If everything is as connected as I felt it was during my nervous breakdown, then perhaps kindness can go much further than we know.

No, I'd rather not say anything at all to young, freaked-out Michelle. I'd rather just pull her close and pet her cropped head. *Don't worry*, I hope my pats would communicate. *That heart inside you will never stop caring, but it will never stop longing for beauty, either. It will never stop craving pleasure, and this will both lead you into terrible trouble and save your life. You will donate money to struggling artists and people who can't pay their hospital bills, and you will buy overpriced wrinkle creams and dresses that are expensive even when on sale. You will be, finally, like most everyone else: part of the problem, always, but part of the solution as well.*

# 13.

# Eat Me

I don't know about you, but here's what I ate growing up: hot dogs. Frozen fish sticks. Hamburger Helper; Kraft Macaroni & Cheese. Deviled ham sandwiches (or regular ham, or bologna and cheese—or, for something really special, *fried* bologna and cheese). Steak-umm—slabs of particle board "steak" that you peel from waxed paper sheaths and throw in a frying pan. The last time I visited my mom she fried me up a Steak-umm. I was shocked they still exist; I thought you could only get them if you time-traveled back to the land of my childhood—1980s New England. But no—you, too, can taste the greasy glory of a Steak-umm if you like. Because the thing is, Steak-umm is kind of delicious. Perhaps my palate is sadly conditioned to enjoy such cuisine, or perhaps it's one of those grody, trashy foods that are weirdly scrumptious— like Spam, or Ellio's frozen pizza, which is basically pieces of cardboard with some shitty cheese and sauce blasted onto it. Okay, I guess it's my palate. Unless you grew up eating Spam, chances are the salty goodness of that canned meat product is a kitschy joke, not sustenance.

The question "What are we having for dinner tonight?" was frequently answered in my household growing up with "Shit on a shingle," or "Fish heads and rice." It was a joke response, but creepily true. Some of these dinners *were* the equivalent of shit on a shingle. But people eat what they eat, and your palate is built from what is presented to you. Once my mother topped a shepherd's pie with a packet of neon orange cheez powder from a box of mac 'n' cheese. Processed foods served creatively—this is the cuisine of my people.

Growing up, everything in my cabinets and refrigerator was canned or boxed, processed to the max. The only fresh vegetables I ever saw were roots like potatoes and carrots, or some corn on the cob in the summer. Anything green was in the freezer or an aluminum tube. Now, I know that frozen broccoli retains as much of its nutrients as the fresh stuff, but ours came with a frosty brick of microwavable cheese sauce. I was so ignorant about the food I ate that the first time I saw a vegetable being grown in the ground I was baffled, then filled with rage. The cucumbers our neighbors had planted looked bizarre to me, just sitting there in the dirt instead of on a store shelf where I usually saw them. Cucumbers were my favorite. I jumped the fence and picked one; instead of eating it, I smashed it on the ground. I often wonder what I was thinking. Did it seem unreal to me, like a fake cucumber, even though it was actually more natural than any I'd ever held in my hand? Was I resentful that this person had figured out how to hook themselves up with free cukes, while we were all buying ours at the grocery store? Or was it just the sad pattern of bummed-out people trying to bring down anyone who tries to rise up a little, plant a veggie garden in a blighted neighborhood? Maybe I was just a kid, pranking. Maybe it was all of the above.

Because of the way my vegetables were delivered to me, for years I thought I didn't like them. String beans, for instance. Does anyone enjoy the soggy, olive-green contents of a can of string beans? It's taken me decades to come around to the fresh stuff, pulled by the handful from a bin at the co-op, roasted with salt and garlic and oil. They bear absolutely no resemblance to the string beans of my youth. Same with spinach. In my house we just never ate it, and being aware of its reputation as a veggie children gagged on, I was fine with that. Now I cannot imagine going without greens. Mornings I blend up a swampy concoction of spinach, its overachieving sister kale, some powdered green probiotics, a giant glug of aloe vera, a heaping teaspoon of bee pollen, bought from a beekeeper at the farmers market, some chia seeds (not sure why but, hey, can't hurt), and a bunch of coconut water. This is so far from the sort of stuff I ate growing up, I do think it might send some part of my psyche into shock each time I drink it. Is it good? Well, that depends on your definition of *good*. In my family, if something didn't taste awesome, you didn't eat it, and awesome was defined as meaty, fatty, oozy butteriness. My family still laughs at me if I mention I'm preparing tofu for dinner, and they'd certainly look upon my morning smoothie as something a doctor would force you to eat before an invasive procedure. ("What's wrong with sugar?" my mom recently demanded. "It grows in the ground!") But somewhere along my stumble to adulthood I began to realize that, while it was important, food tasting good was only part of it. It should also *be* good for you, and maybe even produced in a way that doesn't harm working people or the planet itself.

Growing up, I was a skinny kid, and never had any bullshit flung at me about what I should or shouldn't eat. A big bottle of Pepsi sat in the center of the kitchen table at dinner, and unlimited refills were granted. Still, I became obsessed with the concept of dieting (or "health kicks," as I called them). Inevitably some of this fascination with dieting came from the body-shaming, weight-obsessed culture a girl grows up in. Even if my family didn't send me those messages, the rest of the world did. One thing I always understood was that diets were something females (and Richard Simmons) did, and those females were often leggy white women with bouncy, wild hair, clad in bathing suits and laughing with their big red mouths.

In fifth grade I devised an all-pickle health kick. I really, really loved pickles. I still do, and now I buy the ones with probiotics so I'm actually doing something good for my body while chomping down. But—an all-pickle diet? It didn't last long. That was the summer I watched *The Richard Simmons Show* each afternoon, joining him in his televised workout and then eating a pile of iceberg lettuce, a cut tomato, some Italian dressing, and an English muffin slathered in butter. This was my daily regimen, unless I was hanging out at the park down the street and getting the free lunches the city handed out. My diet ended each evening, when I ate whatever my mom whipped up for us, but after every dinner of Minute Rice and chicken fingers I looked forward to the next day's health kick.

I had a few incidents of passing out when I was a kid, both times on hot summer days when I ran around and didn't eat. I wasn't trying not to eat—I'd intended to get around to it, or maybe I did eat, but not enough. I wasn't a very hungry person, except for the things I especially loved—Italian ice, watermelon, pickles. And not only was I not very interested in food; I couldn't always tell when my body was hungry, and I was able to go seemingly forever without replenishing the reserves. This served me well in my twenties. I was so broke, it just *killed* me to spend money on food (especially when I could be spending it on booze, yo), and I always had enough native energy to run around doing all the superfun things I wanted to do—go to clubs and bars, put on shows, have crazy affairs, run away on road trips. Only now, with older, wiser, and more sober vision, do I see that I was getting *high as fuck* off of low blood sugar.

Low blood sugar affects people very differently. One of the first things you learn about someone you are seriously dating is what happens when they don't eat. I've dated people who rage out, hard-core. Dashiell doesn't get "hangry" like those folks; she gets what I call "hungfused" (I know, it doesn't really work, but it's stuck). Dashiell gets spacey and drifty and floaty and scary to drive in a car with. But I get high. I've done crystal meth, and there is a similarity there. It fosters a slight mania. I feel lighter and brighter; my thoughts seem clearer; everything is faster. My self-esteem reaches delusions of grandeur levels—I *dig* myself! In addition to the variety-pack chemical bender I spent my twenties on, I was also probably really, really hungry all the time, but too messed up to know it.

When I first got sober, I didn't really know what to do with myself. Like most newly sober drunks, I spent a lot of time watching television and, well, eating. Maybe that's what most people do anyway, but when you're an alcoholic it's new to you—you normally spend your time wherever the alcohol is, with your attention focused on obtaining it and imbibing it. Sober, I started to be in touch with my body more and began noticing when I was hungry. And I was hungry *a lot*. My body was going through a massive sugar withdrawal. Though I never had much of a sweet tooth, I'd been ignorant of the fact that I was basically sucking down pints of sugar water each night. When I shut off the taps I found myself starved for ice cream, for Reese's Peanut Butter Cups, for the sort of dismal plastic-wrapped sweet treats that jumble the counters of coffee shops. I didn't care—if it had sugar, I needed to put it in my mouth. After a while my body leveled out, but the sweet tooth stayed behind.

Sometimes quitting drinking inspires you to quit other things as well. I know a bazillion people who cut sugar or dairy or wheat from their diets their first year sober, people who go Paleo or buy a dehydrator and start a raw food diet. Perhaps as alcoholics you have a heightened understanding of your body as a sort of chemistry set. I'd been pouring a little of this and snorting a little of that for decades, trying to strike that perfect balance. A lot of dieting seems like the same thing—what can I put into my body, or never put in my body again, that will make me feel perfect? I'm drawn to cleanses, though I've only ever done one, and it was one that had you eating three square meals a day. I think about the Master Cleanse like I once thought about certain drugs I'd dreamed of trying: What would *that* be like? Would it get me high? Would I feel just so, so perfect, and pure, and healing? As an addict, I kind of get it from both ends—the addict urge to get high off starvation, and the recovered person's desire to get super healthy *right now*, to make up for the wear and tear all that drinking and drugs did on my body. In sobriety I am sometimes shocked to think about what I put into my body—like chunks of heroin from goddess knows where, pulled out of the grimy pants pocket of a grimy man, cut with all sorts of crap. I'd dissolve it in water and snort it up my nose, followed with the grisliest, yellowest baggie of cocaine I'd ever seen. (It came for free with your purchase of the heroin!) Is it any wonder I have chronic mysterious sinus problems now? People think that drug addicts don't love themselves, or else how could they do what they do, bumming a crack pipe off a stranger who looks positively tubercular and proceeding to smoke a drug so gross it's become a punch line? But I think it's more complicated than that. I *did* love myself; I just loved the crystal meth, that glittering pile of battery acid, *more*. For me, once I got sober and exited that haze of obsession and compulsion, I could feel that self-love again, wounded and shaky, fragile and neglected. I pledged to make amends to myself by taking care of my body, whether through regular massages, manipedis, or learning to cook healthful meals and eat them regularly. More or less.

Breakups can send a person on a real cleanselike eating

regimen—or, a not-eating regimen. One friend called it "the personal tragedy weight-loss plan"—you're not necessarily trying to shed pounds, but you're too fucked up and heartbroken to feed yourself. At the end of my eight years with the rapper, I found myself eating less than ever. It felt lonely and uninspiring to cook for myself. Single and left to my own devices, I will eat the exact same snack food again and again. One year it was Tillamook cheddar cheese on Triscuits. Another year it was avocado on tamari rice cakes with cumin-spiked adobo. For many years I lived near a taqueria with shredded chicken tacos I would sometimes eat for three meals a day. After my breakup I ate a lot of almonds and not much else. I found that when I ate food I felt really, really sad. It put me right back into my body, a sack of skin and bones that felt abandoned and heavy and weepy. If I didn't eat, I got lighter and lighter, until I was hovering somewhere above my feelings. It felt great. I lived like this for a few years, eating more than almonds, but never very much.

Sometimes I wonder if I had, or have, an eating disorder. I certainly don't have a normal relationship to feeding myself. But when I look around, it seems like nobody else does, either. I have friends going on and off vegan and gluten-free diets, friends who burst into tears when they try to quit sugar, friends who cleanse five times a year, and friends who pride themselves on living off bacon and meatballs. None of this looks like the textbook anorexia depicted in my favorite eighties TV movie, *The Best Little Girl in the World*, but it all seems pretty disordered. I'm not even sure what the baseline for "healthy" is. Some believe eating whatever you want and not stressing is healthy, but if I eat whatever I want it's a lot of burritos, chocolate chip cookies washed down with giant glasses of milk, ice cream, Oreos, and bowls of buttery popcorn covered in nutritional yeast. And then I feel sort of grody. Eating dinner with Dashiell has been a revelation— when she is no longer hungry she *stops eating*! This is fascinating to me. I don't have that mechanism that tells me I'm full and it's time to wrap it up. No way. As long as the thing tastes good in my mouth, I will keep putting it in there.

Some people believe cutting out all such decadent and trashy food is the way to go, and as attractive as that way of life is to me, it's also shades of orthorexia—anorexia disguised as superrestrictive health kicks. Although my long-ago foray into veganism was definitely orthorexic, it also set me on the right path for feeding myself in the long run. I know a lot of people live healthy vegan lifestyles (I pin your recipes on Pinterest, thanks!), but leaping from a lifetime of frozen pizza and ramen to veganism was too brutal for me. I simply didn't know what to eat. I didn't know how to cook vegetables, having rarely eaten them. I recall eating a raw bell pepper and hoping it was enough. I found a recipe for dal at the back of the book *Animal Liberation*, and it became my signature (i.e. only) dish. I paid attention to what the people around me were eating—one girl had me over for dinner and served pasta with black beans dumped on top of it, plus chopped tomatoes and raw garlic. I ate this every night for about a year after.

Slowly, through copying people and dabbling in health kicks, I learned how to feed myself. And I found that being in a healthy relationship makes me *want* to feed myself. I jumped three dress sizes in my first few months with Dashiell, because I was happy, and I wanted to eat delicious food with her, to cook for her. The more we were together, the more I ate—no more creepy, lonely snack dinners. Now, as a married person, I cook our dinners every single night. It made Dashiell nervous at first. "I don't want you slaving away for me every night," she said. "We can just make some pasta." Left to her own devices, Dashiell eats pasta the way I eat cheese and crackers. Specifically, she eats "herbal pasta," a delicacy from her childhood consisting of pasta, butter, and, I think, paprika. But I love cooking for Dashiell, for a whole lot of reasons. I love that I have become skilled at something—skilled at anything—in my later life. I've always feared my laziness. I don't like learning new things; I get frustrated very easily and want to cry.

But cooking. I'd mastered a skimpy handful of dishes once I'd gotten sober and realized I had to eat; gone were the days of claiming that beer is bread and having a Guinness and a bag of SunChips for dinner, or passing a Bloody Mary off as a salad. By the time I connected with Dashiell, I was dying to impress her with my skills in the kitchen. Don't get me wrong—they're not all that. I'm not a creative cook; I can't raid a pantry and whip together something intuitive and marvelous. I painstakingly follow directions, often making mistakes due to my difficulty painstakingly following directions. But when I am able to bring out some steaming squash-kale casserole, or some flavorful roasted vegetables, or chicken that's been stewing in the Crock-Pot all day, I feel like a hero. I'm so proud of myself it's stupid.

Occasionally, when something very cool has happened to me

career-wise, my mother will cluck her tongue and say, in a mix-
ture of admiration and awe, "You're just a girl from Chelsea. Can
you even believe it?" Like—how the fuck am I not on welfare
with three kids and a shiftless, alcoholic dude on my couch? How
did this *happen*? I get that feeling myself when I do something
like bake a dozen onion bagels from scratch, which happened last
month. A friend of mine had blown my mind years ago by baking
her own bagels. Bagels? *But bagels are something you buy at the
store!* Eight-year-old me rose up in anxious confusion. Um, no.
Anyone can make bagels. And so I did. The tangible result of
them, all burnished and fragrant and plump and delicious, as-
tounded me. I made that! I *am* teachable!

I also like cooking dinner because it is a relief after working
on the computer all day. From sunup to sundown I am in a little
room with my head shoved into my laptop, maniacally typing
away. That's my job. Sometimes I take a break and talk to my
sister on the phone, or field a few texts from friends, though this,
too, is disembodied. I walk the dog, but picking up a pile of
steaming poo isn't how I want to be brought back into my body.
Cooking is. Beholding the perfect butternut squash, both slender
and fat, and putting my muscle into chopping it up; stirring stuff
together—tamari with ginger with wine with oil with some seeds
and ground up this and that, toss some honey in, maybe some
apple cider vinegar—it reminds me of being a kid, playing witch
in the bathroom, when I took all my mother's beauty products
and dumped them together into a bowl to make a foul potion.
Only this potion is amazing! By the time Dashiell arrives home I
have shaken out of the strange zombie state a day at home alone

on the computer leaves me in. I'm a person, a person with a body, a person with a body who wants to sit down and eat with another person with a body. The meal I've prepared is an offering of love, to myself for the work I've done all day, to Dashiell for her own time on the clock, for this time we have to come together as the sun goes down and reconnect and enjoy this life we're so lucky to be building together.

When I'm cooking, I guess I feel whole—body, mind, and spirit all engaged in the creation of something beautiful and temporary. It's rare that my creativity isn't tied to my income, my self-esteem, my persona. This raw little bit of play is allowed to be imperfect. The food is only for me and my beloved, and Dashiell is so happy to not be eating herbal pasta, she'll heap praise on almost everything I bring, unless it's a serious fail, like the too-sweet Indian rice or the too-sour blue cheese pasta. But in the rare case that a recipe's a dud, there's always popcorn with nutritional yeast for dinner. And that's a serious step up from a crusty bowl of Top Ramen.

Sometimes I get a little nostalgic for the trashy food of my childhood, and think it would be a transgressive treat to indulge in some processed food from the big chain grocery store I try not to shop at. And almost every time it's a revelation, though not in the way I thought it would be. I simply can't eat the garbage I used to. And if some MSG-laden McFood manages to trick my tongue into thinking it's tasty, I will soon thereafter feel barfy as fuck. I've trained myself out of being able to tolerate food that isn't good for me, much the way I've trained myself out of being able to put up with relationships that aren't good for me. And the more I think about it, the more connected these things are—food and love, my love for my physical self, my love for Dashiell, what I refuse to put in my body, and, um, *whom* I refused to put in my body. I truly believe that when you start a revolution in one area of your life, prioritizing true health and well-being, that excellent intention spreads to other areas of your life, places where maybe you didn't even know there was a problem. You start to spoil yourself with the better things in life—non-dysfunctional love affairs, French cheese—and suddenly the two-bit Romeos and their Velveeta equivalents just don't cut it anymore. You get used to feeling good in your mind and your body, and so you notice a bit faster when something is making you feel lousy. Through trial and error, you keep coming back around to the stir-fry of bok choy and chickpeas, keep coming back around to the person who is actually nice to you, who knows how to love. Every day I end my hours of work with the perfect, lucky confluence of the two: food that will make me feel awesome shared with a person who makes me feel awesome. What is more awesome than that?

# 14.

# I'm So Vain

When I learn that a person I'm talking to—an adult, sane, together-ish person who manages to make herself breakfast in the morning and leave the house without toothpaste smeared across her face—does not moisturize, the world freezes for a second. Everything I think I know about this person goes tilt-a-whirl. One such incident happened recently, while getting a coffee with two friends, both athletic types who run marathons and whatnot. One makes her living as a life coach, gently and enthusiastically ushering people through nutritious cleanses; the other makes her living by fermenting cabbage into award-winning sauerkraut. (Yes, there are awards for sauerkraut. It's a great big world out there.) These are people who prioritize being in touch with their bods. And yet, the conversations went thusly:

Me: Oh man, I forgot to put on sunscreen again!

Life Coach: Oh, I never wear sunscreen.

Sauerkraut Champion: Yeah, I don't wear sunscreen, either.

Me: Really? But, like, don't you just have a moisturizer with sunscreen in it?

Life Coach: I don't moisturize.

Sauerkraut Champion: Yeah, I don't moisturize, either.

Me: What? Really? Are you serious? But—your *skin*! Your *face*!

Although similar freak-outs have inspired other of my friends to break down and buy their first bottle of Retin-A night cream, the coach and the champ were unmoved.

"I don't have the money for that," the coach said. "I'm just going to have to get old."

Well, we're all getting old, whether or not we're slathering glycolic acid on our faces every so often (or every single day), but to me moisturizing isn't so different from putting turmeric in my rice to give my joints a boost, or exercising to help my ragged brain make new cells. Aging deteriorates every single part of us, and I'm into easing the wear and tear wherever possible. I do the work to help other beloved things hold up against the rigors of time in our material world, so why would I deprive my face—my *face*—of the care I'd give to my computer? (And, for the record, a good drugstore cream doesn't actually cost all that much.)

Back when I was a total drunk I had a friend named Nicky who was also a total drunk. Arguably, Nicky was an even worse drunk than I was, but all that means is her behavior was a little more unruly while she was loaded. A drunk is a drunk is a drunk. Regardless of how much booze she'd downed, how many Oxys popped, how many nights spent lolling in the drunk tank for slapping the cell phones out of the hands of businessmen, Nicky always looked sort of soft faced and innocent. My own skin was splotchy red with dehydration and the various toxins being pushed out my pores; some patches were scratchy dry, and others were pimply oily. Nicky's secret? She moisturized.

"What?" I remember asking. "Are you serious?" Imagining rough-and-tumble Nicky pampering herself was almost comical. But she explained to me that her mother—a single mom, fairly impoverished, working as a librarian in a small town—had always insisted she take care of her skin, going so far as to buy her the complete Clinique cleansing system once a year on her birthday.

"Yeah, you know, it's not a big deal." Nicky shrugged, spitting a spurt of chewing tobacco from her never-chapped lips.

When I finally got sober, I wasn't looking too hot. My hair was so parched it no longer could hold any color, and was a dull, washed-out shade of dark nothing with odd highlights of yellow, green, blue, and red. My skin was lizardy. My first encounter with a pack of sober alcoholics left me flabbergasted. Their skin was *so good*. They had a glow about them, and while much of it was an inner glow from having awesome higher powers and being off the drug train, some of it was just that their skin was really great because they were no longer dumping toxins into their systems. I wanted what they had—nice skin, a face that glowed and smiled. In a state of confused desperation, I flung myself on the mercy of these people, and believed what they told me, because I needed to: that I could stop drinking, that I would still have an interesting life and be an interesting person without booze, that the compulsion to whoosh doctored-up battery acid up my nose would fade. And that if I stayed away from the stuff that had been tearing me down, not only would my life clean up; so would my complexion.

Not spending my money on cocaine and liquor certainly freed up some cash. I spent it on cosmetics. Not makeup, per se. I've never been very good at makeup, though I've figured out how to utilize the basics in a passable manner. What I binged on was creams, serums, toners. A day cream with sunscreen, a night cream with retinol. Something nice with glycolic acid. An eye cream. Lip balms—oh my God, I started a lip balm collection. Vitamin C serum. Vitamin E oil. Tinted moisturizer with SPF. My tiny shelf in the bathroom sagged with the weight of my products. I found a scrub made especially to sand away those little dry bumps I always had all over my arms and legs. I found lotions that smelled like cocoa or fig or verbena or lavender. My ruined hair, my tarnished crowning glory, went into rehab. I splurged on shampoos only sold in hair salons, rich conditioners, oils to smooth my unruly locks. Face scrubs! Body scrubs! I even made one of my own, from olive oil and oatmeal and lavender and powdered goat milk. It looked like I'd taken my breakfast into the shower with me, but my skin felt so nice and soft and it was fun to have made it in the kitchen.

Caring for my body had a very practical purpose: to coax it back to where it would have been if I hadn't spent the past two decades tearing it down. But it was also a metaphor, a ritual, a physical affirmation of self-love. I'm worth caring for, and I'm capable of doing it. It's a reminder that beauty matters, that beauty and I are not separate, and I do not need to banish the concept from my heart. The time I spend lathering and lotioning in the bathroom, time spent alone with my literally naked self, often praying or making gratitude lists in my head, made me imagine exalted lady cultures that probably never existed, priestesses shaving their legs together in worship of some hot goddess.

Vanity is underestimated as a motivator for getting sober. I had an eye on the drinkers who'd come before me, and the ones who were still holding down their end of the bar were looking greasier and greasier as the clock ticked on. And it wasn't just their skin that the chemicals were taking a toll on—alcoholism was ruining their fashion, too. I like to play a game with the people closest to me, especially those who never knew me as a raging, fight-starting drunk. The game is called That Is Who I'd Be If I Hadn't Gotten Sober. We'll be out at a bar or an event, and I'll spot her. Her skin looks kind of mottled and her hair has been stripped and dyed so many times it looks flammable. Her makeup sits strangely on her scaly skin. She's wearing something that was certainly amazing when she first put it on in 1997. Alas, she got so drunk in the intervening years, she forgot to take it off. There she is in her fake-hair scrunchie with the pink streaks, a pair of faux-fur chaps buckled over her latex pants, a studded dog collar tight around her throat. That's who I'd be if I'd never gotten sober. The girl in the hand-bedazzled T-shirt that says GIRLS ROCK!

My impulse toward cosmetic self-care began while I was still drinking, but I was too much of a mess to really follow through. I couldn't help but be alarmed at the deteriorating condition of my skin and hair, but I couldn't deal with the thought that it was my drinking that was the problem. In all problem-strewn areas of an alcoholic's life, they *never* want to admit it's the drinking. When you're in the throes of if, having your face prematurely decay into a scaly, splotchy, hideous mess is preferable to contemplating a life without drinking. I tried to chip away at the problem, buying an antiaging moisturizer from the Body Shop or a bottle of deep conditioner for my raggedy locks. On the last day of my twenty-ninth year, realizing I looked more on the verge of forty than tipping on thirty, I even got myself a facial, my first facial ever.

Where does one even go for a facial, I remember wondering, baffled. With no Internet in the house during these days before Yelp, I pulled out the Yellow Pages and stared blankly at the listings. How did one know if it was a good or bad facial joint one was phoning? What did one look for in a facial, anyway? I phoned a friend who worked in a hair salon, a part-time makeup artist who looked like she regularly indulged in the beauty arts. She gave me the number for a salon and told me not to let them do extractions. Okay, no extractions. What the fuck were extractions? Were they going to pull my teeth or something?

Surprise—the recommended salon was booked for that evening. In fact, salon after salon was booked, because the bazillions of women who *do* get facials on the regs have their standing appointments, or they book in advance. They aren't sitting on a moldy carpet with the Yellow Pages on their laps, needing to make an appointment *right now* because it is the eve of their birthday and if they don't do it *right now* they might lose the nerve it takes to go into such a place—a beauty salon, a place they feel too dirtbaggy to visit—and spend the money it takes to have a professional slap products onto their skin. This whole outing was so far out of my comfort zone, the only way I was getting through it was knowing it was in celebration of my *thirtieth birthday*. I had to do it now, before the moment passed and scarcity issues took over.

I wound up at Elizabeth Arden's Red Door salon. It didn't seem like the place for me—too matronly. My grandmother had Elizabeth Arden products, and the perfume smelled like the urine of an overly pampered French cat. But they had the opening, and so I went. I remember exactly what I was wearing—a Mötley Crüe concert T-shirt that had been so sliced and diced it was a wonder it hung on my body; a thrifted sequined miniskirt whose sequins had long ago dulled and were falling off the elastic, leaving a trail of scales behind me like a molting amphibian; ripped-up tights (not deliberately—tights just ripped, right?) and motorcycle boots a bit too wide for my chicken legs. I felt tense and defensive, ready to be treated badly. Only, I wasn't. The ladies spoke to me in the same soothing spa voice they used on the respectable females, offering me delicious little cups of spa water flavored with cucumber and lemon. They kindly showed me to the locker room and gave me a robe to change into. I was happy to peel out of my street clothes. All snugged up in the fluffy robe, I was just like any other woman enjoying an afternoon of pampering. Except that my hair was blue and dry as straw, my face a mosaic of drug-induced splotches.

The Russian woman who tended to my face told me to relax, and it is hard to disobey a commanding Russian aesthetician. I relaxed. I found that I loved getting a facial. It was so nice to lie down, eyes closed, and feel the helpful hands tending to my face. When she told me she was going to do extractions I felt the awful hot and cold flush of being bizarrely unable to advocate for myself in a service situation. This conflict really interfered with the peaceful relaxation I'd just been experiencing, so I decided to hell with my friend's advice and let the Russian woman extract away. Apparently, there was, like, gold or something buried in my pores, because the Russian woman dug and dug and dug until tears sprang to my eyes. My facial had ceased being relaxing, but I was not unaware of the maxim "No pain, no gain," so I figured if something hurt that bad it must be really necessary, must be doing something really great for my face.

And maybe it was. I'll never know, because after my first facial I went out to celebrate my thirtieth birthday by drinking a ton of cheap well vodka at some long-gone dive bar, following it up with a cocaine bender at a friend's house. Any good the facial had done was obliterated as I snorted bump after line after rail of gasoline-soaked, heavily processed, cut-with-baby-laxative, what-once-was-a-leaf up my nose and out my pores. I wouldn't return to such a salon until I finally gave up chemicals once and for all, years later.

On the eve of my fortieth birthday, when I'd been off drugs and alcohol for almost eight years, I had another cosmetic reckoning. In many ways, this birthday was a reverse of my sad thirtieth. At twenty-nine, I looked into the mirror and saw someone who looked practically forty. Now, at thirty-nine, in many ways the face looking back at me could pass for thirty, depending on the lighting or how much sleep I'd gotten the night before—or how much of my forehead was visible. If the lighting was harsh or I was a tad sleep deprived and my forehead was on full display, it wasn't so much that I looked my age as I looked like Johnny Cash. The resemblance struck me especially hard after seeing the results of a photo shoot I'd done for a literary journal that was trying to up the cultural capital of the humble writer by pairing us with bona fide fashion photographers and doing glamour shots. Mine was expected to be on the cover.

The photographers posed me in the marble interior of San Francisco City Hall in black lace; by a stand of leafless trees in a crazy pink dress; in my own bedroom, topless, with my arms crossed over my chest. When the photos came back I had the same dissociative feeling I always do—*Oh, that's what I look like? I felt so much prettier taking the pictures! Oh well.* But it was compounded by, *Holy shit, what happened to my forehead?* I looked sort of amazing in the photos, in a haggard, cowboy kind of way. *Like Johnny Cash*, I realized. I liked it, and I didn't. I can imagine a woman who, through aging, comes to resemble Johnny Cash in a way that is very handsome and attractive. She is the kind of woman I would have dated, not the kind of woman I would want to *be*. A very forbidden thought occurred to me: *Maybe I'll get some Botox.*

The first time I ever heard of Botox I was on a Sister Spit tour with a dark-humored writer. "Did you hear," she gasped over one of the tabloids she bought in bulk at every gas station stop, "that people are injecting *botulism* into their faces to kill their nerves and stop their wrinkles?" She let loose in an amazing cackle. This was the sort of bizarre news she delighted in. "That's sick," I breathed. I was in my twenties, and thought plastic surgery of all kinds was bad and wrong. I once got into a fight with a gay male comedian who was talking about "getting some work done" in order to keep up his professional appeal. "You're selling out to ageism," I said haughtily, a decade younger than he was. I had no idea what it would be like to watch yourself start to fade and crease in the mirror, how the desire to engage with that process is more gentle, less violent, than I had imagined.

The first person I knew who ever got Botox was another gay male friend, who wrote for television in Los Angeles. He rushed up to me at an event, jabbing his fingers toward his wide, smooth forehead. "Look at this; look at this!" he exclaimed. "I'm raising my eyebrows *right now!*" Nothing on my friend's face moved. His wide, smooth forehead was a like a snow-covered plain in early morning, before any critters had left behind unsightly hoofprints. I was startled by my friend's bold cosmetic action, but not exactly surprised. He once did a performance piece that involved giving himself an enema with a Starbucks triple latte, then reading poetry atop the toilet. He totally *would* go and get Botox. And I totally wouldn't.

Or would I? As the years had eroded my collagen, so had they eroded my resistance to what had initially seemed like an anti-feminist, self-hating procedure. I mean, women who get Botox famously hate themselves, right? But I didn't hate myself. I didn't even hate the wrinkles on my forehead; they had just happened the way anything happens, after forty years of laughing and crying and making funny faces. There wasn't anything as intense as hate happening here—just a knowledge that I'd look better without a Johnny Cash forehead, and a growing, terrifying desire to investigate *Botox*, a word that had become synonymous with *vain, rich, amoral, hideous woman.*

Honestly, the more I pondered the possibility of Botox, the more the taboo around it excited me. I'd always gotten a thrill out of doing things I wasn't supposed to do, whether it was copping drugs on the street or spray-painting a feminist slogan on a wall or having sex in a public bathroom. Some of these outlets for rebellion were thankfully closed to me now, and others just didn't really seem that transgressive anymore. But declaring, as a feminist, that I didn't dig some part of my body and would pay money to have it altered? At that point in my life, it was sort of the most off-limits thing I could imagine myself engaging in.

As feminists we are just supposed to looooooooooove every little bit of ourselves. I get it—it's a radical act to shuck off the reigning corporate-approved beauty standards, say *Fuck You*, the Man, *I'm going to let myself go gray and wrinkly and I'm going to* love myself *in spite of the bazillions of dollars you're spending to convince me otherwise.* I rebelled against the social norm of shaving my legs when I was a newbie feminist, letting my hair grow long and curly down my legs. Guess what. My legs, sticking out of a vintage mini-dress, stuck into a pair of high-heeled Mary Janes, looked absurd to me. Every day I tried and tried to get down with them, beating myself up for being so *brainwashed*, for being a bad feminist. And every day the same word rang through my head as I looked at my scruffy legs: *wrong.*

Not wrong in general. Wrong for *me*. I had friends whose hirsute gams looked tough and cool on them; surely there were people I dated with hairy legs I was hot for. But for me, it just didn't work. Eventually, I caved in and shaved. I felt relieved at the sight of my new smooth legs flashing beneath a pair of cutoffs, but I felt a little disappointed in myself, too. Like I had failed feminism, meaning I had failed myself, and failed all women. *Oh well*, I internally shrugged. *I guess I'm just going to be the kind of feminist who shaves her legs*.

I wasn't alone. As I got older and more worldly I made the acquaintance of all kinds of females whose feminism was a challenge to the strict, neutered beauty standards that second-wave feminism had offered as a bland alternative to the dominant paradigm. These women wore stilettos and slinky dresses; they wore false eyelashes and engaged in occupations that feminists insisted were antifeminist, like hooking and stripping. Not long after I was among them, certain that we were a new kind of feminism—sex positive, femme positive, beauty positive. I do so love to rebel against an oppressive structure. When feminism felt like it was bumming out my reality, it was time to redefine what a feminist was.

So, maybe I was the kind of feminist who gets Botox. *If I can't have cosmetic injectables, I don't want to be part of your revolution.* I pulled up Yelp on my computer and made an appointment with the top-rated Botox doctor in the city. Part of my nervousness about my decision came from the taboo I felt I was breaking, and part from the scads of cash I was about to blow, but I was also concerned about the reality of altering—paralyzing—part of my face, and with a toxic bacteria. I wanted someone who really knew what she was doing.

The Botox doctor had a moon-shaped face, very pale and

wide, with a perfectly smooth forehead. She was super friendly, and her office was hung with photos from the many missions she had done in Africa with Doctors Without Borders. "I recommend Dysport," she told me. "It's cheaper. It's what I have; it's what everyone in the office has." Of course everyone in a Botox doctor's office has Botox. They probably even get a discount. I thought back to the blond receptionist who had checked me in. Her brow was unlined, but she also looked about twenty. For all I knew, she was my age.

Dr. Botox took me into a room and gave me a headband branded with the Dysport logo to hold my hair out of my face. Then she took a series of pictures with a digital camera, and uploaded them to my file on her computer. After analyzing them, she devised a course of action—a light introduction to the neurotoxin, hitting the dents between my eyes and some points along my eyebrow. I was a little disappointed. The addict in me likes for everything to be *extreme*. Botox is a drug, after all, and if there are drugs involved I'd like the highest dose, always.

Dr. Botox loaded up the syringe and drew near, stretching the skin above my eyes and sinking the needle. The injections hurt, as injections do, but not a big whoop after sitting for hours of tattoos. Shortly thereafter, my brow began to tingle; then it grew numb and froze. I remembered my friend in Los Angeles, pointing at his brow while gasping, "I'm raising my eyebrows!" I did the same, flexing my eyebrow muscles and watching absolutely nothing happen on my new, super-relaxed-looking forehead—even though Dr. Botox had ordered me not to do this. Flexing those eyebrows wears the Botox away, and after you went through all the hassle to paralyze them, why keep trying to use them?

Basically, no one could tell I got Botox—in a good way. I didn't look crazy and frozen. I looked like myself, just maybe a little more relaxed, a little less Johnny Cash "Sunday Morning Coming Down." Sure, I was less expressive, but I could use a little less expression, if you ask me. I'm pretty animated. I tried to keep the irresistible "I'm raising my eyebrows!" trick to a minimum, and the Botox lasted for a good six months.

When it faded away, and sensation returned to my brow with the weird tingles of an anesthetic wearing off, I wanted it again, badly. I made a last-minute appointment with Dr. Botox, before she went off to Africa and I went off to my writing retreat in Mexico, which would be followed by Cruise Dude. I figured there would be a lot of squinting in the sun, as well as a lot of photographs snapped, so why not get some more shots?

This time Dr. Botox's injections left a bruise on my forehead that looked like I'd been to church on Ash Wednesday and had a thumbful of burnt palm leaves smudged into my skin. My Botox bruise embarrassed me greatly. It seemed the sort of thing cynical people would hope would happen to a person who opted for the shots, something disfiguring to punish you for your vanity. But I don't think vanity should be punished. When I remember how lousy I looked and felt at my bottom ("bottom," in 12-step lingo, is when you are beat down the hardest by all the gnarly stuff you are putting into your body), and how happy and healthy and attractive the sober folks looked, I know that vanity in part has saved my life. Sometimes a bruise is just a bruise. It faded away before my cruise, and it was great to not crease up my forehead with all the stressed-out bawling I did while fighting with my boyfriend.

I sure would like to get Botox again, but my cash reserves aren't what they once were, plus you can't go injecting poison into your body when you're trying to have a baby. It's not because I think older people are ugs, or want to look twenty-eight forever. So many older people are fucking gorgeous—I'm thinking of Patti Smith here, or Vivienne Westwood, or Yoko Ono. But when I look in the mirror, it's not Patti's striking face staring back at me, or Yoko's (though we do have the same birthday). It is *my* goddamn face, only with Johnny Cash's forehead. I know those ditches in my forehead are the result of too many hours scrunching up my face and weeping, because of bad fights with lovers or a brutal drug crash. Chemicals, at least in part, are responsible for the state of my face. And I continue to believe in the power of chemicals to reverse the damage.

Just you wait. After I'm done delivering my test tube baby via an astrologically planned C-section, then breast-feeding till the kid is nine, I'm going to get *so much* plastic surgery! *Look, kids! Want to see a trick? Mommy is raising her eyebrows, right now!*

# 15.

# Confessions of a Gym Rat

I remember when I first discovered I had a body. The year was maybe 1979, and I had recently enrolled in a dance class—tap, jazz, and ballet at a storefront down on Washington Avenue. As a kid who always had her face jammed in a book, having an extracurricular that took place squarely in the physical world was a brand-new thing. Around nine or ten years old, I hadn't been exposed much to sports—gym class at school was a lot of dodge ball, and once I'd joined a pickup basketball game around the corner. But dance was a whole other world. It introduced me to the leotard—a shirt with its own underwear attached to it! It was like a bathing suit for outside the pool! As I feel best when I am wearing the least amount of clothes possible, something about donning a leotard made me feel free, made me *want* to spin and leap and sashay. I loved the leathery ballet shoes I pulled onto my feet. I loved how the pale pink got so dirty so fast—they were being *used*. They were *working shoes*. I loved standing in a line with the other girls, in my leotard (blue) and tights (purple) and ballet shoes (dirty pink), staring at myself in the mirror. I both did and did not recognize myself. My hair was long and wild. I would forget to brush it and then discover with horror that the locks had wound together in a matted ball at the nape of my neck. A *real rat's nest*, my mother would say as she painfully combed it out. I didn't think I was very pretty, but I was still fascinated with the sight of myself. I existed. I had a body.

I remember one sunny weekend escaping into my mom's room, suited up in my leotard, clutching a giant glass of ice water. Her bed was gigantic compared to mine, the footboard a long, shiny bar of wood that made me think of the barre at the dance studio. I popped Barry Manilow in the 8-track and started *working out*. I was just, like, jamming my foot up on the footboard and streeeeeetching down to touch my toes. I couldn't do a split but I was getting closer little by little, and I loved the feeling in my body, like my muscles were malleable and I could make them limber and strong. I did sit-ups and push-ups and jumping jacks until I was sweaty. I tried a backbend, though it was scary to watch the world go upside down. I practiced my dance routines. I watched myself, red-faced and damp, in the mirror that sat on my mother's dresser. I practiced high kicks, which were actually useless, as I learned in class. I thought the teacher would be impressed by how I flung my leg up, so straight and so tall, but in fact I was supposed to kick it up a little more gently, in line with all the other girls. Bummer. I loved kicking high, feeling the pull down my leg. It had to be good for something.

I stayed in my mother's room for hours, doing this. Periodically I'd walk into the kitchen, practically panting, to refill my ice water, and all the adults would look at me curiously. "Whatcha doin' in there? Ain't she a hot ticket. What a hot shit you are." I swapped out the Barry Manilow for Tony Orlando and Dawn, or Kenny Rogers, and resumed my place at the foot of my mother's bed. I had a body and my body was alive.

It has always been a challenge for a spacey, living-in-my-head girl like me to really *feel* my body. The dancing and exercise did the trick when I was a tween, but in the years to come I would abandon it for other sensations. Smoking made me feel my lungs, those hot balloons. Pot made me tingle. Beer made everything perfect, like the world was at once submerged in water and totally electric. Crushes on long-haired metal boys who looked like girls made me flutter. Eventually I would dance again, spinning to Goth music at all-ages clubs, but it wasn't much of a workout. Exercise? You've got to be kidding me. Once I joined a slightly athletic friend for a jog around a park. I thought it would be funny to jog while smoking a cigarette, but it was hard to jog and smoke *and* laugh. I collapsed on the grass with my pack of Marlboro Lights. With the exception of running for buses, I didn't jog again in public for nearly thirty years.

In my twenties I became aware of a curious distinction: There were people who were "in" their bodies, and there were people who were not "in" their bodies. I wanted to be in my body, because it sounded like the right way to be in the world, but I feared I was not. You know who were in their bodies? People who did yoga; dancers, modern dancers, the bulk of whom tended to be earth signs—hearty Taurus, graceful Virgo, solid Capricorn. I was a poet, an Aquarius, an air sign—mental, scrawny, full of ideas that burst out of me into notebooks and arguments. I didn't exercise—who wanted muscles? Muscles were for meatheads: jocks, frat boys, softball lesbians, people who were not *me*. My physical activity consisted of dancing at nightclubs while drunk, getting into fistfights while drunk, and having sex while drunk. While drunk, I could always feel my body.

Though I was never attracted to competitive sports, I had once loved the endurance of dance and exercise, a sort of private competition with oneself. That childhood pride I had in being able to touch my forehead to my knees or kick my leg *so high* became replaced, strangely, by seeing how much drugs and alcohol my body could endure. There is something pleasurable about things that are grueling, even punishing. Think of obstacle courses like Tough Mudder; think of mixed martial arts, cage fighting, long-distance runners doubled over puking at the finish line. These athletes are coming up against the limits of their physicality, and pushing through them. Brutal, yes, but there is also a feeling of toughness, of pride, a primal exultation in having a body. The shades of this I once felt while doing hundreds of sit-ups to Barry Manilow I later got from staying up all night on glittering rails of crystal meth washed back with vodka and a full pack of Camel Lights, then going to work and completing an eight-hour shift selling books at a bookstore. I was a *machine*! Was there nothing that could stop me? "Sex and drugs are the only time I know I have a body," I remember telling someone, as if this excused and explained my indulgence, meaning I actually required it, a kind of medicine.

If only one could stay young and on drugs forever! As I moved deeper into my twenties, then crawled into my thirties, drugs and alcohol continued to remind me I was flesh and blood, only now by giving my body the shakes, inducing vomit, roiling my guts with—sorry, but I'm trying to keep it real here—the most toxic, chemical-smelling bowel movements I have ever had. My head pounded and my voice grew hoarse from so many dehydration cigarettes. I was *alive!*

At my lowest bottom, my rapper ex-boyfriend and I moved to Los Angeles. It seemed to be a great idea at the time but I now know it was a "geographic." Geographics are these funny things that addicts do. With their world crumbling around them, they feel the way a duck caught in an oil spill looks—dirty, stuck, fatal. What could be the problem? Is it the junky heroin you're snorting every other night? The cocaine celebrations that have moved from New Year's and birthdays to weekends to hey it's Wednesday let's party? Nah. It's probably just your *city*. Your city has bad vibes, man! It's bringing out the worst in you. If you moved you could start over; a brand-new you would emerge, sparkling and fresh like an icky sticky bird bathed in dish detergent by a kindly volunteer. So, my boyfriend and I moved to L.A.

We thought it was a very grown-up move, actually. Leaving the communal punk rock shanty for our very own Hollywood studio—what could be more adult than that? But we were—I was—boozy feral cats who did not know how to live in the world. I sabotaged a job teaching at an art college by showing up still drunk from the night before. Where did I get so drunk, you may ask—raging at some glamorous Los Angeles party in the Hollywood Hills? Ah, no. Try at my kitchen table, consuming an entire jug of Carlo Rossi Paisano—bought on sale at Rite Aid—chain-smoking, alone. My ex tried to sleep in the next room, light from the kitchen and a rolling fog of cigarette smoke spilling over him. "When are you coming to bed?" *As soon as I finish this gallon of cheap wine! Unless I decide to call the Pink Dot and have them deliver a bottle of champagne!*

Lots of grown-ups are alcoholics, but I will posit here that they are not living grown-up lives. My definition of an adult is a person who can take care of herself, who comports herself with dignity, who has self-respect and respect for others, who is capable of dealing with reality and has managed to figure out, at least a little, how people do things—like pay taxes and return phone calls—who has learned that what the designer Tom Ford said is true: "By looking my best, it's a show of respect." Some alcoholics may be able to meet one or two of these criteria, but never many at once and always with that internal trembling, the terrible effort of holding it all together and hoping nobody notices the cracks.

During this sad Los Angeles pit stop, my ex—who was wrangling with his own chemical issues—decided to start working out. As with pulling a geographic, a lot of people who don't want to deal with their drug and alcohol problems think that going on a health kick will fix everything. He got himself a membership at a fitness center located in a huge industrial hangar a few blocks away. He would begin each day with a workout, and because we were locked in a codependent death grip, he would bully me into joining him.

There I was, scraping myself off the futon, my face puffy and my mouth still purple from the previous night's Carlo Rossi. My ex was reading some diet book that makes you start every day with a big glass of water, so I did it, too, even though water is disgusting. After I choked it down, I would make a French press of coffee, pour it into a mug, and be ready to go. It made my ex *so mad* that I drank a giant tower of coffee while working out—it's funny where his anger at my alcoholism manifested—but I was powerfully hungover and *needed* my coffee. And I didn't want to be working out anyway; I was only doing it because I'm super codependent and couldn't say no to my boyfriend.

The gym was like a chamber of horrors, filled with gleaming metal racks for me to torture myself upon. Though my body held faded memories of the sweaty pleasures of physical endurance, I felt only relief that I didn't throw up while negotiating the treadmill. Mostly I sat at the machines, trembling and catching my breath between pumps and lifts, clutching my coffee the way others clutch their water bottles. I would kill time until my ex was done with his workout, and then stumble home and cry in the shower.

Shocker—changing cities didn't make me feel any better, and Los Angeles sucks without a car. We returned to San Francisco, and within a year or so I was ready to reckon with my drinking. All the while, I never stopped codependently following my ex to the gym, first to the Chinatown YMCA, where Ping-Pong was considered physical activity, then to the Embarcadero YMCA, where the elliptical machines looked out onto the San Francisco Bay. I had stopped putting poison into my body, and slowly my body was coming back to me. Working up a sweat helped squeeze decades of accumulated toxins from my pores a little quicker. No longer depressing my nervous system with booze on the daily, I suddenly had a bunch of excess energy. Sleeping was hard, as I'd become accustomed to not so much drifting into a slumber but passing the fuck out. *And* I was still drinking coffee at emergency hangover levels, even though I was hungover no more. Working out gave me a place to put all this antsy new energy, and made falling asleep a little bit easier (though I still gobbled down herbs and supplements to help shut off the whir in my mind).

Other things were happening to my body, things I wasn't quite as aware of in my newly sober haze. The exercise was releasing endorphins, which I needed badly, coming off a booze-induced depression and into the stark screaming anxiety that is life with all its edges intact. Exercise also increases the production of brain-derived neurotrophic factor, a protein that makes you smart and sharp and helps your memory. Every single person benefits from the exercise-related production of this magic stuff, but for people who have been dousing their systems in booze it's even more crucial: Studies on poor little rats have shown that drinking a bunch of booze actually ruins your brain's ability to churn out BDNF. Here is scientific proof of what we all already knew—drunks are dopey and foggy and can't remember shit. But working out can reverse that. The combination of exercise and getting off the sauce not only gave me my body back; it gave me my brain back!

It's no wonder so many former boozehounds join what I call

the "get sober, get buff" lifestyle. When my ex and I split up I no longer needed his codependent peer pressuring to hit the gym; addict that I am, I'd become addicted to working out. I'm not kidding. Just as people can get hooked on sex and shopping and eating, they can get strung out on exercise. My sober body was especially starved for feel-good chemicals, and a half hour on the elliptical let loose a storm of endorphins and enkephalins and endocannabinoids, all of which mimic the effects of various drugs on your nervous system. I felt rad, and I was hooked on feeling rad. It also didn't hurt that after decades of neglecting my body I was suddenly becoming fit and strong. My postworkout flush had me glowing all day.

After my ex and I split, I switched gyms, moving from the rather posh YMCA downtown to a scuzzy place folks I know had dubbed the Prison Gym, as it resembled the sort of grimy, bare-bones workout space one might find themselves pumping iron in whilst incarcerated. I loved it. I mean, I wish it had been cleaner. I did fear picking up MRSA or some other frightening antibiotic-resistant flesh-eating bacteria each time I lay down on one of their grubby mats to stretch. And I did have my cell phone stolen from my locker by a gang of homosexual teenagers. (Thanks for nothing, comrades!) But the skater dudes who worked the desk were cute and helpful, the monthly rate was dirt cheap, and my fellow exercisers were a refreshingly motley crew. No yoga moms here, no tight-assed gym queens, no muscle-headed athletes. There was the elderly woman in the Pope John Paul II sweatshirt who wore her rosary while she worked out her forearms; the woman with the Satanic tattoos, severe black hair, and the largest bosom I had ever seen, who I was sure had captained an all-girl street gang in the past. There were lots of writers trying to bring some tone to their scrawny writer physiques. And there were bunches of sober drunks I knew from around town. My favorite was rather handsome, in a Dennis Hopper way, and I had a special fondness for him after hearing him tell a friend that his "old lady" had tossed his yoga equipment out the window during a fight. This was not what you'd expect from a biker who had dollar signs tattooed on his eyelids. One afternoon I saw him watching me as I struggled with an ab machine. The Prison Gym's equipment was pretty busted, and many of the old machines had been built during an era when women didn't work out as much. It was hard to figure out how to fit my tiny, five-feet-three-inch frame into the chair and use it in a way that wasn't actually hurting my body.

I grew tense watching Eyelids watching me. I just *knew* he was going to come over and man-splain the best way to use the machine. I broke off eye contact and put a scowl on my face—what I do when I'm hoping to ward off a helpful man. As much as I admired my eccentric gym-mates, I didn't want to strike up a friendship with any of them. I was there to get buff and get high on endorphins, not to buddy up with a probable ex-con. But then I stopped. In 12-step we're taught to be teachable. So many drunks aren't; we think we know everything. I know that non-drunk humans can have this problem, too, and in general it's great to remember to be teachable—open, flexible, approachable. I decided to give Eyelids a chance.

I was right. Just as my bitch's intuition (bitch's intuition: the sixth sense that tells a lady when her lover is cheating on her and also when a strange man is going to approach her) had told me, Eyelids wanted to show me a more helpful way to use the busted ab machine. He ripped the seat off a different busted machine, stacked it on top of the ab machine's seat, and voilà! I was now at the correct height to work out my core without throwing my back out. I thanked Eyelids, my stomach got ripped, and the two of us became friendly. "Hey, Muscles!" he'd shout at me in the street. "Lemme see; lemme see!" I'd flex my wimpy peanut muscles at him and he'd give me a high five. This would never have happened at the Y. I went there for years and no one ever spoke to me except to scold me for dragging my gym bag around with me when I forgot to bring quarters for the lockers. At the Prison Gym, the lockers were free. They also had no doors, which is how the Gang of Baby Gays stole my Android, but oh well. You make sacrifices for an interesting life.

After years of working out, it has become a solid part of my life. I might fall off—especially with round after round of IVF treatments, which require no sudden moves while waiting for a zygote to hopefully implant itself into your soothing, serene uterus—but I always get back on. While living in my eleven-hundred-dollar birthday apartment I'd hoof it into the Castro and plunk myself down on the rowing machine beside a batch of brawny gym queens. Now I'm living out by the ocean with my husband-wife-spouse-person. (Dashiell's a female, but she looks like a male model and I just can't figure out what to call her!) It's the most suburban place I've ever lived in my life, and there are no gyms close by, prison-esque or otherwise. But there is the sea.

In the morning I pull on the running shoes Dashiell bought me after I horrified her by trying to hike in a pair of thrifted cowboy boots. *What do you think cowboys hiked around in?* I'd asked her, and she admitted I had a point, but she still bought me a pair of hideous, embarrassing hot-pink-and-neon-green sneakers. I became somewhat less ashamed of them after I watched Texas senator Wendy Davis do her feminist filibuster in the exact same pair, but still. Running shoes aren't really my style. Neither is the athletic headband I stretch over my ears, or the weird thin black gloves that keep my hands warm, or the fanny pack I stuff my house keys and cell phone in. When I go jogging in the morning, I look like someone else. Tali wanted to see, so I texted her a picture of me, cozy in the giant BOSTON hoodie I stole from my sister.

*You better wear a punk T-shirt or something; you look like a yuppie,* Tali texted. To which I replied, *I got a neck tattoo, bitch. I don't need to prove shit!* My tattoos really come in handy sometimes, like when I get a little nervous about what a suburban yuppie I've become.

The first time I jogged on the beach I worried I would hate it. In spite of this love letter to exercise, I often find myself counting the minutes till my workout is done. Always the addict, I want instant gratification—endorphins ASAP—and on lazier days those twenty minutes on the elliptical can feel endless. At the gym I distracted myself with the banks of TVs hanging from the ceiling, blaring *Real Housewives* or Rachel Maddow. What would I do on the beach to make my workout fly by?

Well, I would be on the *beach*, face-to-face with the motherfucking *ocean*. What is more glorious than running alongside this big, heaving, wondrous mass of liquid life, with the morning sky a pastel watercolor of lavender and periwinkle? Nothing. Nothing in the whole world. The roar of the waves is hypnotic; the sight of the surfers in the butt-ass-cold Northern California water, handling the brutal waves, was majestic. Seabirds scattered in a flock as I approached, making me giggle. There were men in waders, fishing, their poles jammed into the sand. Once there was a pod of dolphins. Dolphins! Dolphins are about as close as we come to unicorns in real life. I stood on the shore and watched their fins break the surface, dozens of them. I was so jealous. I wished I wasn't completely terrified of the ocean and could be out there with the animals like the surfers and the paddleboarder and that one hard-core swimmer.

At the end of my beach jog I felt *amazing*. Sure, I'd just started a new course of antidepressants, and the Zoloft was just kicking in, but it wasn't only synthetic. Jogging became a habit, and as with all habits I would lapse occasionally, sick with a cold or busy with a morning meeting. On those days I just didn't feel as awesome. I woke up anxious. I entertained gloomy-doomy thoughts about my future. But on days that I ran alongside the ocean, forget it. Life was fantastic. Jogging produced in me a peacefulness, an ability to accept it all as it is. And after a lifetime of childishly chasing various highs, the ability to feel content where I am strikes me as strikingly adult. On my way home from my runs, I scan the shore for treasures, bringing home a shell or a piece of sea glass, a sand dollar or a special stone. I lay them out on my front steps and see them as I come and go. These tangible bits of beauty remind me of the beauty of my runs, of the planet, of myself. The way I've allowed myself to be transformed by life is gorgeous, and sometimes it's hard to remember when you get caught up in the daily chaos of texting and e-mailing and cooking and cleaning. When I see this pile of treasure I remember these morning jogs, just me and the ocean, me in my body and the ocean in its depths, alive and grateful, grown-up but still a bit forever young in the face of its ancient tides.

# Acknowledgments

Gigantic thanks to Lindsay Edgecombe, without whom this book would not exist. Thank you for your belief and enthusiasm and sharp eye, and for always having my back. To Kathleen Napolitano, also for her belief and enthusiasm and sharp eye, for helping me structure the original manuscript from a rambling tangent to something legitimately readable. To the many beloved people who have helped me grow up: Kathleen Black, Ali Liebegott, Alexis Persyko, Tara Perkins, Beth Pickens, and Tara Jepsen. And to the biggest reward for all lessons learned, Dashiell Lippman. Thank you for your constant support and highest-quality love.